J·A·M·E·S
GARNER

Other books by Raymond Strait

Mrs. Howard Hughes
The Tragic, Secret Life of Jayne Mansfield
This for Remembrance: The Rosemary Clooney Story
Lanza: The Mario Lanza Story
Star Babies
Lou's on First: A Biography of Lou Costello
Hollywood's Children
Alan Alda: A Biography
*Queen of Ice, Queen of Shadows: The Unsuspected Life of
   Sonja Henie*

J·A·M·E·S
GARNER

RAYMOND STRAIT

ST. MARTIN'S PRESS / NEW YORK

Design by Paolo Pepe

Library of Congress Cataloging in Publication Data

Strait, Raymond.
    James Garner, a biography.

    1. Garner, James.   2. Moving-picture actors and Actresses–United States–Biography.   I. Title.
PN2287.G385S77   1985   791.43'028'0924   [B]   85–2671
ISBN 0–312–43967–9

First Edition

10 9 8 7 6 5 4 3 2 1

for . . . Charles Farley . . .
friend and compatriot

Acknowledgments

A very special thanks to those who were kind enough to grant the author interviews. Some, of great length, were given with great patience and candor: Roy Huggins (who not only was cooperative, but made suggestions that bore enormously valuable results), Jimmy Lydon, Les Martinson, Jack Kelly (Jim Garner's co-star on "Maverick"), Arthur Hiller, John Sturges, Burt Kennedy, Jack Scagnetti, Michel M. Grilikhes and Harold R. Belknap (editor and publisher, *The Norman Transcript*, Norman, Okla.).

Other important contributors: Kenneth Norris, Doug McClelland, Sandi Freeman (and Cable News Network's "Freeman Reports"), Diana Markes, University of California Department of Special Collections (Dr. Robert Knutson and Ray Holland), Warner Brothers Studios (especially Kimberly Brent), Ronald Neame, Edward Anhalt, Dennis Weaver, Jim Mahoney, Metro-Goldwyn-Mayer Studios Legal Department (Herbert Nussbaum, Esq., and Donna Shurk), Maggi White, Ralph Nelson, The Academy of Motion Picture Arts and Sciences' Margaret Herrick Library, The American Film Institute's Louis B. Mayer Library, University of California at Riverside Library, University of California at Los Angeles Humanities Library, Paramount Pictures, Inc., ABC Televison Center, Standard & Poors Register of Corporations, Directors and Executives, International Alliance of Theatrical and Stage Employees, Screen Actors' Guild, Directors' Guild of America, Custom Tailors' Guild of America, Fleetwood Publications of London, *Filmgoer's Companion*, *New York Herald Tribune*, *Weekly and Daily Variety*, *Hollywood Reporter*, *Washington Post*, *The New York Times*, *Popular Science*, *This Week*, *Parade*, Triangle Communications, *Book of TV Lists*, *Motion Picture Almanac*, *Film Facts*, *Time*, *Look*, *Life*, *Los Angeles Times*, *Los Angeles Herald-Examiner*, *Los Angeles Daily News*, *Photoplay*, *American Weekly*, *Seventeen*, *Motion Picture*, *House Beautiful*, *Toledo Blade*, *Limelight*, *Motion Picture Herald*, *Esquire*, *Movieland-TV Time*, *Labor*

Week, Newsweek, Associated Press, *Los Angeles Mirror, Cosmopolitan, Screenland, Movie Life Yearbook, Screen Album, Feature Films, Movie Stars Annual, Billboard, Cash Box,* Motion Picture Association of America, *Entertainment Weekly, Coronet, Motor Trend, TV Guide, Modern Screen, Hollywood Life Stories, Hollywood Citizen News, Film Comment, Saturday Evening Post, San Fernando Valley Magazine, Drama-Logue, Hot Rod, Panorama, Detroit Free Press, Santa Monica Evening Outlook, Good Housekeeping, Playboy, The New Yorker, Hollywood Studio, Architectural Digest,* Marie Torre, David Scott, Jan P. Norbye, Gabe Essoe, Jack Bagby, Nancy Curbin, Hank Grant, Amy Archard, Jim Hoffman, Fred D. Brown, Mavor Moore, Bob Thomas, Leslie Taubman, Erskine Johnson, Vernon Scott, Howard Thompson, Murray Olderman, Abe Greenberg, Sheilah Graham, Pete Martin, Jerry Asher, Cameron Shipp, Bill Tusher, Dick Kleiner, Guy Newton, Earl Wilson, Carolyn See, Dick Wells, Patrick McNulty, Cecil Smith, Dorothy Manners, Joan Schmitt, Paul Gardner, Morton Moss, Sidney Skolsky, Walter Winchell, Al Stump, Doris Wedge, Kit Snedaker, Muriel Davidson, Arnold Hans, Dick Lochte, Arnold Roth, Charles Champlin, Lee Winfrey, Rona Barrett, Jean Vallely, Daniel Menaker, Morrie Gelman, Marilyn Beck, Dave Kaufman, Ellen Torgerson, Jerry Buck, Howard Rosenberg, Charles Parker, Samir Hachem, Mary Beth Murrill, Beverly Linet, Richard West, Arnie Friedman, Cameron Curtis McKinley, Janice Fuhrman, Greg Baxton, Dave Wallace, Gary Deeb, Rick Du Brow, Cam Bentley, Ron Base, Robin Leach, Roderick Mann, Jenny Andrews Harwell, Gail Williams, Jo Weeden, Adam Dawson, Peter J. Boyer, Carl Connor, Robert Ward, Kevin Thomas, John J. O'Connor, George Christy, Patte Barham Boyne, Leo Guild, and Kirk Crivello.

"I don't do futuristic pictures, and I don't do horror. That seems to be all they're making these days. I don't have any particular sense of my image, but whatever I do has to have a sense of humor about it. There is nothing worse than the steely-eyed sheriff. Brave bores me. Smart intrigues me. I'm very wry and off-beat. I'm not going to make you fall down and laugh. I don't do comedy. I do humor!"

James Garner in the *Detroit Free Press*, January 17, 1981

J · A · M · E · S
GARNER

I

In 1928 Oklahoma was still a raw-boned territory in the minds of most Americans. It had only been admitted to the Union a little over twenty years earlier, in 1907. In 1834 a large area north of Texas had been set aside by the United States government as "Indian territory" and had eventually housed many Indian tribes, including Choctaws, Creeks, Seminoles, Chicasaws, Quapaws, and the ones most known to populate the region, the Cherokee Nation. It was not until oil was discovered that the Oklahoma Territory became of interest to white settlers and investors.

It was into this setting that James Scott Bumgarner emerged on April 7, 1928. His parents, Weldon and Mildred Meek Bumgarner, were by no means wealthy people. Nor was Mildred physically strong. Weldon Bumgarner, on the other hand, was a hearty man who was no stranger to hard work. He made ends meet, but just barely, by driving a laundry truck for a firm in Norman.

After James was born, Mildred was never well again. Her health worsened rapidly, and she soon took to her bed for good. In hopes of improving his wife's health, Weldon left his job in the city and bought a small country store about nine and a half miles east of Norman in an unincorporated area that was not even listed on the map. It is now called Denver, Oklahoma. At the time the little store was a mail drop. The family lived behind the store, and Mildred kept to herself more and more.

Jim recalls, "She was sick all of the time. From the time I was born she was ill. I never saw her much because she was bedridden all of the time. Later, when it really got bad, she became a Christian Scientist and moved into Norman to live with my aunt. All of a sudden there was a funeral and the funeral procession passed on the road that went from Norman to Shawnee, Oklahoma—and right by the store where we lived on that old country road. I remember passing by the store as part of the funeral procession and couldn't figure out why we didn't stop, because that's where we lived."

The funeral party continued on to the cemetery. Afterward, young James, his father, and his two older brothers returned to their home and the small store on the old road. It was to be a short stop for the boys—and a low point in Jim's young life. He was five years old and had barely known his mother. To all intents, he was an orphan, though he did have love. Plenty of it. He came from a big family. What he lacked following the death of Mildred was any kind of real supervision.

In a magazine interview, one of his childhood friends, Bill Saxon, recalled Jim as a young boy following his mother's death. "There was no semblance of family. Jim's father was a man with an eye for the ladies and in his day he was every bit as handsome as his son is now. It didn't seem to bother him if the women were loose or tied—just as long as they were willing."

Mr. Bumgarner meant well, but he knew more about merchandising than mothering. He just didn't have the domestic ability to keep house, manage three growing lads, and run the store at the same time. The boys were soon farmed out to various relatives in Norman. Jim went to live with his uncle and aunt, John and Leona Bumgarner. There, he had plenty of family support; some sixty of his relatives lived in Norman, a small community where everybody knew pretty much what everybody else was doing and what their problems were.

More like Tom Sawyer than Little Lord Fauntleroy, Jim easily gained the affection of the female members of the clan. Many women seem to like the kid with scuffed shoes, bruised knuckles, and scraped knees, and Jim filled the bill to perfection. He always seemed to be in some minor scrape, often just short of the law. But though he liked to have fun, he never got into any trouble with the authorities. He had a healthy respect for the law.

He was still a little boy who had lost his mother and was shuttled about from one place to another with no real sense of direction. And now he had not only his brothers but his cousins to compete with. He learned from a very early age that it was going to be James against the world and that the world gave little or no quarter.

It didn't take long for Jim's hurt and anger over being deprived of a mother to turn into cockiness. One early schoolmate describes him as having been "somebody who seemed to feel cheated and was out to let the world know that nobody would ever do that to him again."

After a decent period of mourning Mildred's passing, Weldon remarried. His second wife, Wilma, was not the mother he wanted for his children, but it was difficult to be a man alone with three young boys and he wanted them all to be together again under one roof. Following his marriage, the boys moved back in with their father and his new wife, from all accounts the archetypal wicked stepmother.

The three boys seldom agreed on anything, and a healthy

sibling rivalry prevailed. When Jim was five his brothers were seven and nine and they looked on him as something of a pest who always wanted to tag alone. However, no matter how many disagreements there were between them, they were unanimous in their belief that their father did them no favor by marrying Wilma.

"She was a damn no-good woman," according to Jim's older brother Jack. "She was mean and beat the hell out of us. She was meaner to Jim than to myself and Charles and I don't know why."

Neither did Jim, but he supports his brother's assessment of their stepmother. A strict disciplinarian, Wilma seemed to think that all boys were "bad" and deserved punishment, and that none was more deserving of the switch—her favorite means of correction—than young James.

"I was the recipient of whatever was handy," Jim recalls, "but she had a real affinity for the spatula when it came to me. She would make us go out and cut the willow switches she was going to whip us with and we knew better than to get little ones. If she wasn't satisfied with the size of them, we were sent out to get larger ones, or worse—she went out and made her own selection." Jim felt that she never treated him fairly.

"She loved to beat us on the butts," he declares with some stifled bitterness. "As I said, switches were her first line of offense, but with me she preferred spatulas. Oh boy, she was great with the spatula. She'd use boards or sticks or whatever, but her eyes really lit up when she had a spatula." Young James' rear end was commonly covered with big red welts. He didn't like being whipped, but he kept silent for a long time. He'd heard over and over that this was the Depression. Times were hard and folks had to make do as best they could to survive. His father was barely able to support them. The boys ran barefoot all summer to save shoe leather for the cold winter months when shoes were needed, but like all country kids, they saw going barefoot as a privilege, not a deprivation.

James's young life was hectic. His only consolation, if it can be called that, was that his family was economically no worse off than almost everyone else he knew. At that time, relief was common, and welfare lines were long. His father had too much pride to accept handouts from the government or anyone else. But the Bumgarners were themselves generous. When an old man came along the dusty country road during a thunderstorm, he was fed. When he asked if he might stay in their storm cellar for the night, he was made to feel welcome and a part of the family. "He stayed on with us," Jim says, "until I was seven years old. Even after that, when the store burned down, old Pop Gunther still stayed there."

If the Bumgarners were generous it was partly because, like their neighbors, they had so little. During the thirties, Oklahoma was not only hard hit by depression but was almost at the center of the dust bowl that had left the heartland of America barren and created the great drive of humanity from Oklahoma to California. Thousands upon thousands of families packed up their meager belongings, strapping mattresses on top of old rattletrap cars that looked as if they might not make it ten miles, much less over a thousand miles to California. These "Okies," so deftly described by John Steinbeck in his classic *The Grapes of Wrath*, went looking for the promised land only to discover there was more promise than land for them.

Such was the Oklahoma of James Garner's youth. He went to school because he had to—his father believed in education. But he was never an outstanding student. One reason he had difficulty with school was his own sense of justice. If a teacher was wrong, he didn't hesitate to say so, which got him into a lot of trouble. (His older brother Charles was the scholar of the family and went on to become a teacher himself, a considerable achievement for a boy from the dirt farms of dust- and Depression-ridden Oklahoma.) Jim was athletic like his other brother, Jack, who was good enough at baseball to become a pro in the Pittsburgh Pirates organization and later a manager in the Pirates farm system.

Jim Garner's early education took place in a one-room country schoolhouse. He and his two brothers often rode the family horse to school, which was a little more than a mile away from their home. Other times, they walked. They were not unlike other kids growing up in rural areas of the country in the thirties. "We were poor, I guess, but I never saw it that way. We were what we were and that was that. We didn't know anything different. It didn't mean a thing that we didn't have anything. Nobody had anything. I'm sure it has impacted my life in some way, but I'm not sure how."

Although he has since become nostalgic about farm life, when he was a child Garner hated it. He felt unsettled and thought only of "doing something else," Indeed, his whole life has been rooted in "doing something else," a desire that doubtless began during his father's second marriage. There were other wives—four or five altogether, according to his son Jack—but Wilma was the one who made the most vivid impression on Jim. There simply had to be something better than what he was stuck with.

If there was any stability in his preteen life, it came from his grandmothers, Abbie Meek and Lula Bumgarner. When he needed honest answers to his questions, he went to one of them. He loved and was loved by them intensely. No matter what he did wrong, to them it was either somebody else's fault or exaggerated out of proportion.

But there was little they could do to help him with the struggle between him and his stepmother: He would have to resolve that matter himself. This he did when he was fourteen years old. One day, according to Jim and his brother, Wilma decided it was time Jim be punished again with her spatula. For the first time he openly took issue with her.

At fourteen, Jim was a big boy, very big for his age. And he decided that he was too much of a man to have a woman beating him who wasn't even his own mother.

Wilma swung at him with the spatula she had been holding in midair above her head. As she came down toward his face he instinctively defended himself by hitting her, knocking her across the kitchen. She hit her head against a shelf and was dazed. Before she could regain her balance, Jim pounced on her and with his large hands locked around her throat began to throttle her. He might well have committed murder had his father not come into the kitchen to find out what all the commotion was about.

"What the hell is going on in here?" he demanded, pulling Jim off his stepmother. His brother Jack had followed their father into the room.

Weldon's initial reaction was to side with his wife. He knew about Jim's temper and his discontent. But all he saw at the time was his overgrown son trying to choke his wife. Consequently, Jim got his punishment, much to Wilma's delight. While his father and Jack held him down, Wilma beat him with a spatula. It was the most humiliating day in his life. He couldn't understand why his father believed his stepmother and not him. He was filled with hatred for the woman and contempt for just about everybody else.

While Jim went off by himself to recover, his father began to think about what had happened. He realized that he hadn't really pursued the issue before taking action, which was certainly unfair to his son. The more he thought about it, the more he felt guilty for having made so abrupt a judgment without having heard both sides of the story. Finally, he approached his wife and asked, "Just what did the boy do?"

"Something." Wilma had no better answer than that.

A huge fight between husband and wife ensued, and didn't end until Mrs. Bumgarner moved out a couple of weeks later and was never heard from again.

It was back to square one: Weldon, trying to keep house for his three teen-aged boys, had an eye out for every skirt that passed by. It was an untenable situation, and he knew it. He hadn't been and still wasn't capable of taking care of his boys by himself. It was not that he was a bad father—he truly wanted to be an example to his boys—but he had difficulty just dealing with life and work and expenses without the added responsibility of man-sized boys who were not as yet of legal age.

Within two months after his wife's unceremonious departure, Weldon Bumgarner went to California to look for work. Before he left he made sure his boys were properly provided for. Jim was placed on a farm in Hobart, Oklahoma, where he was to work and attend school. He didn't like the work and in a couple of months abandoned farm life and moved back to Norman to live with an aunt. For all practical purposes he was on his own.

He already knew how to drive, having taken his father's car without permission and learned the hard way—by trial and error out in the countryside where there were no stop signs or traffic cops to interfere. Therefore, without difficulty he obtained not only a driver's license but a chauffeur's license as well. It was summer and school was out, so he gladly accepted a job as the driver for a clothing salesman from the

Curlee Clothes Company. He spent several months on the road touring Texas with the salesman and learned a lot about life and business.

His employer was an elderly gentleman whose penchant for Scotch and milk aggravated his ulcers. Jim became not only his driver but also a sort of valet-goter, learning the ropes from someone who knew them all.

"I did a little bit of everything for him. He wasn't allowed to smoke, but I doled the cigars out to him, one at a time. We stayed at all the best hotels in Texas, where he would entertain buyers while they sat around and drank expensive liquor." By the time the bottle had been passed around a few times all too often it was Jim who did the selling, not the salesman. He was quickly accumulating an education that far exceeded anything he might obtain in the public schools.

During the winter he returned to school in Norman, but the following year he was back on the road again, this time with another salesman who covered the Oklahoma territory. Jim was becoming a self-sufficient teen-ager. A road career, however, was not yet in his immediate future. Though he did not particularly relish it, he still considered school a priority, for he was smart enough to know that he would need some sort of education if he intended to get ahead.

While school was in session, he worked at a variety of jobs, his immediate goal being financial independence. His aspiration was to become wealthy. It never occurred to him that he would find a place in the limelight. Actually, he shied away from any kind of recognition, preferring to remain in the background as long as he had a source of income. This was very heady stuff for a young man of fourteen who was considered a bit rowdy and stubborn to a fault. Most people did not understand his motivations: He had endured more than his share of suppression and was determined to control his own life without interference from anybody, well-meaning or otherwise. He had learned what it meant to be a "have-not" through the loss of his mother and the poverty he had grown up in. Even Wilma had taught him a valuable lesson: to resist domination by the whims of others, to stand up for what you believe to be right no matter what others think.

He worked hard, stocking grocery shelves, felling trees for a telephone company, working with sheetrock and bricks, carrying hod, and even putting in some time in a chicken hatchery. He had a job for a while at the University of Oklahoma in Norman that required him to get up at 3:30 in the morning to sweep out the university's administration building before going to school. "The only time I ever quit a job was because I was bored with what I was doing." Mundane duties have always driven him up the wall. If he had a reputation for not staying on the job very long, he also possessed a sense of pride. He *always* worked. One of his grandmothers once commented, "That boy doesn't have a lazy bone in his body."

In an interview with *Seventeen* magazine while his series "The Rockford Files" was high in the television ratings, Jim described himself as an introverted kid who kept pretty much to himself. Following his father's departure for California he lived for a few months with an aunt, but he felt restless and uncomfortable. He was a man in his own eyes. He was already six-foot-three, his height today. "I looked like an old 4F to the sailors stationed in Norman," he says, and he literally "had to fight the navy every day."

After a while, he left his aunt's house and moved in with his buddy Jim Paul Dickenson. "His mother operated a big rooming house in Norman. Because her son and I were such good friends she refused to take any money for my room and board. She was real nice people." Although he would not accept gratuities from anyone, he accepted Mrs. Dickenson's generosity as if it came from a mother.

Over the years it has been rumored that Jim did not get along very well with his brother Jack. Whether this is true or not, he did criticize one of his brothers in one interview. Looking back at his youth, he commented, "My father was a volunteer fireman for twenty years in Norman. Because of that they gave him a small pension. Charles, my oldest brother, took that pension when my father moved to California and went to live upstairs over the firehouse. Jack lived with another relative. I had aunts and uncles all over town, and I had my grandmother if I was really in desperate need. But I always thought I could take care of myself. One thing I never did. I never took money from my father. I thought that was wrong. But one of my brothers would take everything he was given. He was always smarter than I was."

Jim declares that his youth was never as rough as it sounds. There were good times, too, some of them at school because of sports. "They thought I was a good football player and so did I. As long as I was able to keep my grades up, I could play football. That was the best incentive I had to crack the books." But even sports could not keep him interested in textbooks for long. From time to time his grades faltered, and he could not play football until they came back up.

By the time Jim was a high school freshman he was less introverted. "I played varsity football and had a terrific time with my pals." His dozens of kinfolk were concerned about a boy of his age being out on his own. They felt there were too many opportunities for him to get into trouble. Jim didn't see it their way. He felt capable of supervising himself.

"They needn't have worried so much," he says. "I did mischievous things like breaking streetlights with rocks on Halloween and stuff like that." One game he and his friends were obsessed with was called "Ditch 'em." It was played with automobiles. A half-dozen or so drivers would line up. The lead driver would take off and would try to evade the others, who were always in hot pursuit. The idea, according to Jim, was that "everybody else would try to stay up with the guy in front. I loved it. You'd drive wherever you wanted, all over town and even out in the country, trying to lose the guys behind you. There was a lot of hell-raising, hootin' and hollerin' and squealin' of tires, but we never hurt anybody."

In a small town a boy's car gets as much attention—often more—than his sweetheart. Thus for the most part Jim and his friends were all good drivers. "It wasn't as dangerous as it sounds," Jim laughs. His interest in formula racing, which would emerge during his career in films and bring him to national recognition as an amateur racer, probably developed at this time.

Jim has been frequently described as a hypochondriac. Even as a kid in Norman he was prone to injury. As a pre-schooler he once fell down a flight of stairs and nearly killed himself. Although he hardly remembers the event himself, family members have told the story so often that he knows it by heart. Experiences like these fostered a genuine fear of pain that has stayed with him.

In football he also suffered many bumps and bangs. A big teenager, he was an easy target for tacklers, who seemed to take great pleasure in singling him out and hitting him harder than others. Bill Saxon recalls that Jim was always "a bit of a show-off and a real sissy when it comes to pain."

During the summer of his fourteenth year, Jim made a trip out to California to visit his father. He didn't stay with Weldon, however, but with an aunt, and immediately got a job at an A&P grocery store. By summer's end he was back in Norman, still dissatisfied and restless. He moved back in with the Dickensons, who were always happy to see him and make him feel like family.

Living at Jim Paul's house offered him both security and, at long last, permanence. These friends acknowledged his maturity and allowed him the freedom he felt he needed— freedom from always being told what to do. At the same time his adopted family offered warmth and support.

It was wartime, and Jim and Jim Paul, anxious both for adventure and to participate in the war, decided that maybe they ought to join the Merchant Marine, where they would receive room and board and excellent pay while being less at risk than their older counterparts fighting with the armed forces around the globe.

"The two of us went down to Houston to try to ship out with the Merchant Marine. We figured it would be a cinch." Neither of them gave much consideration to getting hurt or killed. "Hell," Jim says, "we didn't think about casualties. Boys who went off to war were heroes and came home with medals. I was big and if a truck was to hit me I figured it would bounce off, but I never thought anything was going to happen to me—not ever."

But something did happen. Though he liked the Merchant Marine, was a good worker, and got along with his buddies aboard ship, he didn't take to the sea. He suffered from chronic seasickness and couldn't shake it no matter how hard he tried. He finally had to abandon his sailing career for something on terra firma.

"I traveled a lot in those days. Jim Paul and I got robbed down in Texas and headed out to California to ship out again, but I didn't stay at any one thing very long. I guess I must have had five or six dozen jobs of one kind or another when I was a kid. I just couldn't make up my mind what I wanted to do, but I knew there was something for me somewhere and one day I would find it."

Jim finally decided to head west. Nothing much was happening in his life, and he had liked southern California on his first visit there.

Although he couldn't possibly have known it at the time, this decision was eventually to change a hulky country boy of scant means into a wealthy television and motion picture star.

II

Jim Paul Dickenson accompanied Garner to the West Coast. They parted company there when Dickenson decided to ship out again with the Merchant Marine at San Pedro. Jim then moved in with his father, who by this time was making a decent living in the carpet-laying business. His son worked with him for a short time but became entranced with Hollywood High School and decided to return to school. His interest in Hollywood High had more to do with the gorgeous girls on campus than with the halls of learning. It is little wonder. His feelings were reciprocated. Jim Garner was as handsome as any Hollywood leading man and naturally attracted girls. He considered it one of the fringe benefits of being mature before his time.

He wanted to play football at Hollywood High because without sports he didn't consider school worthwhile, but his gypsy ways interfered with his plans. He didn't often bother to attend class, preferring an afternoon at the beach or just to wander about town seeing the sights. Consequently he was kicked out of school. Under California law at that time one was required either to graduate or to attend school until aged eighteen, whichever came first. Since Jim was barely seventeen, he ended up in the Frank Williams Trade School.

Weldon had once again married, and Jim had a better rapport with his second stepmother than with his first, so family squabbles were rare. Since his father was now able to support him while he was in school, if he worked it was because he wanted to, not out of necessity.

Though he made bad grades at Hollywood High School, and, by his own confession, "preferred the more glamorous things of life, such as pool halls and going fishing and hunting," his show business career started there. The Jantzen Company, a sportswear manufacturer that was then, as now, famous for its bathing suits, sent a company representative to Hollywood High looking for young, "all-American" boys to model their products for magazine ads. The football coach recommended Jim, and he was chosen. He had never posed for anything other than a family photograph made with a Brownie or box camera in the backyard but was assured that that was no problem, since his appearance in a bathing suit would be eye-catching. Sex appeal was as important an aspect of advertising in the forties as it is in the eighties, and though most of the emphasis was on female models, men too were exploited in this regard.

"It wasn't bad," Jim says. "They paid our way to Palm Springs for five days at a time to do modeling sessions for which I was paid a very large fee—twenty dollars an hour." For him, it was an unheard-of sum, and he had trouble reconciling himself to it. He had difficulty comprehending the idea that he was making more money than his teachers at Hollywood High.

When Jim left Hollywood High he also vacated the football team. But he didn't abandon football. He transferred his talent to a team representing the Hollywood Boys' Club.

When Doc Lefevre, the football coach at Norman High School back in Oklahoma, heard that he was playing football for the Hollywood Boys' Club he quickly got on the phone. The Norman team was desperately in need of players; Lefevre had been advised that recruitment had to increase if he was to keep his job. In Norman they take their football seriously.

It was the nudge Jim needed. He had already considered taking his modeling earnings and returning to Oklahoma to think things over, and the coach had given him a reason to do so. He would go back to school, play football, maintain good grades, and generally behave himself. He was welcomed back with open arms but, as he is quick to point out, "I wasn't paid any money because that's illegal." However, he admits that he had the use of a credit card at a clothing store and that he lived comfortably even though he wasn't working very much.

Jim had enough talent as a journeyman punter and linebacker that a scout for the University of Southern California made him an offer to play for that prestigious school, known for its outstanding football teams. But though he liked playing football, he didn't care enough for academics to stay in school to do it. Consequently, when he turned eighteen he quit school and started to drift throughout Texas, Oklahoma, and on to California. He never lacked money, always managing to find a job quickly and to accumulate enough money to facilitate a move when the time was right. At one point he became something of a stevedore, loading freight not onto steamers but semi-trailer trucks. Loving the outdoors, he found it a challenge to work in the oil fields of his native state and in Texas.

He was riding on a breeze, having a good time without any real thought of what tomorrow might bring.

Still, he knew that he was going nowhere—and fast. There was no hope of a professional football career; he'd been injured while playing for Norman High both before going to

California and upon returning, and during a brief hitch in the Oklahoma National Guard he had severely injured his right knee during maneuvers. And though he had worked at an impressive number of jobs, none of them really led anywhere.

His aimless existence continued until sometime in 1950 when the lure of California's beaches and golden girls brought him back to Los Angeles. He again went to work for his father in the carpet-laying business, doing temporary jobs on the side.

Nothing was permanent, a fact vividly impressed upon him when the Korean War broke out in 1950. Legally, he was still a resident of Oklahoma, and he became the first draftee from that state to be inducted into the service during the war. He went into the U.S. Army Infantry as a foot soldier assigned to the Fifth Regimental Combat Team of the Twenty-fourth Division in Korea, where he spent five months and sustained two wounds.

Studio biographies have always listed them as "wounds suffered in action," but because several versions of the incidents have been related by various writers and by Garner himself, they have sometimes been regarded as a kind of joke or publicity stunt. Far from it. Jim did receive two injuries. The first was more embarrassing than painful, but the second was serious.

"I was wounded," he relates, "the second day I was in Korea." While bringing up the rear of a patrol party, he was hit by a shard of shrapnel. "I got hit in the hand and on the edge of my eye." When he got back to the field dispensary he sat down and started picking out the tiny pieces of metal. An officer approached him and said, "Don't do that yourself. Go on inside the dispensary and have them do it. Hell, man, we'll get you a Purple Heart."

Jim obeyed the officer and was officially listed as having received the Purple Heart—though he never did receive it. He sustained his second injury sometime later when his combat team was surprised and overrun one night by Chinese troops. "We spent the whole night pulling back, just trying to cut our losses," he explains. They had started out with 130 men. By morning the attack had left them with 30 tired and worn stragglers just trying to survive. About 6:30 in the morning his group met up with another unit that had also been through a horrendous fight the night before. Together they watched an encouraging event. "We got there just in time to watch some of our navy fighter planes blowing the shit out of the Chinese positions and we were yelling and screaming encouragement to them."

Just then, an AT–6 spotter plane flew over their position, and because Jim's group was not displaying the orange air panels used for identification, the pilot of the AT–6 notified the main squadron that he had discovered a "troop concentration." As a result, all hell broke loose.

"Within a few seconds there were navy Panther jets unloading 20-millimeter rockets at us. I immediately got hit in the butt and my rifle was blown up." Rocket explosions splatter white phosphorus in all directions, so to avoid suffering burns, Jim jumped out of his foxhole and took off without any sense of direction. "I went over the side of a cliff and must have rolled end over end a hundred or so yards down the side of the mountain." He suffered a dislocated shoulder and busted up both his knees. The navy jets sustained their bombardment without letup, so Jim lay low, trying to avoid getting hit again. Having been splattered with white phosphorus, he was in a lot of pain, with serious burns on his neck and back.

A soldier from the Republic of Korea had rolled down the

hill with Jim, and once the planes left the two men climbed back up the hill, where they discovered that the rest of their companions had moved out. They were alone behind enemy lines. Neither of them spoke the other's language, but each understood the predicament they were in. Looking around they spotted an encampment of Chinese soldiers numbering close to two hundred. The Chinese also saw them. "It was the damnedest thing you ever saw," Jim says, "because we walked right on by them and out of sight towards our side of the battleground." The ROK soldier still had his gun and from a distance the Chinese must have thought he was a North Korean soldier with an American POW.

Six hours later, the two men heard the sound of American tanks approaching. The Korean soldier then gave Jim his gun and took Jim's helmet. In case there were some anxious fingers on the trigger, it would look as if an American was bringing in a prisoner.

Jim thought little of his burns. He was more concerned about his injury-prone knees, which were horribly swollen. After some time he recovered and was transferred to a postal unit in Japan, where he spent the next nine months practicing what would become a way of life for him in "Maverick," "The Rockford Files," and dozens of films. He became what is known as a "dog robber"—someone who operates just barely within the law, if *law* is loosely defined. Nothing upsets a soldier more than not getting his mail or not getting it on time. Jim found himself quartered with the base post office in a war-ravaged factory greatly in need of refurbishing. To accomplish that end, he devised a plan that guaranteed the delivery of materials and furniture: He withheld mail until he got what he wanted. Thus, using his influence with a Graves Registration outfit, he managed to have a bar built and stocked with the best alcoholic beverages, plus ice (which nobody else had).

There were other accomplishments: "I built us a theater in the biggest room in the shoe factory, put in hot water and showers, and, miracle of all miracles, managed to have a swimming pool built. It all started from a pile of rubble that used to be a building." To have the swimming pool built inside, he begged, threatened, and cajoled. An outside pool would have drawn too much attention to an unauthorized project and would have been overrun by outsiders. The building had a small basement that, when cleaned up and cemented, served as one of the finest enlisted men's pools in the Far East Command.

Jim was finally given an honorable discharge. In retrospect, it is surprising that they took him in the first place, considering his numerous football injuries and troublesome knees.

With his military career behind him, Jim returned to civilian life and Los Angeles, where he found a job waiting for him with his father. He went back to laying carpet, if only to have an income. He never did like the work, but he had to support himself somehow.

Through military GED tests he had managed to obtain a high school diploma and two-year college certificate, which enabled him to go to college if he wanted to. After a few months of laying carpet, he wanted to. Once again he took to the road, returning to Norman and enrolling at the University of Oklahoma. Though Jim was more interested in playing football for Oklahoma than studying, his previous injuries ruled out the slam-bang action of contact sports. He tried to make a go of college, but without sports to enliven his spirits he only lasted one semester. He hung out at pool halls after school, won a few bucks on the tables and at cards, and "stole whatever I could from the register," while collecting an additional $20 a week in GI benefits.

Six months after arriving at the University of Oklahoma Jim was back in Los Angeles at his father's house again. Weldon welcomed back his gypsy son. He told his son not to worry about food and lodging; he could live at home, but for God's sake get a job that lasted longer than a few weeks or months. What he really wanted was for Jim to stop drifting from state to state and job to job and settle down. Jim agreed to try, but his good intentions weren't enough.

During one of his visits to Los Angeles, while attending Hollywood High School, he had worked at a Shell service station on the corner of Hollywood and La Brea. Just down the block, at the Gotham Drug Store, a fellow named Paul Gregory jerked sodas. He and Jim had struck up an acquaintanceship when Gregory came to the station to buy gas. Gregory's ambition was to become a producer. He had encouraged Jim to consider an acting career, but Jim had just laughed at the idea and had declined Paul's offer to become his agent. He didn't particularly care to be on exhibition. "I had never cared for fan magazines or night clubs or any of the things that were associated with being an actor or movie star." Fan magazines in particular would come to be one of his pet peeves after he achieved stardom.

After returning to California, Jim was driving around Hollywood one afternoon considering his father's advice when he noticed a big sign reading: PAUL GREGORY AND ASSOCIATES. He hadn't seen Paul since the old days but had read somewhere that he was now producing plays and was getting good reviews in national magazines for one of his productions, *Don Juan in Hell*, whose stars were Charles Laughton and Agnes Moorehead. Jim decided to drop in and see him if only to say hello, though he did remember that Gregory had thought him to be the acting type. It was a decision that would lead to momentous change in young James Bumgarner's life.

Paul Gregory welcomed him. He and Jim sat and talked for over an hour. Jim asked him if he still thought he might make it as an actor.

"I certainly do. Take a good look at yourself. Listen to yourself. I think you could do very well if you took what you've got and learned to act. You could have a big career," Gregory said.

At the time Jim had nothing else to do except lay carpet, and he couldn't see doing that all his life, so he agreed to give acting a try. He signed a contract with Paul Gregory and vowed to himself that if he didn't succeed as an actor in five years he would abandon the whole idea and try something else.

Jim's decision paid off. Though he didn't know it at the time, Paul Gregory was an important man. Gregory was associated with Charles Laughton and was being heralded as a rising star on the Hollywood scene. He was endowed with all the accoutrements of Hollywood success, which had impressed Jim and had led to his decision. A very private man not given to living it up, he could often be found at a party sitting alone in a quiet corner observing others rather than trying to be the center of attention. But he understood the power that such a life-style signified.

But Jim's decision did not mean overnight stardom either. It didn't even mean immediate employment. Like any newcomer he was sent out on interviews. When he did cold readings at Universal and Columbia Pictures, his lack of dramatic training was obvious. Neither studio was interested enough to offer him a significant contract, though Universal did offer him a stock contract that was not very promising. It was his good looks that attracted Universal. At the time, Universal was building a stable of youthful actors and actresses—including Troy Donahue, Susan Kohner, John Saxon, and Rod McKuen—and was on the prowl for young talent, especially handsome young men.

Paul Gregory discouraged Jim from signing the Universal contract. He was aware that studios often signed up dozens of contract players, most of whom did not last past the first six months, and felt that Jim had too much going for him to sign that kind of deal. He knew that the path from aspiring actor to star was long and difficult, and he had no intention of short-cutting it. Furthermore, he knew better ways—and quicker ways—to get his new client work.

Jim's encounter at Columbia Pictures had left him in a fighting mood. The Columbia talent coach, Benno Schneider, told Jim: "I don't know what you've been doing, young man, but you really should go back to it. Just because you're young doesn't mean you can be an actor." If Jim had any second thoughts about acting, Mr. Schneider erased them. He now had a challenge that he would meet no matter how long it took.

Jim was fortunate to have an agent who was also a producer, for if his agent were producing a play, he could give his own clients some of the parts available. Paul Gregory was indeed producing a play for Broadway. He had attended the reading at Columbia and had disagreed with Schneider's assessment of Jim. On the basis of that reading, he decided to give Jim a chance in his production of what would become a hit play and later a hit movie. He was producing *The Caine Mutiny*, and Jim was hired at $40 a week to give cues to Lloyd Nolan, one of the stars. He was also assigned to understudy another star, John Hodiak. Jim likes to tell how he appeared in 512 performances and never spoke a line of dialogue.

This is what happened. Once Nolan knew his lines, Jim was assigned to cue Henry Fonda, another of the stars in the production. Eventually Paul gave him a part as one of the judges in the court martial who sat with the other judges merely observing the proceedings. Jim not only sat and observed the staged court martial but enthusiastically observed the actors who held center stage. The play's director was not only a master director but also a master actor—Charles Laughton. To learn from experts like Laughton, Fonda, Nolan, and Hodiak was more than any novice actor could ask for. Jim might not be a college graduate, but he was smart enough to know the opportunity being offered him.

Henry Fonda fascinated him, and he spent hours just watching the way he moved. "It was an experience just watching the way he sat down," Jim says, "but what I most absorbed from watching him was his concentration and professionalism." Jim admits to having borrowed liberally from Henry Fonda when acting in his own films. "I copied much of what I saw in Fonda when I made the film *Support Your Local Gunfighter.*"

Jim sought and received sound advice from the stars of the play. John Hodiak, who became a good friend, gave him pointers about his personality and about how he presented himself on stage. "Jim, you must remember that you have a friendly personality. Ninety-nine out of a hundred people instinctively like you. Forget the one percent who don't. You won't change them. So, that means that ninety-nine out of a hundred in the audience will also like you." This advice couldn't help but give Jim's ego a lift, and it stood him in good stead throughout the years. He has said, "I don't act, I react to what someone else does. People want to see someone on the screen who they enjoy. I've tried to give them that by being natural and part of the scene whether it was in films, television, or on the stage. If an audience gets the idea that you're acting, you're finished. You've got to look real and I think that comes from being real."

Charles Laughton was especially kind to Jim. As a superstar before the phrase was ever invented, Laughton could have well ignored the young man without lines, but he didn't. He was always willing to give advice to an aspiring actor.

Jim was made to feel welcome in New York, but he would never be really comfortable there. It simply was not his kind of town. A kid from Oklahoma might feel comfortable in southern California, but the staccato pace of New York City was too stressful for Jim. The very first night the play appeared on Broadway, Fonda, Nolan, and Hodiak fixed Jim up with a blind date who turned out to be a gorgeous model named Barbara Walters—no relation to the newswoman of that name. He studied briefly at the Herbert Berghof School of Acting, and he also auditioned for two plays, *Bus Stop* and *Black-Eyed Susan*, but declined to appear in either one. "I just couldn't do it. Not then," he states matter-of-factly, "but I could now. I'd just blaze through it and that would be that." At the time Jim couldn't be his own champion. It was the worst attitude an actor could have, and he would have to overcome it if he intended to stay in the business.

Jim was approached by Twentieth Century Fox to do a screen test while he was in New York but decided that if he were to do a screen test it would only be in Hollywood. He reasoned that the two coasts were highly competitive and that while New York was the center for theater, it was Hollywood that ruled the motion picture industry. His reasoning was amazingly acute, given how long he'd been in the business.

Although the film executives in New York thought Jim was a bit crazy to turn down their offer, he bade New York farewell when the play closed and returned to California, where he had his father and a sense of home and security. Actors by nature are not very secure, but Jim never considered himself an actor and probably still doesn't. Family meant security to him more than a job, and what he really needed at the time was to be with his father. He was not far removed from the gypsy who pulled up stakes every three or four months and moved on to what he hoped would be greener pastures, taking his home with him.

While considering what to do now that he was unemployed, Jim took up Twentieth Century Fox's offer of a screen test. Nothing came of the test, but the studio did convince Jim that any actor with a *Bum* in his name was destined to become a loser before he had a chance to make it. It suggested that he drop the *Bum* and use Garner for a last name. Henceforth he was known as James Garner—a name soon to become famous in America.

Exciting things were happening now that Jim was back in Hollywood. Paul Gregory was preparing a road tour of *The Caine Mutiny* and offered Jim one of the starring roles, that of Lieutenant Maryk. It was to be a national tour and would be directed by Charles Laughton. Would he take the job? Absolutely. "I would never have turned down an opportunity to be directed by Charles Laughton whether it be on the stage or on a street corner. I was tickled to death to have that chance. It was a big step up in my five-year plan."

Rehearsals began and Jim struggled doggedly. He had great difficulty projecting his voice and was still so introverted that he had trouble letting go and expressing himself. He was worried that he might not be able to bring off the role after all. Laughton thought differently. He watched and listened carefully as Garner went through his lines during rehearsals. Finally, he asked Jim to join him for lunch at his house. Jim suspected that Laughton was preparing to fire him tactfully. "I wasn't very good in the role and I knew it," Jim admits.

Laughton, however, had no intentions of dismissing Jim from the cast. He merely wanted to give him some advice. "James," he said benevolently, "your problem is that you expect to be bad and are afraid to express yourself. Rather than fail, you do nothing. Don't be afraid to be bad. I've noticed you trying to go straight down the middle of the road. There are no highs and no lows in your performance. Don't worry yourself about being laughed at or disliked. Just give the performance naturally and you'll do just fine."

Jim said he would try and Laughton assured him that if he did anything wrong, "I will let you know." From that point on Jim's difficulties diminished. He learned from Laughton to rely on the director to correct mistakes and just to go out and do the best he could with a role, not worrying about anything else.

He was on the road for several months, playing in Arkansas, Louisiana, Texas, and his native Oklahoma. It was a greater learning experience than the original Broadway production had been because he now had a good part with good lines and the best direction possible. More than ever, Jim Garner was becoming a committed actor.

III

When Jim returned to Los Angeles he brought with him several months of practical acting experience. The national tour of *The Caine Mutiny* was certainly important, but he had also learned a lot from his original role. It took a great deal of concentration to sit through the play without speaking any lines, for he still had to register emotions when reacting to the actions of the other actors. This experience taught him how to listen and also to allow the other actor a fair share of the limelight. This was something he brought to later roles even after becoming a star.

If few people know that Garner posed for Jantzen at sixteen, even fewer are aware that in 1955 he made a Winston cigarette commercial and survived on the money he made from it for almost a year while he made the rounds looking for work.

His money was running out and there were no new modeling jobs in the offing. Fortunately Jim was a man people easily remembered once they'd met him. He was the all-American guy—tall, dark, and handsome, with an incredibly good physique. He dominated any room he entered, his presence overpowering everybody else in any group he might chance to be with. His attributes included a loping stride, an easy swing of the shoulders, and a casual, infectious grin—

the same attributes that had endeared him to his female relatives back in Norman.

He had even more going for him than he realized. Several people at Warner Brothers had noticed him, including director Richard Bare and William Orr (Jack L. Warner's son-in-law). As a result, he was hired to appear in a couple of segments of one of the most popular of the Westerns that were the rage on television at the time—"Cheyenne." "Cheyenne" star Clint Walker was a looming figure on television in the mid-fifties. His character was a Western adventurer in the aftermath of the Civil War—a mean drifter who fought tough men for a misunderstood look or a pretty girl and to whom shootouts were second nature. The series clearly distinguished the good guys from the bad guys, but it was sometimes difficult to tell which one the Clint Walker character was. The series began as part of a trilogy called "Warner Brothers Presents." In addition to "Cheyenne," there was "Sugarfoot," which starred Will Hutchins, and "Conflict," an anthology that featured various actors and had been the springboard for the character played by Will Hutchins in "Sugarfoot."

Garner's "Cheyenne" roles led to a contract with Warner Brothers, where he started at $200 a week. Roy Huggins, one of Hollywood's most prolific writer–director–producers, was also under contract as a writer–producer at Warner Brothers when Garner came on the lot for the first time. Thus, Jim came within Roy's domain at the start of his career in television. Roy has excellent recall of the time.

"Jim was under contract at Warner Brothers," Roy states, "and the pressure was always there to use a contract player. I used him on a couple of segments of "Cheyenne" and he was bad. I mean literally bad. I knew it. He knew it and so did everyone else. Bad because Jim is only good when he is doing the thing that Jim does so well. He's like Cary Grant.

Grant did a film directed by Clifford Odets, *None But the Lonely Heart*, in which Grant played a role that was not a Cary Grant role. This is a long time ago, 1944 I believe. It wasn't a comedy and so it wasn't a Cary Grant picture. It was heavy drama. It bombed and Cary wasn't very good in it. Jim wasn't very good in any of the things he did in the beginning. On "Cheyenne" he was barely adequate. That's all.

"The producers on the lot were doing their best not to use Jim because he was not an accomplished actor, and they were all looking for tried and proven talent. Jim couldn't play leading men or heavies or anything that required that kind of dramatic training. That sort of casting wasn't in his genes in the first place and I doubt he would have been right for those roles even if he had had the training. He wasn't a man who could be plugged into just any part."

Roy was producing "Conflict" at the time and decided to use Jim in a small role. The segment was called "The Man From 1997." Charles Ruggles played the man from 1997 and Garner was given a small role as a con man. "I had written some lines," Roy declares, "that I didn't think for a moment would be read so that they were funny, because they were typical con man lines. Dry lines that had to be read by a man with real understanding of that kind of humor. Dry. Throwaway humor. What was to become Jim Garner kind of humor."

Roy firmly believes that no one does this kind of humor better than Jim. "No one ever did it better. Cary Grant in his own romantic way was able to read drily humorous lines, but no one I've ever seen could play that wry kind of sly humor and do it the way Jim did to make it really great. But I didn't know that at first. One day I was sitting in a project room watching 'dailies' and a little scene came on the screen. Then a guy came into the picture reading that dialogue the way I had written it to be read and never expected to hear it read.

In fact, it was better than I had expected. Here was someone who had an instinct for that kind of wry, from left field, sort of subtle dialogue. It was not just big yuks. Jim Garner has never gotten big yuks. He had created a character based on his capacity to do that kind of humor and I looked at it and said, 'My God! I didn't think he had any talent and the fact is, he's got extraordinary talent and we've never used it because we never knew what it was.'"

Jim's con man was a fellow who couldn't ever quite tell the truth but was nevertheless charming. Roy Huggins said to himself, "I've got to do a series with this guy in which he plays that role."

This didn't happen right away. The studio wanted Jim to get as much experience on the lot as possible. He was somewhat wasted in his early roles. His first film was called *Toward the Unknown*. The cast included William Holden, Murray Hamilton, Charles McGraw, Virginia Leight, and Garner's old friend from *The Caine Mutiny*, Lloyd Nolan. Mervyn LeRoy directed the picture, one of his less memorable ones. It was an independent production done by William Holden's own Toluca Productions, and was co-produced by LeRoy. The story concerns Maj. Lincoln Bond, played by Holden, who aspires to becoming a test pilot while living with the stigma of having broken under communist brainwashing during the Korean War. The film was supposed to model the flight test center at Edwards Air Force Base in California, where experimental test pilots climbed aloft in jets and rocket-propelled aircraft to probe not only outer space but the limits of man himself. It had originally been entitled *Air Flight Test Center*.

Shot on location at Edwards Air Force Base, ninety miles from Warner Brothers Studios, the film was to be as authentic as possible. Jim played Maj. Joe Craven, and Karen Steel was cast as Polly, his wife. Housing was scarce and many of the cast and crew found themselves doubling up in hotel rooms. They were even told by the studio to "bring your own alarm clocks." Due to maximum security, no visitors were allowed on base except families of the stars, and then only after clearance from the base commander himself. Security ID badges were required at all times.

Jim's role was so small that he did not have to report until the film was in its twenty-sixth day of shooting—more than halfway through the shooting schedule. According to studio publicity releases, two very impressive appearances on "Cheyenne" led to his being signed for this film and to his being given a long-term contract at Warner Brothers. Interestingly, in light of future contracts, his contract for the picture called for him only to be "featured on the screen."

It was the fifties, and the Motion Picture Association of America, under the ultraconservative leadership of Eric Johnston, operated a censorship bureau that was politically in line with the House Un-American Activities Committee and with the activities of Senator Joe McCarthy. Consequently, the MPAA saw fit to excise from the film the expression "Nuts!" and Bill Holden's use of the word "Hell!" as totally unacceptable to the association's standards of morality.

Although Jim was not singled out for praise by the critics, after he became famous as Brett Maverick the studio re-released the film to capitalize on his television fame. Generally, however, the critics had very little to say about the film, and very little of what they said was good. But the film was important for Jim because it was a start in the right direction. Perhaps the critics weren't paying attention to him, but Warner Brothers executives were. William T. Orr, head of television production at Warner Brothers, had great faith in Jim, and Roy Huggins wanted him as the star of a series that he was currently preparing. Orr had great influence with his father-in-law Jack L. Warner. He was also much-liked and respected as a production chief throughout the television industry. Consequently, Jim had several well-placed proponents for him at Warner Brothers Studios.

Garner went directly from *Toward the Unknown* into a very bad Tab Hunter picture, *The Girl He Left Behind*. Most of the critics felt that the picture should have been left behind. The picture was shot on location at Ford Ord, California, with the cast and crew headquartered at the San Carlos Hotel in Monterey. Jim drove his own car from Los Angeles to the shooting site and did his own driving while there. He was cast as Preston, Jim Backus as Sergeant Hanna, and a young David Janssen as Captain Genaro. The female lead was played by Natalie Wood, who would later co-star with Garner in one of his better films.

The film was adapted from Marion Hargrove's novel of the same name and was filled with Hargrove's particular brand of military humor, which had been so popular in his previous book-to-film project, *See Here, Private Hargrove*. Although the film was given a mediocre review and Tab Hunter thoroughly panned, the *New York Times* critic Bosley Crowther said, "There are laughs aplenty in this picture, which Warner Brothers has made with David Butler directing. But there is also an air of something wrong. We wonder what would happen to a draftee if he acted the way Mr. Hunter does?" James Garner contributed significantly to the picture's lighter side.

Unfortunately, strong objections by the Motion Picture Association of America led to many cuts, eliminating any semblance of real life from the picture. The association's Geoffrey Shurlock advised Jack L. Warner that he must eliminate Natalie Wood's line, "Remove your hot hand from in under my rib cage," as well as any reference whatsoever to narcotics and hypodermic needles. Expressions like "Broad jumper" and "She was a dry socket" were totally forbidden.

"Screw up" was too suggestive. "Ruffed bustard" was not to be handled in such a way as to sound like "rough bastard."

Even at the studio itself there were doubts about the picture. Frank Rosenberg wrote a memo to Jack L. Warner on May 3, 1956, in which he indicated his concern. "I feel especially duty-bound," he said, "to express my deep concern with which I view the box-office future of *The Girl He Left Behind* as it is presently being prepared." The sneak preview on October 18, 1956, at the Huntington Park (California) Theater confirmed Rosenberg's concern.

None of this really affected Jim's future with the studio. He was not expected to carry the film. That obligation fell to Tab Hunter and Natalie Wood, whom the studio was hoping would capture young America's romantic fancy. It was merely experience for Garner. He was a contract player being used whenever and however he could be used. Under the star system, actors were supposed to be kept busy while they earned their weekly salaries. When the time came, if they merited it, they would be given more important roles. If they did not live up to expectations, they were simply dropped as contract players when the next option period came around. It happened routinely.

Being closely observed by your employers can have either a positive or a negative effect on an actor's career. In Jim's case it appeared to have both. Though he was not being utilized in worthwhile pictures, he *was* being kept busy, honing his craft and learning from seasoned actors.

In November 1956 he began his third picture of the year, *Marshal of Independence* (later changed to *Shootout at Medicine Bend*). Randolph Scott headed the case, which included veteran actor James Craig and newcomer Angie Dickinson. The picture dealt with peaceful citizens of the Quaker persuasion living in a Nebraska valley. When murderous gunslingers invade their serenity they are forced to take up arms to defeat them. Randolph Scott played the good guy, Capt. Buff Devlon, who, with his two pals, Sgt. John Maitland (James Garner) and Pvt. William Clegg (Gordon Jones), helped bring quiet back to the valley.

Although the National Legion of Decency gave the film its approval, rating it "morally unobjectionable" for general patronage, the MPAA had a number of objections. They asked that Warner Brothers "exercise great discipline in staging" the film so that "the finished picture not be excessively brutal in its overall effect upon the audience." The association was being severely criticized at the time for "the amount of brutality in our pictures" and therefore was asking the film companies to adhere more closely to the standards set down by the Motion Picture Code. It hoped that Warner Brothers would respond to its objections to this film.

For instance, in one scene, it was considered bad judgment on the part of the film's producers to permit Scott to hit an Indian with a tomahawk more than once in a fight. It was hoped that such scenes would be merely suggested—that is, done off camera. "Consequently," they said, "may we suggest, that so far as possible you indicate out of frame the specific acts of people being killed." In another scene Devin suggests to Clegg that if a woman he is interested in is the right woman she won't want money. Clegg responded "Who wants the right woman?" Totally unacceptable to the protectors of morality in the MPAA.

There were strong objections to several men being completely nude in a bathing scene although no below-waist nudity was revealed. The MPAA censors preferred the men to be "attired in underwear." In another scene, which takes place in church, the minister is reading to his congregation from the Bible. He speaks the following lines: "Behold there came wise men from the East" as three seminaked men walk into the group. The MPAA thought this "entirely disrespectful and very likely to offend the religious sensibilities of members of your audience."

The scene considered most unacceptable was the following:

DEVLIN: "*Fifty plates of sow bosom! Sow bosom? Sow belly?*"
PRISCILLA: "*I prefer bosom.*"
DEVLIN: "*Well, matter of fact, so do I. More refined.*"

Most of the critics focused on Randolph Scott who was at the end of his career and hadn't been active in pictures for some time. The premise of the film was a good one and Jim's performance adequate. Yet it looked as if he were going to spend his entire career as "the other male lead" or "the leading man's best friend." In fact, the most notable mention of Garner's activities regarding the picture concerned an injury he sustained on the second day of filming. The nature of the injury was never disclosed, and the picture was not interrupted because of it.

To date he had modeled swim suits, performed in a stage play, appeared in supporting roles in Warner Brothers' various television enterprises, and been cast in three films—nothing earth-shattering and nothing that would indicate his potential as a star. What he needed was a film role that would give him some national attention. He certainly had all the attributes of the current breed of stars but for some reason audiences had yet to discover him.

Yet the foundations of Jim's future success had already been laid a few years earlier—not in Hollywood, but in Japan, and quite by chance. James Garner wasn't even in show business in 1951 during the Korean War when two old friends met one day at the Tokyo Foreign Correspondents'

Club. Josh Logan and James Michener had worked together closely during the months when Michener's *Tales of the South Pacific* was being brought to the Broadway stage by Rodgers and Hammerstein as the hit musical *South Pacific*. Logan was the director of *South Pacific* in New York.

During their chance meeting in Tokyo the two old friends spent a great deal of time discussing one subject. Logan was eager for the famous novelist to write a book set in modern Japan that would give the world an inside peek at that country's unique theater arts. The result of that meeting was James Michener's best-selling novel, *Sayonara*.

When casting began for the motion picture *Sayonara*, the role that would eventually become Garner's was far down the list in importance. The two lead characters were an American air force officer and a Japanese woman who fall in love. Rock Hudson led the list of those being considered for the part of the racially prejudiced Southerner, Maj. Lloyd Gruver. Other possibilities included Paul Newman, Jeff Hunter, Don Murray, Tab Hunter, William Holden, Barry Coe, Lee Phillips, Glenn Ford, Montgomery Clift, Cornel Wilde, Kirk Douglas, and Gig Young.

Josh Logan wanted Audrey Hepburn for the role of Hana-ogi, with whom Gruver falls in love. Rock Hudson's name was dangled before her and her agent Kurt Frings. In August 1956, while in New York, Logan sent a telegram to Steve Trilling at Warner Brothers in Hollywood regarding the possibility of securing Miss Hepburn's services. He informed the studio that he had spoken to director Billy Wilder in Paris, who had suggested he contact Audrey Hepburn immediately. "I decided," he told Trilling, "to wire Hepburn at Hotel Rafael in Paris full details including fact Bill Holden and Rock Hudson interested. Suggested starting date late fall and asked if I should send script. So far I have had no reply from her or Frings." He even suggested that her husband, Mel

Ferrer, could play Nakamura, a role that eventually went to Ricardo Montalban. For whatever reason, Audrey Hepburn declined the role and it went to Miiko Taka, a young actress from the Japanese community of Los Angeles. She was hailed as the find of the year.

Of course, Marlon Brando eventually got the lead, and his performance made film history. On the basis of Garner's previous assignments it didn't seem likely that he would be chosen to play Brando's buddy in this picture. Twenty-five actors of varying degrees of stature in the motion picture business—all of whom were better represented than James Garner—were up for the part of Captain Bailey. They included David Janssen, Gary Merrill, Darren McGavin, Robert Sterling, and Ronald Reagan as well as a young actor named John Smith who was represented by Bill Shiffrin (known to employ every gimmick possible to draw attention to his clients). As late as December 11, 1956, a few weeks before principal filming—filming that involved the major stars—was to begin in Japan, Jim had not yet tested for the part. Others had, including John Smith, David Ford, Larry Blydon, and Efrem Zimbalist, Jr.

John Smith was the likely choice—or so it seemed to everyone except James Garner, who really wanted to break out of the mediocre fare Warner Brothers had presented him in. He knew about the wrangling that had gone on with Audrey Hepburn and gossip had it that if the studio signed Hepburn he, Garner, might even get the lead.

"I knew that both Josh Logan and William Goetz [who produced the film for Warner Brothers] thought the ideal matchup would be Marlon Brando and Audrey Hepburn. I also was aware that to get them both was somewhat cost prohibitive since each wanted such a large salary. The budget wouldn't allow for the demands of them both. I also knew, if they opted for Audrey Hepburn I had a good shot at the male lead and I really wanted it," Garner recalls. "I still had the second male lead in mind in case it didn't work out the way I hoped it would." While most actors in Jim's position would have been nervous wrecks, he was as casual and cool as he has always been.

John Smith was equally sure that he would play Bailey, although he had not as yet been signed. Garner, with his usual forthrightness, went to the Warner Brothers front office and talked to casting director Solly Biano. "Solly," he said, "in case I don't get the lead, I don't see why the studio would go out and pay fifteen hundred bucks a week when they've got me here on the lot for nothing."

Biano had other problems. "Look Jim," he said, "don't talk to me. Go see Josh Logan."

Following Biano's advice, Garner not only spoke with Logan but also with William Goetz, the producer. The two were still trying to decide whether to go with Marlon Brando and an unknown Japanese girl or to keep trying for Audrey Hepburn and a lesser-known male lead.

"They finally decided on Brando and the Japanese actress," Garner says, "and so I put in my pitch for the Captain Bailey role." He was very blunt with the two men. By then he had been tested and felt he had done a good job. "Look," he said, "you've seen my test and you know what I look like. I'm also sure you know that I can play this part, so why should you pay so much money for John Smith? I'm already under contract at the studio for two hundred and fifty dollars a week, so I come a lot cheaper and I know I can do a hell of a job in this part."

Whether it was for his brash approach or because the movie-makers actually felt he was the best man for the part, he got it and of course acquitted himself admirably.

The cast finally chosen to make the picture was outstanding: Marlon Brando, Miiko Taka, Red Buttons (who won an

Academy Award for his performance as best supporting actor), Patricia Owens, Ricardo Montalban, Myoshi Umeki (also winning an Academy Award for best supporting actress), James Garner, Kent Smith, and Martha Scott.

Principal photography did not begin until early 1957. The advance forces had moved in December to the location sites at Kyoto, Kobe, and other places in Japan. Garner left Los Angeles on January 8 and arrived in Tokyo January 10 via Honolulu. Brando, who was already in Japan, specifically requested that he be notified of Miiko Taka's flight number and arrival time in Tokyo so that he could meet her. Brando's fondness for Asian women was well known in Hollywood, and Warner Brothers encouraged the possibility of romance between their star and his Japanese leading lady. It didn't matter that Brando was at the time engaged to marry Anna Kashfi, with whom he had been having an affair for quite some time. Jack L. Warner wanted as many photographs of Marlon and Miiko together as possible.

Brando had often stated that he held little esteem for Josh Logan's previous credits, which included such giant Broadway successes as *South Pacific*, *Mister Roberts*, and *Fanny* and the films *Picnic* and *Bus Stop*. According to Kashfi, now Brando's ex-wife, Brando accepted the role merely to get back to Japan where he had created such a sensation making *Teahouse of the August Moon*.

Sayonara was an important picture for Josh Logan, who had suffered a serious nervous breakdown a couple of years earlier but upon recovering had thrown himself back into directing both on the stage and screen. He had done two plays and two films in barely two years. The question was whether Logan could withstand the pressures of such a major undertaking. He had suffered previous breakdowns, and many of his friends felt it was because he worked too hard on too many major productions. When Brando was selected for the lead there was concern. Brando could be very demanding of his directors. Although Logan permitted him to make changes in the script, Brando so rewrote it that Logan had to withdraw his consent, considering the new material to be offensive.

Regardless of temperament, Marlon Brando was one of the biggest and most sought after stars in the motion picture industry. He was "bankable"—that is, any picture he appeared in was expected to make money—and consequently very powerful. If he didn't want someone in one of his films, then another actor was chosen. Jim Garner was thus lucky to grab the role of Brando's air force sidekick in the picture.

Sayonara dealt with interracial marriage and was made when Brando's public involvement in what became known as "causes" was just beginning. He was looking for what he called "moral satisfaction" from this picture. He already had the audience, which gave him the platform from which to denounce prejudice and bias. Josh Logan wanted him to feel comfortable in the part, which was why he had given him permission to make changes in the script. For whatever reason, Brando, who did not easily acquiesce on any issue regarding film making, gave in to Logan when the director explained that the production company needed the full cooperation of the United States Air Force and felt the brass might be offended by some of Marlon's changes.

Nonetheless, it was Brando's picture, and no one was more aware of his prominence than Jim Garner, who was extremely nervous during the shooting of the first scene he had to do with the great star. The two of them were seated in a taxicab. Jim's hands were wringing wet and he fidgeted nervously. Brando noticed and asked, "What's the matter?"

"Well," Jim drawled, "this is my first good picture and I'm a little nervous."

Brando assured him there was nothing to be nervous

about, but that he understood the feeling. "Don't worry," he said. "I'll be there and I'll help you out if you run into any problems." And he kept his word.

"Marlon Brando," Jim says, "was the nicest person you'd ever want to know on a set. He went out of his way to be helpful and to make sure that I was comfortable." Brando became Jim's constant coach, even going so far as to show him how to do a scene, and Jim was in Brando's debt ever after. Jim's easygoing manner complemented Brando's intensity and helped him relax. Jim never tried to upstage the star or take pot shots at his temperament, exhibiting none of the nastiness that is sometimes exhibited by some of Brando's more celebrated co-stars.

Jim can't praise Brando enough. "I think he is the best actor we've ever had. He was a man who didn't just trust everybody to select his material. That's why he had so much confidence in Elia Kazan, who directed him on Broadway in *Streetcar Named Desire*. I'll always have great affection for the man because he was thoughtful and considerate of my position when we made *Sayonara*. Others may complain about working with him, but I found him an absolute joy to do scenes with."

The picture was not without its problems. In some instances Brando was the source of the difficulty, other times he was not. Jim Garner was never directly involved in the turmoil. He merely did his job.

IV

Trouble had already begun when Jim arrived on the set to begin filming the picture. Leon Roberts, the wardrobe man, had collapsed on the set at 9:30 A.M. and was rushed by ambulance to Japan Red Cross Hospital, where less than an hour later he was pronounced dead from a heart attack. It cast a pall over the entire company; innately superstitious movie people on both sides of the camera saw Roberts's demise on the first day of shooting as ominous.

The company was beset with problems. By the seventeenth day of shooting the film was already six days behind schedule. Mechanical failures were the biggest headache. Trucks broke down constantly. One of the planes they used was out of commission part of the time, and the weather was never predictable and generally bad. Due to the fading light in the afternoon, they were often forced to close down production as much as two or three hours ahead of time. Though Garner shot most of his scenes in one take, Brando rarely went with less than four or five takes. After twenty-six days of shooting they were nine days behind schedule.

Numerous problems also had to be ironed out with both the military and the MPAA. In December of 1956, before the picture began principal photography, Jack L. Warner had

written to Gen. Laurence Kuter, commander of the Far East-
ern Air Forces at Fuchu Air Station in Japan, requesting cooperation. He cited his and General Kuter's "very dear friend
General Arnold." Arnold had been the commanding general
of the U.S. Air Forces in World War II.

Kuter responded by praising Warner Brothers for their fair
treatment of the armed services in past motion pictures, but
was hesitant to cooperate on this particular film. He said, "I
judge that the *Sayonara* story reflects far from favorably on
the Air Force and its personnel. I do not believe it desirable
or fair to use Air Force facilities and personnel to support it."
He indicated that he had gone directly to Air Force Headquarters in Washington for further instructions.

William Goetz and Logan were on the verge of panic. They
were in Tokyo waiting to start production and without air force
cooperation there simply wouldn't be a picture. Goetz wired
Warner Brothers' executive Steve Trilling, declaring that "besides air battles this puts us in terrible position regarding trucks,
personnel and food to outlying districts. . . . Hope you can do
something and quickly as time most important."

Meanwhile General Kuter kept himself busy outside of
Japan and was unavailable. He left the matter to one of his
assistants.

The problems were finally ironed out, but not until
Warner Brothers made some significant changes in the script.
The MPAA had its usual objections to language. The phrase
"Damn jet!" was felt to be objectionable and its omission was
requested. "What the hell!" was another undesirable line.
The association was adamant that "This saintly girl" not be
used when referring to a prostitute.

Marlon Brando continued to work "his way." On March 7
the shooting call was for 8:30 A.M. Everyone stood around
and waited until Brando showed up at 11:25. The principal

photography was finally completed on April 19, 1957—nine days behind schedule.

Josh Logan kept up a constant flow of correspondence between the Japanese location and Jack Warner at the Burbank Studios. He was delighted with the film's initial progress and in late January of 1957 wrote to Warner, enclosing some photographs he had taken at a party that Bill Goetz had hosted in honor of Brando on his arrival in Japan. He was particularly pleased that Brando was not sullen or moody. "He was having such fun," he said. "He was in such an expansive mood that I think it bodes well for our picture. Notice the way he is giving the once-over to Miiko Ataka. It was the first time he had seen her in any kind of repose." He assured Warner that "Marlon is all we dreamed of and more because he looked so very handsome in the uniform and has lost a lot of weight."

In February Warner wrote to Logan in the same folksy manner and told him that he was delighted with the dailies. He was particularly pleased with the new Technirama Process being used to film the picture. His major concern seemed to be that there had been "considerable illness in your company." He added, "Judging from the stills there must have been jolly times for Marlon and the Geisha girls. . . . I wish I could be the assistant cameraman or your assistant rather than be here behind a desk."

Everyone connected with the film was sent out on personal appearance tours to promote the picture. Even Brando opened up to the press. In one interview he may have alienated the entire southeastern part of the United States. "I felt," he said, "that I could enhance the cause of brotherhood a little. *Sayonara* is the love story of a jet ace and a Japanese girl. The South seems to be the seat of most prejudice in this country. I thought maybe if I could play this role as a Southerner then maybe some of the people down there would see themselves in a similar situation—a self-identification."

The picture was given a sneak preview for theater owners around the country. Irving C. Ackerman of Ackerman/ Rosener Theaters in San Francisco wrote Jack Warner in ecstasy following a San Francisco screening in July 1957. He described the picture as "superbly presented lavish spectacle, a completely novel theme, a touching, tender, and suspenseful love story together with a seasoning of just the right element of good comedy. The fact that the film contends with a present-day somewhat controversial subject should bring big box office by creating a desire to witness the film. . . . You have another *Giant* on your hands."

Josh Logan was concerned about the music. Irving Berlin wrote the title song, and Logan didn't want it schmaltzed up like an overly sentimental dance number. He cabled Warner Brothers from Hawaii in September and said, "I would hate to cheapen this picture by one of those cornball arrangements of a popular song into the titles."

Before the picture was premiered, however, Warner Brothers did some wholesale cutting in their publicity department. This prompted the Screen Publicists Guild's New York office to fire off the following wire to theater owners:

THIS WILL ALERT YOU TO FINANCIAL DISASTER FACING YOUR FORTHCOMING ENGAGEMENTS OF SAYONARA BY WHOLESALE WIPING OUT WARNER BROTHERS ADVERTISING PUBLICITY DEPARTMENTS NEW YORK. FANTASTIC FIRING OF VIRTUALLY THE ENTIRE UNIONIZED NEW YORK STAFF PLUS PUBLICITY MEMBERS IN HOLLYWOOD ENDANGERS SUCCESSFUL RUN OF SAYONARA. ENTIRE LABOR MOVEMENT PREPARED TO VIGOROUSLY PROTEST. SUGGEST YOU

URGE WARNER ORDER IMMEDIATE REINSTATEMENT
PUBLICISTS, AD MEN, ARTISTS TO AVOID SAYONARA
DEBACLE.

Jack L. Warner was unfazed. He proceeded with plans for
the picture's world premiere, to be held at Warner Brothers
Studios in Burbank, California, on December 5, 1957.
Nothing was spared to present a gala worthy of the studio's
biggest picture of the year. The entire wall adjoining the
north gate at Warner Brothers, which measured 213 feet, was
decorated with Japanese motifs. Tropical plants, tapestries,
oriental prints, and other Japanese artifacts were lit by a bank
of multicolored spotlights as the select guests passed the gigantic display to enter the studio. It was estimated that one
million watts of electrical power were used to illuminate the
galaxy of stars who came to the premiere.

Warner Boulevard, which fronted the Warner Brothers
Studios, was renamed Sayonara Boulevard for the event.
Capitol Records' recording star Gordon MacRae recorded the
title song, and the company bent over backwards to see that it
was released in time for the premiere. The premiere, like the
film itself, was a smash hit despite all the difficulties, which
included union problems. Russell V. Downing, president of
Radio City Music Hall, telegraphed Jack L. Warner following
Sayonara's opening as the theater's Christmas and New Year's
feature picture.

THANK YOU SO MUCH FOR YOUR KIND TELEGRAM,
WHICH ARRIVED ON THE OPENING DAY OF SAYONARA.
IT SEEMS AS IF WE HAVE HAD NOTHING BUT SNOW,
RAIN, SLEET, AND NOW FREEZING WEATHER—TO SAY
NOTHING OF A SUBWAY STRIKE TO HARASS US EVER
SINCE WE STARTED. OF COURSE IT HAS HURT, BUT

THE BUSINESS WE ARE DOING UNDER THE CIRCUM-
STANCES IS A TRIBUTE TO THE STRENGTH OF
SAYONARA AND THE CHRISTMAS SHOW. OTHERWISE IT
WOULD HAVE BEEN NOTHING SHORT OF TRAGIC.

Jack L. Warner wrote personal notes to all the critics and columnists, thanking them for their reviews and to the television and radio hosts who accommodated the stars of the picture while on tour. Jim received numerous plaudits. *The New York Mirror* conservatively wrote, "James Garner is pleasant and likable as the Marine Corps [*sic*] Captain who becomes a buddy of Gruver's." It was a big boost for the handsome young co-star; he had received good to excellent notices in his first important film. His future looked bright.

There was one negative review, which came from *Time* magazine. *Time*'s owner, Henry Luce, was an old friend of Jack L. Warner, and the studio chief took what was for him an unprecedented action by writing directly to Luce to complain. The review began, "*Sayonara* (Warner) is a modern version of *Madame Butterfly* which has gained in social significance but lost its wings—Puccini's music." It became increasingly critical, with such comments as, "Brando is supposed to be a Southerner though his accent sounds as if it was strained through Stanislavsky's mustache." Warner was incensed.

In his letter to Luce, he declared, "You must know that I do not object to reviews generally, but the unfairness of your review on our great motion picture *Sayonara* . . . has caused me and our entire organization great stress." He went on to delineate the costs of producing the picture, plus advertising, promotion, and other costs, and concluded by pointing out that "we have a staggering investment in excess of $7 million in this motion picture. You can readily see therefore how serious this situation really is to us." What he was doing, really, was pointing out the importance he placed on a *Time* critic's opinion and its effect on the box office.

Luce was unmoved. He responded in friendly fashion, but like a father gently admonishing a child he said, "I do not feel in a position to criticize *Time*'s critic. Not being able to go to the picture myself I sent a most trusted assistant who describes herself as a pretty uncritical movie lover. Alas, she was not enthusiastic about this particular picture."

Sayonara made millions. The new camera techniques and Technirama processing afforded a unique insight into Japanese culture, which had never before been captured so accurately in a commercial motion picture. Moreover, they did it with great glamour and beauty. The Japanese were extremely cooperative during the three-month filming schedule. It was the first time that either an American or Japanese film company was permitted to film on the magnificent grounds of the Imperial summer palace in Kyoto. Warners' was also allowed to film sequences involving the principals in the Kabuki, Noh, and Bunraku theaters, which could not have been duplicated elsewhere.

The producer of the picture, William Goetz, hailed it as a cultural breakthrough for the two countries, former enemies who were now attempting to establish a friendship. "It was apparent to me," he said, "that differences between governments and their diplomatic representatives have no relation to the feelings between peoples of different countries. As a result, we left Japan with new friends and a new appreciation of the Japanese people as a whole."

The film was nominated for nine Academy Awards, including best picture and best actor. It won three—two for supporting roles and one for art direction.

James Garner was the real winner. He had appeared prominently in a picture with one of his idols, Marlon Brando, and the picture was with few exceptions deemed a smashing success. Warner Brothers executives were pleased with the performance of their new contract player on the big screen. He had no reason to feel anything but elated. His five-year plan was now forgotten; his days of moving from town to town and job to job were over. From now on the only moving he would be doing was from picture to picture and location to location—which probably satisfied his hunger for movement more than he ever thought it would.

He was learning important lessons about the way Hollywood does business. A good journeyman actor, he reasoned, could always work and make an excellent living if he didn't go overboard with salary demands. "I always worked a little cheaper," he says, "because I saw big stars pricing themselves out of a job all too often. I'd rather be working steady than to be a star without a paycheck." The film moguls appreciated Garner's views on salary, although they would eventually find out that at times his notion of "cheaper" and theirs were not the same.

The original "Maverick" television script was sent directly to Jim while he was still on location in Japan with *Sayonara*. Budd Boetticher had already been signed for a minimum of two weeks to direct the series at $1,000 a week.

When he returned home from filming *Sayonara*, James Garner was returning to more than a television pilot. He now had a real home to come back to. In 1956 he had given up the single life, opting for a wife and family.

Although he has seldom made a public display of his political beliefs, Jim is not devoid of strong political opinions. During the summer of 1956 he found himself at the home of Jess Kimmell, in Hollywood, in the midst of a political rally for Adlai Stevenson, who was running the second time for president of the United States on the Democratic ticket. He was at poolside, where a number of youngsters were playing, and soon found himself engaged in a game called "Monster of the deep" in which he became the monster. He got along well with the children, and they apparently enjoyed having an adult take the time to play games with them.

At that time he noticed a beautiful young woman sitting by the pool watching him cavort with the children. He left the children after a while, swam over to her, looked up from the pool, and said, "Hello." They spent the rest of the afternoon talking and "falling in love at first sight."

What ensued surprised them both. He was a man who had always been his own boss. He shunned attachments, including marriage; he'd never really been close to any one woman for very long. In fact, with women he was really rather timid. Beautiful women made him feel especially uncomfortable. Furthermore, having a family was not a part of his plans. His own family life had been so transient, and the loss of his mother while so young, however repressed, was so painful that he did not want the responsibility of a family. In fact, he rarely discussed his mother's death with anyone. Yet he found it easy to talk to Lois Clarke.

Still, he was wary of commitment. A person who has always been concerned for the welfare of others, he didn't want to risk fathering a child that might be orphaned. And Lois was a woman of independent means. She knew how to take care of herself. She wasn't the least bit interested in marriage, certainly not to an actor whose future was so unpredictable.

But at poolside they talked more than either had intended. Jim learned that Lois was a divorcée and the mother of an eight-year-old daughter, Kimberly. Kimberly was presently a patient at Los Angeles Children's Hospital, where she was recovering from polio. Lois was concerned about her child's prognosis, not romance.

Yet they agreed to see each other again. It never occurred to Jim that he would fall in love with a woman who was the mother of a growing daughter who was seriously ill. Love proved far more infectious and durable than either had imagined. They were together every day after that first meeting, and two weeks later, on August 17, 1956, were married in a civil ceremony at the Beverly Hills Courthouse.

Theirs was a marriage facing difficulties right at the start. Though they were very much in love, Jim and Lois hardly knew each other. Lois had her hands full with Kimberly's convalescence and physical therapy. Jim was just embarking upon his acting career and would soon be separated from his new wife and stepdaughter to fly to Japan for the filming of *Sayonara*. There was a further difficulty, related by Jim's brother Jack in several interviews. "Lois was Jewish and Jim and I had grown up in an area where we knew one Jew in town and everybody poked fun at him, calling him 'Jew Richard.' That we were able to overcome that kind of experience and not be prejudiced when we grew up was something special. My father had other views. He alienated her from the rest of the family."

Despite differences in background and whatever family disapproval there may have been on either side, Jim and Lois made a pact to rely on each other and to share both the good times and the not so good—and there would be many of both. From the outset of his marriage, Jim Garner was a caring, loving husband. He always let Lois know where he was, what he was doing, and when he would be home. When he decided to get married he knew it was to be a lifetime commitment; he was determined not to emulate his father in this regard. One wife, one family—that was enough for him. He had never been promiscuous when he was single, and so he was naturally a loyal, devoted husband.

Jim now had not only a wife but a stepdaughter. Being a stepparent is one of the most difficult jobs in the world. For Jim, working out a relationship with Kim was much more difficult than dealing with a new wife. He loved Lois and she loved him. He accepted her child, but would she accept him?

At first she didn't. Her loyalties were to her father, not some stranger her mother had met and married after a two-week relationship. How could she be expected to accept him so easily when she knew absolutely nothing about the man her mother had married and he knew even less about her?

Although Garner has always discounted anything written about him in fan magazines, he has never denied the truth of an article by Jim Hoffman that appeared in the October 1959 issue of *Photoplay*, which discusses his initial contact with Lois's daughter. It states:

> . . . *at first he babied her. After all, she'd just come home from the hospital, she had some difficulty walking, so he handled her gently and with great patience. But he just couldn't get through to her.*
>
> *One day Kim came home to their small apartment, disturbed by a problem she was having at school. He tried to find out what was bothering her, but she wouldn't tell him. Babying didn't work; so finally, in desperation, he blurted out: 'I can't stand this; please say something—anything!' But she said nothing at all. Then he did something he never thought he'd do, that he didn't even feel he had the right to do. He took her over his knee and spanked her. She didn't cry, she didn't*

*whimper. She didn't say anything, but when he was fin-
ished she darted out of the house into the street, leaving
a very stunned and confused James Garner wondering
whatever had compelled him to take such action. Within
half an hour she was back in the house, happy and bab-
bling as if nothing had happened. She went into great
detail about what had been bothering her and accepted
his fatherly advice. Later he found out where she had
gone when she stormed out of the house. What she had
done was go to a neighbor's house, where she boasted
that, "Jimmy spanked me! My father really cares about
me!"*

Jim has a reputation for becoming very frustrated when
problems arise that he can't solve. Such frustration leads to
anger, which he has always tried to stifle. On occasion he
gives vent to it, as he did with Kim. There is no question that
he learned to care for the child as if she were his own.

Lois understood that Jim often had to be away from home
while filming because she worked in the film industry herself. When she met Garner she was employed as a secretary
for Mark Stevens Productions. She knew that if an actor went
on location, it could be for a few days or perhaps for months.
Against her better judgment she had married an actor; she
didn't walk into it blindly. If anything, she was better
equipped to deal with the situation than most women would
have been. If she didn't know him, she certainly knew the
precariousness of the business he was in.

Hollywood in 1957 was a comfortable place for a man like
James Garner to be working. Regarding film making, it was
probably more conservative than it would ever be again. The
repercussions of Senator Joseph McCarthy's anti-communist
witch-hunts could still be felt. It was the era of Dinah Shore,

Chevrolets, baseball, mom, and apple pie, and ghosts of Roy Rogers and Gene Autry rode the range nightly on network television. The Western dominated the airwaves. "Gunsmoke," starring James Arness, was number 5 early in the year but jumped to number 1 by October. "Gunsmoke's" popularity carried with it several other Westerns: "Tales of Wells Fargo," starring Dale Robertson, number 3; "Have Gun Will Travel," starring Richard Boone, number 4; "The Life and Legend of Wyatt Earp," starring Hugh O'Brian, number 6; "General Electric Theater," hosted by Ronald Reagan, number 7 (although this show sometimes featured dramatic formats, it was by the late fifties essentially a showcase for Westerns); "The Restless Gun," starring John Payne, number 8; "Cheyenne," starring Clint Walker, number 12; "Wagon Train," starring Ward Bond, John McIntire, Robert Horton, Frank McGrath, and Terry Wilson, number 15, and "Sugarfoot," starring Will Hutchins, number 16. Nine out of the top twenty shows in the ratings were Westerns. In between was sandwiched such family fare as "December Bride," "You Bet Your Life," "Alfred Hitchcock Presents," "The Tennessee Ernie Ford Show," "The Red Skelton Show," "Father Knows Best," the ill-fated "Twenty-One," plus the perennial favorites "The Jack Benny Show" and "The Ed Sullivan Show."

Thus, during prime time the networks were saturated with the Marlboro look, cowboys and Indians, white hats versus black hats, horses, guns, and saddle sores. If a new Western series was to be introduced, it would have to be completely different from anything that had ever been done before. Many of the shows were based on fact; for example, "Gunsmoke" concerned the life and times of Matt Dillon, a legendary sheriff of Dodge City, Kansas. Although Roy Huggins is credited with conceiving the idea for "Maverick," a memo dated December 18, 1957, sent by Jack Emmanuel at

Warner Brothers to Bryan S. Moore, also at Warners', related the following story:

In response to your inquiry as to the origin of "Maverick," to the best of my recollection the following series of events took place.

After reading certain source material such as Aces & Eights *by L. P. Holmes,* The Gentle Grafter *by O. Henry, and reading several volumes of* The Get Rich Quick, Wallingford *books as well as other volumes such as* Sucker's Progress *by Herbert Asbury,* ELO Kid Weil *by W. T. Brannon and Joseph R. Weil, and an extensive amount of other materials supplied to me by our reading department, I concluded that it would be a good idea for us to do a series about a gambler after a quick buck from the South during the period 1876–1886—the basic theme being that he cheats cheaters.*

I advised Bill Orr of this in a memorandum along with suggestions for other series. At that time, approximately the first part of December 1956, I suggested that we try to use the title "Cameo Kirby" as I thought the Booth Tarkington novel and play were in public domain. Bill agreed that this was a good idea and we did a copyright search on which there is correspondence between Dinty Moore, Morris Ebenstein, and myself. We found that "Cameo Kirby" was not in public domain by reason of a 20th Century Fox copyright.

When I informed Bill Orr and Roy Huggins that this title could not be used, Roy Huggins suggested the title "Onyx O'Neil" which as I recall Bill didn't care for. Roy subsequently made an oral submission of a story based on 'Onyx O'Neil' to Finlay McDermott for a feature. Later the story was bought for our "Maverick" series on

July 5, 1957 (but not as the pilot due to the fact that in conferences between Bryan Moore, W. T. Orr, and myself, we decided that we needed to base the series on an unexploited property of Warner Brothers owned subject in order to avoid serialization rights).

Roy Huggins then going over Warner Brothers' unproduced properties chose an unproduced book called War of the Copper Kings *by C. B. Glasscock.*

In accordance with a memorandum in our files dated February 5, 1957, I received a call from W. T. Orr asking me for the definition of the word Maverick, *which I gave him. There was some discussion about the use of this word as a title thereafter, and shortly it was definitely decided to use the name. I'm not exactly sure who thought of the name* Maverick *for our central character.*

On January 7, 1957, James O'Hanlan was assigned to do the teleplay on The War of the Copper Kings; *the situation of 'The Apex Law' was contained in the Glasscock book and used in the plot of the pilot. The characters and situations were developed by James O'Hanlan and Roy Huggins.*

It is my contention that the protagonist, Brett Maverick of our "Maverick" series, is the same young unmarried gambler that roamed the west in the period of 1876–1886 that I originally conceived and described to Bill Orr under the name of "Cameo Kirby."

Roy Huggins's first draft of "Maverick," which was presented to Warner Brothers' television production chief, William T. Orr, as a series presentation was as follows:

"Maverick" is a new hour-long dramatic series which will start on the ABC network this September [1957]. It ·

concerns two brothers—Brett and Ben Maverick [later changed to Brett and Bart], handsome, dashing young men in their late 20's—and their adventures in the West following the Civil War. Out on the trail the Mavericks may look like tough, two-fisted cowboys but in town they are fashionably dressed, suave and debonaire, whether coolly outbluffing an opponent at a gambling table or charming a lady in a parlor, Rhett Butlers with boyish smiles. Brett and Bart were raised in Texas by their father, a retired Mississippi River gambler from whom they learned every trick of the gambler's trade and something more: a hatred for cheaters and a respect for honesty in gambling. The father is dead now and since the war the brothers have been making their living as gamblers. Unable to resist a challenge, particularly a challenge to right a wrong. Both of them love to "cheat a cheater." Brett says, "No one is easier to win from than a cardshark if you know his twist."

This trick provides a formula for many "Maverick" scripts. A dishonest person or crook tries to use Maverick for an illegitimate purpose only to be outwitted and see justice done in the end. The Mavericks will readily use the con-man devices they know so well, whether in handling cards or verbal trickery, to serve a worthy cause. Persuasive and likeable, they can sway a crowd as easily as they can sway a single man or woman.

An interesting swindle scheme or method of cheating is a good basis for a "Maverick" script. However, a sound Western story that lends itself to the character of the "Maverick" preface is more than welcome.

Most of the scripts will concern only one of the brothers because an hour show with the same central character appearing weekly is a production impossibility. We are *using the device of two heroes, alternating them each week in the same sort of story. One week we'll feature Brett Maverick and the next week his brother Bart. Warmly devoted to each other, they are of the same reckless temperament. Occasionally we'll do a story in which both brothers appear. In these instances the two roles should be as nearly equal as possible. The Mavericks' exciting adventures in the West are the by-products of their never-ending search for the scar-faced man named Grimes, their fellow-captive in the Union Prison Camp during the war. Grimes had done some informing that had cost the lives of two boys from the Mavericks' home territory. Released soon after because of his service to the enemy, Grimes had told irate neighbors that the Mavericks were to blame for the boys' deaths and [that] they had hastily left for parts unknown.*

Branded as traitors upon their return home at the end of the war, the Mavericks realized that they would have to track Grimes down in order to clear their reputations. While the search is referred to upon occasion it is not a major part of the story line nor is it a grim quest for vengeance. For the Mavericks, with their lust for life, their humor and their ability to attract both adventure and beautiful women, are not grim young men. They are enjoying their travels and their escapades immensely. Brett neatly sums up the search for Grimes when he says, 'It isn't that I want to go back home so much—the important thing is to be able to go home.'

So—Brett and Bart Maverick roam the West gambling and engaging in audacious enterprises and winning by honest means except when the swindler really asks to be taken. And if a little of the swindler's money 'sticks' to their fingers—occasionally—well, Brett and

Bart are only human and their efforts are usually in a good cause.

Experts at talking their way out of a jam, the brothers can use their fists or even resort to a gun when words fail. No models of irritating perfection, they are vital devil-may-care young men whose virtues and faults we expect will form a basis for one of the season's most intriguing Western drama series.

The Mavericks' character was almost James Garner personified, and such was the situation he faced immediately following his return from Japan and *Sayonara*.

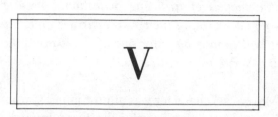

V

Before Jim shot the first scene of "Maverick" another plum fell into his lap. Charlton Heston was set to star in a film called *Darby's Rangers* for Warner Brothers. The first day of shooting was rapidly approaching in April, and the studio still did not have a signed contract from Heston. Agitated with Heston's foot-dragging the studio sent him a telegram, setting 5 P.M. on April 19, 1957, as the deadline for his compliance. Otherwise he was off the picture and the studio's contract with withdrawn.

Heston sent the following telegram to Warner Brothers on April 19:

IN RESPONSE TO YOUR TELEGRAM TO MCA SETTING 5PM TODAY AS THE DEADLINE FOR ME TO SIGN AND DELIVER YOUR PROPOSED CONTRACT IN CONNECTION WITH DARBY'S RANGERS, I AM COMPELLED TO INFORM YOU THAT I CANNOT ACQUIESCE TO SUCH INASMUCH AS THE CONTRACT APPARENTLY CONTAINS TERMS NOT A PART OF THE DEAL MCA MADE WITH YOU ON MY BEHALF. I AM READY, WILLING, AND ABLE TO BOTH SIGN AN EMPLOYMENT CONTRACT AND RENDER MY SERVICES IN CONNECTION WITH DARBY'S RANGERS IN ACCORDANCE WITH THE TERMS ORIGI-

NALLY AGREED UPON. HOWEVER, WITHOUT AT-
TEMPTING TO COMPLETELY ITEMIZE THE POINTS AT
ISSUE ONE OF THE SUBSTANTIAL DIFFERENCES AP-
PEARS TO BE THE CONTRACTUAL WORDING COVERING
YOUR OBLIGATION TO ACCOUNT FOR AND PAY ME ON
THE BASIS OF 5% OF THE WORLD GROSS RECEIPTS
DERIVED BY YOU AND YOUR SUBSIDIARIES AND
OTHER OF YOUR DISTRIBUTION ORGANIZATIONS. I
UNDERSTAND THERE IS NO DISAGREEMENT AROUND
THE DEAL IN THIS RESPECT BUT THERE SEEMS TO BE
A DIFFERENCE OF OPINION AS TO WHETHER THIS
PHASE OF THE DEAL AS WELL AS CERTAIN OTHER AS-
PECTS ARE PROPERLY DESCRIBED IN THE CONTRACT
IN QUESTION. I HOPE THIS CAN BE SATISFACTORILY
RESOLVED BY BOTH OF US SO THAT WE CAN MAKE A
PICTURE THAT WILL BE MUTUALLY ADVANTAGEOUS. I
CERTAINLY AM DESIROUS OF THAT.

Desirous or not, the studio considered Heston's response to
their offer to be negative and it was withdrawn. In the meantime, there was a picture to be made, and it was already in
the final stages of preproduction, with shooting set to start
shortly.

James Garner has always considered April his pivot month.
He was born in April, wounded in Korea in April, and in
April 1957 he learned that he was to become a father for the
first time. So he must have considered it the good luck of his
birth month when Warner Brothers gave him a new seven-
year contract and the lead role in *Darby's Rangers* that had
originally been intended for Heston. It would not be the last
time that he would by default inherit a prize assignment of
another star.

Still Garner felt he had been cheated. The "Maverick"
television pilot was completed by the time shooting actually

began on *Darby's Rangers,* and it was only after he had signed to do the picture that Jim found out that the "Maverick" series had been sold to a network. He relates how he was signed to a new seven-year contract. "At 5:30 in the afternoon on the day Heston was given as a deadline to sign for the picture I was called in by the studio brass. I was told to report to the television executive offices, not motion picture. They told me what a great guy I was and how they wanted to give me a raise for being such a good boy. I was making $250 a week. In a few months my contract would call for an increase to $350 a week. But they were all heart. They wanted to give me the $350 raise right away and as a bonus they would extend my current contract another year and a half, which created a new seven-year contract."

He turned them down. He wasn't exactly sure what the studio was up to but he'd been in the business long enough to know that studios weren't altruistic. They didn't give actors hefty raises prior to option time without an ulterior motive.

A compromise was effected. Warners' offered Jim $500 a week. He couldn't say no. His wife was pregnant with their first baby and Kimberly was just out of the hospital from her bout with polio, so expenses were way up.

On Monday morning he discovered why the studio had wanted him to extend his contract and accept $350 a week. He had been given the Heston role—a starring role. But with the new contract, he would not have to be paid a star's salary. He didn't like the devious methods they had used on him but he figured he would bide his time. "I thought," he says, "if "Maverick" is sold as a series and the movie does well, they'll tear up my old contract and write a new one. I had a lot to learn."

Darby's Rangers was a story of American troops in World War II—all volunteers. It was a true story, based on the career and exploits of Col. William Orlando Darby, who was considered among the most outstanding and brilliant combat commanders in World War II. Darby's Rangers, as they were known, were usually selected from thousands of applicants from two of the best trained and finest divisions in the army. They were among the first American troops overseas, and their heroic exploits were brought to the screen in this picture. The production notes of the film state, "In North Africa and Sicily and elsewhere the Rangers carved a glorious chapter in American military history." It was learned, after he was chosen for the role, that Garner bore an uncanny resemblance to the real Colonel Darby.

Singing star Ella Logan (the only one to entertain the Rangers behind the battle lines in Italy, and adopted as their favorite) presented James Garner with a Ranger patch to wear in the film. The patch had been presented to her by Col. William Orlando Darby a few weeks before he was killed in action.

The idea to do a picture based on Colonel Darby's life originated with Hollywood producer Robert Arthur in 1950. The film would be directed by Rudi Fehr—his first directorial assignment at Warner Brothers. He wrote Warner a note thanking him for the opportunity and promising his best efforts in December 1950. By August 1951 Sheilah Graham was reporting in her gossip column that Errol Flynn would play the lead role, but for whatever reason the picture idea was shelved until 1957.

If ever a film was plagued with turmoil and discontent, this one was, though it did have its lighter moments. Actor John Hudson's aggressive agent, Bill Shiffrin, hired a helicopter and had it hover over Warner Brothers Studios for twenty-five minutes. The helicopter carried a one hundred-foot-long streamer that proclaimed: JOHN HUDSON FOR DARBY! It created such a furor that director Mervyn LeRoy had to stop shooting No Time for Sergeants on the back lot. The FCC was called to see if some federal rule wasn't being violated but finally the director, William Wellman, phoned Shiffrin and said, "For God's sake, send the man in to see me but get that goddamn sign out of the air."

Hudson did not get the part, nor did Robert Stack, another of Shiffrin's clients, who was also up for Darby.

Further controversy arose when Tab Hunter, who had starred in *Lafayette Escadrille*, which had been directed by Wellman, was wanted in a co-starring role opposite Etchika Choureau because the two had produced such good chemistry in the previous film. Hunter (having just achieved great popularity after playing several leading rolls and making a million-selling hit in his first recording, *Young Love*), refused the role, complaining that the part was too small.

The two most powerful gossip columnists in the history of Hollywood went after Hunter. Louella Parsons announced his suspension by Warner Brothers in her column of May 2, 1957: "No movie. No records. That's what it amounts to in the case of Tab Hunter, whose first record, "True Love," sold over a million. Tab refused to do *Darby's Rangers* and since Warners' has him under exclusive contract there isn't a thing he can do without permission. Heretofore Jack Warner has let him do TV and records for Dot but he feels Tab owes a certain allegiance to his Warner bosses. Tab's pretty bitter about the whole thing, but I'm betting it will all be worked out and Tab won't have to go out in the garden and eat green worms." It wasn't worked out.

Hedda Hopper was more vicious: "Tab wouldn't play in it because he didn't think the part was good enough. I'd like to ask how a fellow as young as Tab gets that way."

Of course, Jack Warner had been on the phone with both these charming ladies. One of his charges was misbehaving and he intended to punish him for it. In his book *My First 100 Years in Hollywood*, an indication of Warner's feelings about Tab Hunter was expressed by his asking the question, "I wonder whatever happened to Tab Hunter?"

Dennis Hopper, another of the petulant young actors of that era and also a Warner Brothers contract player, became so upset when he didn't inherit the Tab Hunter role that he threatened to ask for his release from Warner Brothers. Jack Warner considered him just another young whelp and gave the role to Edd Byrnes instead. (Byrnes would become a household name as Kookie on the television series "77 Sunset Strip.")

As far as the public was concerned, the picture would stand or fall with the performance of the star; the public rarely blames a writer or director for a picture's failure. The MPAA, on the other hand, was primarily concerned with language and situations. Its objections to the movie began with the lyrics to a marching song in the film entitled "The Roger Chant." The lyrics were all right except for two lines: "We love our women hot," and "We trained like hell." It further objected to what "appears to be an illicit sex relationship" between two characters, the "knifing of a dummy" on camera, and the expression "For God's sake," which was deemed unacceptable as being "an irreverent use of the name of God."

The Department of the Army insisted on evaluating the screenplay—a form of censorship. After reviewing the screenplay submitted by Warner Brothers, they gave the following evaluation:

1. *This office has reviewed and evaluated Warner Brothers feature motion picture estimating script of the movie* Darby's Rangers . . . *and makes the following comment:*
   A. GENERAL COMMENT: The script in its present form is entirely unacceptable to the Department of the Army. When this project was reactivated on January

10, 1956, it was hoped that Warner Brothers would produce a moving picture that would adequately portray the exploits of the Rangers and those of its Commanding Officer, Colonel Darby. Instead, the present script is a loosely woven pattern of Ranger training and combat interspersed with an overabundance of sex. It is unfortunate that the Ranger story with all the material available has been fictionalized to a point where the prestige and esprit de corps built by these men in combat is completely lost.

B: SPECIFIC COMMENT: It is suggested that the screenplay could be considerably strengthened as follows:

(1) The role of Colonel Darby should be built up to portray the type of leader he really was or bring in his leadership through the eyes of his men.

(2) The love interest should be commensurate with the rest of the action so that it does not overshadow the combat sequences.

(3) It is understandable that not all of the Rangers' combat exploits can be shown but a more comprehensive account by the narrator or montages could improve the situation.

(4) The ending including the Battle of Anzio can be greatly improved. The death of Colonel Darby should be taken into consideration in relation to the impact he and his men had on future Infantry training. Perhaps a training sequence with a superimposure of Colonel Darby might prove an effective ending.

2. This office believes that the story of the Rangers could be a truly great motion picture enhancing the prestige of the Army. No other unit in Army history exemplifies such high standards of individual courage, initiative,

ruggedness, fighting ability, and achievement. We be-
lieve a portion of Colonel Darby's message to his men
most adequately expresses our position. "We the living
Rangers will never forget our fallen comrades. They, and
the ideals for which they fought will remain ever present
among us for we will understand the extent of their he-
roic sacrifices. They will never be considered dead for
they will live with us in spirit."
3. This office is ready at any time to discuss changes in
the present script with the producer or its representatives.
It is hoped that Warner Brothers will, in this case, un-
derstand the Army's position and be amenable to discus-
sion relative to a script revision.

Though Jack Warner wasn't about to allow it, what the
army wanted was a documentary. It was particularly upset
with the love interest between one of the characters and an
Italian girl. Even religion was an issue. The army felt a wedding scene was objectionable because the priest "questioned
the couple whether the children would be brought up as
Catholics." They wondered whether it would be played as
comedy and whether everyone in the audience might laugh
except the Catholics.

Interservice rivalry also came into the picture. There was
one scene in which Colonel Darby says to General Truscott:
"The marines are all committed to the Pacific. The army
must have a specifically trained, highly skillful force to land."
The army preferred that "you do not mention the marines as
the inference is the army's infantry is not properly trained for
such landings. . . . If you must mention a commando, we
would prefer you use the British commandos as a comparison."

Despite all of these difficulties, production of *Darby's*
Rangers went ahead. The cast was rounded out with Etchika

Choureau, Jack Warden, Joan Elan, Stuart Whitman, Torin Thatcher (who was a lieutenant colonel in the British forces in World War II), Edward Byrnes, Venetia Stevenson, Peter Brown, Murray Hamilton, Adam Williams, and Corey Allen. Additionally, William Wellman, Jr., son of the director, who had portrayed his own father in *Lafayette Escadrille*, received his second film part as a serious young infantryman. It was not generally known around Hollywood that the senior Wellman had been a hot-shot pursuit pilot with the famous Lafayette Escadrille during World War I, was shot down in battle, and sent home with a broken back. Wellman was an excellent war picture director and had to his credit the great air picture *Wings* as well as *Island in the Sky, Men with Wings, The High and the Mighty, Beau Geste, Battleground*, and the *Story of DiAngio.*

Wellman ran his productions like a military camp. He immediately took the title of "general" for the duration of production and, as such, saw to it that the principals, the extras playing rangers, and the crew received an intensive and grueling daily workout. Real Rangers were on the set as drill instructors to assure accuracy. They included Sgt. Richard Sandlin (who had served in Korea in the Fifth Regimental Combat Team with Garner) and Second Lt. Ola Lee Mize (who won the Medal of Honor in Korea, having killed more than eighty Chinese soldiers). The overall military technical advisor from Fort Benning, Georgia, was Col. Roy Murray.

A bulletin was posted on the set and a copy sent to everyone involved in the picture, to be observed on the first day of shooting. It was signed by order of Colonel Murray, who was technical advisor on the film.

TRAINING SCHEDULE FOR ALL DARBY'S RANGERS ACTORS UNDER THE COMMAND OF GENERAL WILLIAM WELLMAN.

HEADQUARTERS, FIRST RANGER BATTALION,
APO 464 U.S. ARMY

Monday, April 15, 1957:

0800 *Wardrobe fittings, welcoming of troops and orientation to their mission, introduction of technical advisors and the staff. Welcoming of the troops by General Wellman.*

0930 *Ranger film footage taken at Fort Benning for orientation and inspiration.*

1000 *Assembly of actors to squads, issuing of weapons, alignment of platoons. Uniform fatigues, rifles, packs, etc.*

1100 *Close order drill conducted by Sgt. Sandlin.*

1200 *Lunch*

1300 *Weapons training. How to hold and carry an M-1 rifle, the BAR mortars, tommy guns, etc.*

1400 *Weapons training continued. How to load and reload and fire all basic weapons.*

1500 *Small unit tactics—assault section in action, position of riflemen, automatic weapons men in squad maneuvers crawling on ground, running for cover, covering fire, etc.*

1600 *Unarmed combat (demonstration by Sgt. Sandlin and Lt. Mize) group participation.*

This was just opening day. A new set of orders was posted each and every day of the production.

Prior to the beginning of principal photography a unit was on location in Culver City simulating battle at night. An interoffice memo cautioned, "The City of Culver City had had many complaints about late night explosions and firing there . . . being very strict about stopping this at 10:30 P.M., although regular photography can be done all night." Even the Air Pollution Control District required the studio to secure a special permit when explosions produced smoke.

Filming began in early May, and principal photography was completed on June 21, 1957. It was shot in forty-four days on a forty-five-day schedule. The Anzio Beach scenes were shot on location at Camp Pendleton, south of Los Angeles, while the exteriors of the Scottish countryside and hillside battle line were filmed at the Warner Brothers Ranch. Wellman's "generalship" attracted other Warners' stars to the set. Alan Ladd, who was filming *The Deep Six*, dropped in both to observe the "general's" command and to congratulate Garner on his elevation to stardom. Bette Davis spent half a day watching Wellman direct scenes. It was her first visit to her old studio in many years. Wellman was quite a showman and got lots of publicity by running the set like a military outfit.

Warner Brothers went all out to publicize the shooting of the picture. Nobakuzu Kishi, the son of the prime minister of Japan, watched a reenactment of the Battle of Anzio as the guest of Wellman and Garner. The director and star also hosted the fifteenth anniversary of the Southern California Survivors of Darby's Rangers.

Louella Parsons was one of the first to comment favorably on *Darby's Rangers*—and James Garner. "The talk of the town," she chirped, "is James Garner, who came over so big at the sneak preview of *Darby's Rangers*." *Variety* commented: "Garner is especially effective as the officer dedicated to his rangers, lending authority and understanding to the role. His initial star assignment is a theatrical feature." And the *Hollywood Reporter* also raved about Jim and his "quiet, hard-bitten authority as the commander."

These comments were made before the film was released to the general public. In the meantime, Garner went immediately from being Colonel Darby to filming episodes of "Maverick." Roy Huggins remembers well the beginning of "Maverick."

"I created 'Maverick' for Jim Garner," he states, "but it was Garner who created the character. He was a con man who would lie at the drop of a hat. A pretty girl could come running up to him on the street and say, 'I need help.' Jim would point and say, 'The sheriff's office is right over there, Ma'am.' He was the antihero. Don't get involved. But do it with charm so you get away with it and I did 'Maverick' and 'Maverick' worked."

The show was not an easy sell by any stretch of the imagination. "God," Roy exclaims, "we had all kinds of trouble with it. First of all, it was the most unorthodox of all the Western series already on the air, which right away put it in the category of being 'new.'"

The networks have always complained that they want fresh, new products, but in the final analysis, when money counts, they have always preferred something that has already been proven. "Maverick" was a show that not only had not been proven, it had never even been tried. Finding a sponsor was only one of the numerous problems that accompanied the launching of the show. There were problems with the studio, too.

"I convinced the studio that we should do it," Roy explains, "and they went along, I believe, because I was able to do the pilot as an episode of 'Conflict.' It didn't cost them anything. I had come up with a story. In fact, I had to come up with two stories. The first one I invented, so they would have owed me a royalty. The studio turned that idea down. They said, 'No, we won't do it. You have to take a published story.' So I looked through their list and found a story with a bit of history about the copper mines. I used that and was able to attribute the story, although the story wasn't from the book. The idea was from Glasscock's book, so he received credit for being the writer of the first 'Maverick' story, which was actually the second one. We did it but it was a hard sell. It sat on the shelves for a year."

The only reason it sold was because Henry Kaiser, the industrialist who made his millions in steel and Liberty Ships during World War II and went on to establish a conglomerate of industrial plants, happened to see the pilot.

"Kaiser," says Huggins, "was a bit of a con man himself. I think he saw himself in 'Maverick' and he said, 'I want that show.'"

All of Kaiser's friends advised him against buying the show. He phoned one of them, Art Linkletter, from Hawaii to ask whether or not he should sponsor "Maverick," to be aired on Sunday nights between 7:30 and 8:30.

"I would absolutely advise you not to do it, Henry," Linkletter told him. "There are a zillion Westerns already on the air. Besides, you'll be up against three top-ten shows in 'Ed Sullivan,' 'Steve Allen,' and 'Jack Benny.' I guarantee this 'Maverick' show will die like a dog." Linkletter loves to tell just how much or how little faith Henry Kaiser had in his opinion.

It was like going up against "Dynasty" plus "The A-Team."

"Henry didn't know anything about television," Huggins reveals. "He just liked the show and wanted to sponsor it. He said, 'I want to do it. I like that character. I like that show.'

"So Henry bought that show and never looked back. He didn't become a megamillionaire by not taking a chance once in a while.

"I had faith in the show, but I'm not too sure about the studio at that point. Kaiser felt it was a winner all the way simply because he liked it. So we went on the air with

'Maverick' on Sunday night, September 22, 1957. Our show was on ABC. The first half-hour was covered by CBS with 'The Jack Benny Show.' At eight o'clock we competed against 'Ed Sullivan' on CBS and 'Steve Allen' on NBC. It was enough to discourage any newcomer."

There was no feed-in from the news because in those days the news came on much later in the evenings on Sundays. The show had to stand on its own. And it was Roy Huggins's responsibility to see that it did.

Huggins decided early on that one star alone would not carry the show. The studio agreed. There would have to be an additional character—Brett's brother, Bart Maverick. By the time an actor was selected to play that role, Garner had already filmed eight or ten segments of the series.

"I alternated between Jack Kelly and James Garner. I had known Jack Kelly. He was in a short-lived series at Warners called "King's Row." He was a very nice guy and a very funny man in person. He's the most wonderful person in the world and much funnier in person than Jim Garner. He is also quite an intelligent man. Very literate.

"The truth is I didn't think I could get twenty-six shows on the air with only one actor. I didn't think I could make it because it takes more than a week to shoot a show. Actually, we had eight working days to put the show together, and so every week I was losing anywhere from one to four days and I was looking toward the end of the season and saying, 'Hey, I won't make it. I will be up to air date by the time I've done about nineteen shows. So I have to have two Mavericks.'"

Jim Garner has been compared to Clark Gable on numerous occasions because of his innate sense of humor. Huggins believes that analogy to be erroneous. "I don't think Gable did this kind of humor. Garner has it over them all because he is effortless. That's the magic word. Gable was not effortless. He worked to make humor. His humor is strained.

Garner doesn't work at it. It is in him. I'm sure he never thinks about it. He just knows. It's a down-deep feeling in his gut somewhere. He knows how to read that funny dialogue and very few people even know how to write that kind of dialogue. How often has Garner gotten the kind of thing he does well? Not often."

It is the unanimous opinion of everyone connected with the series that James Garner was "Maverick," not Jack Kelly. "But I'll tell you an interesting thing," Huggins explains, "and this is why the show later won an Emmy. We never lost a single member of our audience when Kelly was on. It was Garner one week and Kelly the next—and once in a while I'd put them together. Jim's shows never got a higher rating than Jack's. Maybe a seventh of a point difference once, but that means nothing. I know very well just instinctively that it was Garner, however, who made the show succeed. Nevertheless, Jack Kelly, every other week, got the same forty plus share. And it was always enough to win the time slot and be in the top ten after the first year."

VI

The first episode of the series was entitled simply "Maverick."
Budd Boetticher was the director, but for reasons that remain
unclear Les Martinson took over directorial duties for one or
two days of the shooting. The episode starred James Garner,
Edmund Lowe, John Litel, and Leo Gordon. The famous
thirties cowboy star Bob Steele had a bit part on the final day
of filming, as did Kermit Maynard, whose brother Ken was
another famous cowboy actor. The episode ran as part of
Warners' "Conflict" series. The first regular episode of the
series began shooting on April 23, 1957, and was directed by
Richard Bare. Appearing in addition to Garner were Joanna
Barnes, Dick Reeves, John Russell, Claire Carlton, and John
Qualen.

Jim's recollection of the "Maverick" pilot differs from that
of Roy Huggins. He recalls that it was a remake of an earlier
Errol Flynn film called *Rocky Mountain*. He swears that he
even wore the coat and vest that Flynn had worn. "They
used stock shots from the Flynn movie, so my clothes had to
match up." According to sources at Warner Brothers, both
men were right. They did indeed use stock shots from the
Flynn movie, but the story was conceived by Huggins and
had nothing to do with the original Flynn film.

Although Jim has tended to shun interviews over the years,

he had managed to obtain a lot of publicity from small gestures. Never one to overlook his popularity back in Norman—anything he does will be picked up by the Oklahoma City papers, which are distributed statewide—he has always welcomed the "folks from back home" when they come to Hollywood. During the summer of 1957, while he was working on the first season of "Maverick," some youngsters from Norman came to California expressly to see their home town success story. Eddie and David Massey and their six-year-old brother Mark were entertained by the Garners. Jim took the two older boys to the set for the day, and young Mark—studio rules prohibited the presence of anyone under twelve on a shooting set—was entertained by Lois at the Garner apartment in the San Fernando Valley. The boys returned to Norman with considerable praise for their hosts, and the Oklahoma newspapers ran it throughout the state as a great human interest story—and it was. Many stars are known to snub fans. Jim has never done that.

While Garner was under contract at Warner Brothers (and later when he made films for other studios) he was expected to give interviews arranged for him by the studio. In the fifties fan magazines were the source of most interviews. Jim hated them—and still does. But whether the stars liked it or not, the studios cooperated completely with the fan magazines because of their importance in keeping Hollywood within the purview of the young fans, who have always had the most influence at the box office.

During the early days of "Maverick," therefore, Jim sat through dozens of interviews, most of which caused him a great deal of discomfort. Asked about his formula for success at the time, he said, "I've never felt there was a magic formula, or a great talent that singled me out for special privileges. I just think through luck and circumstances, I got around to doing what I'm best equipped to do. That's all."

Jim was learning that stardom—or the climb to stardom—involved more than acting in front of a camera. Now he *had* to talk about himself. Jim found it embarrassing. But he also used these interviews as a means of airing his grievances on everything from fan magazines to studio executives to television producers, whom he often accuses of stealing from him. He may have caused studio publicity departments considerable difficulty, but magazine writers have loved the controversy he has generated simply because he says whatever is on his mind without worrying about the consequences. He really doesn't care what people think about his opinions.

Most interviewers want the same information, he complains. "They want you to analyze yourself for their benefit, then they write what they want to anyway. I don't know how many people can be totally objective when they are talking about themselves. I see myself as a combination of a lot of things. I dream a lot and I love it. But don't think I always take my dreams seriously. It is just a lot of fun and I don't see any reason to change that."

Garner was immediately in the national spotlight with the introduction of "Maverick." ABC had taken a big risk with what was considered a totally untried product—and one with a major sponsor. But ABC was "the new kid on the block"; it hadn't gone on line on a regular basis until August 1948. If anybody in the industry could afford to take chances, it could. Everything else it had put up against Ed Sullivan had failed. Even NBC couldn't conquer him, and it had been competing with CBS since the advent of network television in 1941, when both networks were granted commercial licenses for their stations in New York. ABC had been trying to catch up throughout its early years.

Nobody expected "Maverick" to knock its competitors out of the screen—not even ABC. Yet the show was an immediate success. Jim therefore became a recognizable face. People began to ask about him, and they listened to what he had to say. As the star of a Sunday night prime-time series he was an important voice in the industry. He therefore had to reassess the relationship between his personal and his professional life.

Interestingly, the result was that his family became increasingly important. Lois was a down-to-earth woman who wasn't swayed by stardom, which was good for Jim. Although he never took himself too seriously, it was still nice to come home to a wife who provided a totally different atmosphere from the one he had been working in for twelve to fourteen hours a day. From her perspective, he was like any other man; he came home from work expecting a good meal and lots of love and affection and understanding. That's exactly what she gave.

After their initial difficulties, Jim and Kimberly truly became father and daughter, and on his days off from the studio, it was not unusual to find the entire family enjoying the attractions at Disneyland. All three enjoyed family outings. For Jim, it was as if he were reliving his childhood through Kimberly. When Kimberly was thrown from a horse and was afraid to ride again, Jim took her out to director Budd Boetticher's ranch, and under Budd's gentle guidance she overcame her fears and they rode together. Excursions to Budd's place and to the homes of other friends increased as Jim's popularity soared, for it was no longer easy to show up in public places and have any privacy.

It was on the set of "Maverick" in the first year of the series that Jim's temper began to make an appearance. But he never took it out on others—only on himself. He developed the habit of smashing his fist into a wall, a door, or whatever was nearby when he became frustrated. Today the little finger on his right hand has a pronounced crook—the result of numerous breaks caused by assaulting hard objects with his fist. He shrugs it off as the result of everyday events.

Writing stories for "Maverick" was not easy. The producers were forever looking for new stories. As early as July 1957 the studio was aware of the problem. In an interoffice memo from Jack Emmanuel to Roy Huggins, the frustration was evident:

> *Despite the fantastic amount of our coverage for "Maverick" we have failed to come up with enough suitable stories for this series. Of necessity we are going to be forced to develop some of our own stories and the best method of doing so in my opinion is to develop our own springboards or premises, base them on well-known swindler or gambling incidents and then talk to writers who have had experience and a background of writing and selling original stories.*

Racetrack stories were high on Emmanuel's list. Great racetracks existed during the 1870s from Missouri and Kansas west to Montana and Colorado, and even in California. Quarter horses were then at their height of popularity. One of the favorite methods of cheating in quarter horse races was to disguise a thoroughbred as a quarter horse and enter him in a race. There were fabulous characters from the racing world who could provide the focal point of a show: Pittsburgh Phil, Yellow Kid Weil, Harry Fink, Bet-a-Million Gates, Colonel Bradley, Arnold Rothstein, and a dozen or so others.

Land scandals, fleecings over railroad rights, and mining frauds were other possiblities. For instance, penny mining stocks were popular at the time and were sold all over the world through large exchanges in Denver, Reno, Carson City, San Francisco, and every other major city of the West.

Swindles were so common that at one point the federal government had to step in and enact prohibitions against fraud by mail. These types of swindles were incorporated into the stories written for "Maverick." The material written for ordinary Westerns simply wouldn't work—that's what made "Maverick" unique.

Roy Huggins was very protective of the writers with whom he worked, and he was particularly solicitous of Marion Hargrove. Marion had been with "Maverick" almost from the beginning. On one particular segment there was considerable correspondence between Huggins and Jack Emmanuel. Huggins recalled that he had first told the story that the segment was based on to Hargrove in June 1957. In his memo to Emmanuel of June 27, 1957, he stated, "I would like to say here that my secretary specifically recalls that no contribution was made at that time. I asked Marion if he would like to do the story and he said that he would," but Huggins insisted that "I told the story for the first time to Marion Hargrove on June 3 or 4."

One year later, when it looked as if Hargrove would not receive any credits for the episode "The Jail at Junction Flats," which aired during the second year of "Maverick," Huggins wrote to Emmanuel regarding Hargrove. On January 29, 1958, he asked, "Will you please advise me as to what can be done to avert a possible injustice to Marion Hargrove on our 'Jail at Junction Flats' story." He went on to state, "As you will see when you read the script, we are using almost nothing from the purchased story but the idea of getting a man out of jail to get the money." He wanted Hargrove to receive the credit and residuals. Huggins' attitude reflects the "family syndrome" Garner and others have discussed when talking about their shows, which is so important to the inner workings of a series.

It was during the first year that a brother for Brett Maverick was hired. Jack Kelly, who eventually became Bart Maverick, describes himself prior to that auspicious assignment as "a relatively unknown success." He was probably making $50,000 a year and had appeared in everything from "Jane Wyman Theatre" on television to the "innocuous film" he was finishing in Hong Kong when the call went out to find a brother for James Garner. Kelly recalls the sequence of events.

"The film was called *Hong Kong Affair*, and it starred Jack Kelly. I was instrumental in getting the leading lady replaced by my then wife, actress May Wynn, who was traveling with me. Interestingly enough, she took her name from the character she played in the movie version of *The Caine Mutiny*. It certainly beat Donna Lee Hickey, which was her real name.

"Anyway, I got a long distance call from my agent. We were running over schedule on the picture and I thought, 'Well, maybe they've replaced everybody in the picture'— and they should have and started from scratch. However, he asked, 'When the hell are you getting back to Los Angeles?'"

"I said, 'Whenever we finish this dog. Why?'

"'Well,' he continued, 'There's a goddamn television series going at Warners' and they want to see you for one of the leads.'

"'What kind of a series?' I asked.

"'It's a Western. It's a gambling thing and they've got some guy named Jim Garner in it,' my agent said.

"'Who the hell is Jim Garner?' I asked."

In retrospect the coincidences were extraordinary. "Very weird," Kelly says. "My wife got her name in the film, Garner was picked out of the jury box to work at Warner Brothers, and now I'm getting a call on location in Hong Kong. It was like tying together the top of a potato sack with a drawstring."

Jack Kelly was no novice to the movie industry. He was the younger brother of Nancy Kelly, a major motion picture star of the thirties and forties who worked into the fifties. In 1956 she was nominated for an Academy Award as best actress in *The Bad Seed*.

"I was no stranger at Warner Brothers," he declares, "having starred there in a very ill-fated, short-lived television extravaganza called 'King's Row,' which had been a great motion picture starring Ann Sheridan, Ronald Reagan, Bob Cummings, and Claude Raines. Warner Brothers did a lot of resurrecting in those days. They had taken films like 'Cheyenne,' 'Casablanca,' and 'King's Row'—each a major financial success on the big screen—and made them into television series. We alternated every Tuesday night for Chesterfield. Robert Horton (of 'Wagon Train' fame) played the Ronald Reagan role to my Robert Cummings. We lasted six performances, I think. Something like that. So Warner Brothers was aware of Jack Kelly."

Of the forty people who supposedly tested for the Bart Maverick part, Jack Kelly is the only one anybody ever remembers. Not even he knows who the others were. "They were unidentifiable competition," he laughs.

When he returned from Hong Kong, Kelly went over to Warner Brothers in Burbank and met with Bill Orr and Hugh Benson to discuss "Maverick." Bill Orr said, "We'd like you to test for our new series, 'Maverick.'"

Jack shook his head. "I'm not going to test. I just left this studio six months ago. You know whether I can act. You hired me before. So what's the problem?"

Jack has a dislike of testing and with good reason. "Every time I tested I lost the part. I'm dynamite on first readings. You bring fifty guys in a room and if they were casting Mary Magdalene, I guarantee they'll give me the job because I can read it cold. But tell me I've got a week to prepare for a test and you can forget it. Acting is an insecure business to start with, so I'm screwed before I get started."

Sid Gold, Jack's agent, was beside himself, but Jack was adamant. No test. The studio acceded to his wishes. "They finally told me to go down to wardrobe and get suited out. They didn't want a look-alike, which would have been totally impossible anyway. Jim is much taller than I am. I'm six feet, he's six-three. Anyway, I went to wardrobe and was fitted out with one of those Errol Flynn plantation owner outfits.

"When I went on the set for the first time to do a scene with Garner, he was doing a show that featured a camel. I waited until he finished with the scene."

Between scenes there was to be some interaction between Jim and Jack—a chance to see how they worked together. "I was dressed like a goddamn idiot," Jack recalls, "with this great big plantation hat and ice cream suit. I could own the whole cotton field and a couple of pieces of watermelon on top. In that garb, I began to size up Garner. Before we were introduced I just sort of looked at him. I didn't know him from Adam so I asked an assistant director who the lead was."

The assistant director motioned to Garner and said, "The guy in the black hat."

Jack stood off to one side kind of digging his toe into the dust on the street, waiting. When the time came for him and Garner to have their conversation, Jack said, "Hey, Mister Garner! It is a thrill to meet you. I hear this show is gonna be a balls-on, fucking success. That's what Bill Orr and all these guys are telling me."

Garner looked at him strangely.

Jack leaned closer as if to whisper and said, "Would you do me a favor and stand in that fucking hole when you start talking?"

Jim almost collapsed with laughter. Everybody on the set

relaxed. It was going to work. "We didn't have any preface to each other's attitude," Jack says, "but our conversation was crazy." The two men improvised their dialogue. "I'm so happy to be considered for this," Jack said. "I understand you were in *The Caine Mutiny*." It was that kind of back and forth nonsense, both making up dialogue as they went along. The two stars were clearly compatible.

After about ninety seconds of repartee, Jack said, "Excuse me just a moment, Jim." He turned to the camera and said, "Mr. Warner, you know me through 'King's Row.' You owe me one. Give me the job. Thank you very much. Thank you, Jim. Thank you, gentlemen. Bye bye." Afterward he was told when to report for work on the series. He would be Bart Maverick.

His initial rapport with Jim was very good. "It continued to be good," he recalls. "The only thing that maybe could have jeopardized it was still down the road apiece when we went on strike."

Jim and Jack did not work together immediately. Jim had already completed eight or ten episodes, while Jack was starting on his first, which meant he had some catching up to do before he actually appeared on camera with Jim.

"The show still wasn't on the air yet," says Jack. "We were still in preparation. So far as I was concerned, however, the only negative aspect of 'Maverick,' which I've learned to understand and worked very hard to overcome, was my being known as Maverick's brother. Jim Garner was Maverick. I was his brother. From the standpoint of theatrical superiority it was degrading, debasing, and horrible.

"Interviewers understood and it was never in our discussions unless it was a paper like the *National Enquirer*. It was the public at large who didn't understand. They always saw him as more important than I was and that hurt because I was carrying the same load as he was. I was painfully aware of it. As a result, there was one thing I asked to be taken out of my contract with Warner Brothers. They had a clause in all their contracts in those days that specifically prohibited you from hiring outside public relations. Everything was handled by the Warner Brothers publicity department and I suppose the other studios had the same clause.

"So the studio permitted me to hire my own public relations firm and I picked a high-grade outfit to try to right this injustice. It was very tough to do, but I knew the public's attitude."

There was no problem on the set. Jim and Jack never discussed this issue, though both were aware of it.

"As the winner in the battle of the Mavericks without having to lift a finger, Jim didn't need to say anything. But I regard that man with a genuine appreciation. I'm not talking about his acting ability. I'm not talking about his stardom. I'm talking about Jim Garner. That sonofabitch! He's perfect!" Jack says with great affection.

There was no waiting—Jack reported for work right away. The shows became interchangable. "I did a lot of shows without Garner where the script read 'Brett-Brett-Brett.' Shows that were written before I was even signed. The only difference I've ever seen between the two 'Maverick' characters, if a difference can be measured, is the personality of the individual playing. I'm certain that later there were some of the scripts which said 'Bart-Bart-Bart' that were handed to Jim."

Jack was always less intense on screen than Jim, which he attributes to personality differences. "He would be whatever Jim Garner is—a goddamn Cherokee football player. Handsome stud dude from Oklahoma. What you see in Garner is what you get."

Jack was different in other ways from Jim. Coming from an acting family, he understood the "old Hollywood" and the protocol that went with it. He loved giving cast parties and did so frequently. "I did give cast parties at the end of a 'Maverick' segment from time to time. I was very social in those days." He still is, as mayor of Huntington Beach, California. But he doesn't recall Jim's giving parties. "I have no idea if he did or didn't really. I certainly wasn't invited to any, if he did."

Jim and Jack would sometimes see each other at lunch or when making up—each would be working on a different script at a different location at the studio—but didn't socialize otherwise. Jack is quick to point out that he doesn't consider it a slight that Jim never invited him to parties or to his home. "It was no big deal to me. Our minds were in other places than trying to get to know each other socially because it was not important. It was a job." But they did have one common interest away from the studio—a neutral ground—in that they both were great golf buffs. "That's the closest I ever came to Jim Garner on a personal level," Jack states without emotion. "He was always a much better golfer than I. His brother Jack is a golf pro and he must have picked up some pointers from him. As an amateur, Jim is very good."

Jack firmly believes that they were a team that could go on forever or be successfully revived at any point. "I don't care which of the films we did together for that series, you'll see the chemistry we created. One can speak of Abbott and Costello, Clark Gable and Spencer Tracy—any team in the business at any time, and you watch these two characters together—Brett and Bart Maverick—you can't help but ask the question, 'Why the hell isn't the celluloid burning?' And we never prepared for anything. Not so much as sitting down over a bottle of Scotch planning the scenes. It just fucking happened."

Ross Martin and Robert Conrad, from the "Wild, Wild

West" series, were suggested as comparable. "I'll buy that," Jack says. "They were interwoven into every sequence, which is the only difference. When Jim and I played together we played off each other in the same manner as those two did. They just did it every week. We did it, too, and it was never at each other's expense. We did it all without planning. If there was a joke—a Jack Benny reaction, which is nominally an explosive joke—it ended up as if we were choosing sides with the handle of a baseball bat. We totally supported each other, no matter who reaped the harvest. Fortunately for my career, the Maverick brothers were never a team even though we did a show together. We were never a "Laverne and Shirley." We would have bowled over any team in the history of movies or television and the beauty of it is that we never had any coalition whatsoever regarding our preparation creatively. We just knew whatever it was instinctively and we did it."

"Maverick" was not a success by chance. A lot of research went into its conception. Would it work? Who would watch it? Who would sponsor? Henry Kaiser hadn't stood on the sidelines and told Warner Brothers, "Make 'Maverick' for me." A complete study was done of the Nielsen Ratings to see what was selling and why. The Nielsen Television Index of January 2, 1957, showed that the Western was the most popular program category on the air, "regardless of program length," carrying a Nielsen AA rating of 27.1. The top half-dozen program types were, in order: Western drama, situation comedy, variety (30 minutes), general drama, suspense drama, and variety (60 minutes).

When "Maverick" entered the prime-time television arena Warner Brothers was riding high with "Cheyenne," an excellent precedent for the introduction of "Maverick." The technical skills and production facilities used by Warner Brothers on "Cheyenne" had resulted in impressive ratings. At the time, "Cheyenne was second only to "Disneyland" in the Monday-to-Friday ratings. On Tuesday nights in the 7:30 to 8:00 P.M. time slot, "Cheyenne" was reaping a 27.0 rating, or 39.7 percent of the viewing audience. Its competitors were far behind. Warner Brothers was thus known as the studio that produced popular "adult" Westerns. The Nielsen study proved that adult Westerns had an appeal that transcended age, sex, class, or geographical location of the viewer. They were the shows that were known as "family entertainment."

These shows appealed to sponsors as well. Westerns were sponsored by manufacturers of pharmaceuticals, cereals, dog food, cigarettes, office equipment, automobiles, dates, coffee, heavy and light appliances, flowers, cake mixes, toothpaste, electric shavers, dessert mixes, baked goods, and canned and frozen meats. No other category of program had such a wide sponsorship.

Warner Brothers' success in television could be credited to one man—William T. Orr, who was head of television production. He took over when the big movie studio had two floundering shows on television: "Casablanca" and "King's Row." The studio was spending a lot of money on television with little to show for its investment. Under Orr's capable management the situation was turned around in a hurry. He knew how to bring in a series on budget. He made a deal with ABC closely linking the Warner Brothers television product with that network. At one time the studio was producing seven and one-half hours of prime-time television weekly—a remarkable amount. Their shows were class productions: "Cheyenne," "Maverick," Bronco," "Wyatt Earp," "Colt 45," "Jim Bowie," "The Rifleman," "The Lawman," "Sugarfoot," "The Rebel," "77 Sunset Strip," and "Surfside Six"—and these were just their ABC shows. Metro-Goldwyn-Mayer may have been able to boast having the most movie stars this side of heaven, but Warner Brothers was creating stars for the small tube faster than anyone could imagine. Their star creations for television included Jack Kelly, James Garner, Clint Walker, Ty Hardin, Hugh O'Brian, Wade Preston, Scott Forbes, Chuck Connors, Johnny Crawford, Will Hutchins, Nick Adams, Efrem Zimbalist, Jr., Van Williams, Troy Donahue, and Diane McBain. Furthermore, many producers and directors were involved in several shows. Roy Huggins had a sort of behind-the-camera repertoire company that included Les Martinson, Marion Hargrove, and Douglas Heyes. They all worked on "Maverick" during its first two years.

Because of the immediate inroads "Maverick" had made on its staid old competitors on Sunday nights, Jim Garner became known as "Jim the giant killer." Warner Brothers was about to capitalize on his success by Christmas, when it came time to release *Darby's Rangers*. No longer did people ask, "Jim who?" Everybody in the country knew who Brett Maverick was. Garner was, by now, a much bigger star on television than he would ever be in the movies. But Warner Brothers wanted to cash in on Jim's television popularity by sending him on tour across the country to promote *Darby's Rangers*.

It was expected that Jim would be popular along the way, but nobody—least of all Jim himself—had even the remotest idea of the love the American public had for this loping, seemingly lazy rascal from Norman, Oklahoma. An education in public relations was in store for Warner Brothers (who thought they knew everything there was to know about fame) as well as their new star.

VII

At no time did Warner Brothers expect "Maverick" to unseat Ed Sullivan or Steve Allen in the ratings. They felt their best chance for success was during the half-hour when they would be on opposite Jack Benny. He was considered the weakest of the "Big Three" on Sunday nights. By November, however, the rules of viewing television were being tossed out the window. Trendex, an important rating system, came out with its weekly report, which showed that "Maverick" had not only caught up with Sullivan, Allen, and Benny but had actually passed them. Jim couldn't believe it—there had to be a mistake. His show had knocked out Goliath and his two escorts. "I don't know how it happened," he said, once the dust had settled. "We hoped to do well. I mean any rating at all next to Sullivan would mean something, but what has happened is fantastic."

Such was the situation when Garner arrived in Philadelphia. *Darby's Rangers* opened there at the Stanley Theater on January 21, 1958. It was a gala world premiere. Movie people complained a lot during the fifties that television was hurting the film business. If so, *Darby's Rangers* was the exception. People came out in droves, more to see James Garner than *Darby's Rangers*. Most of the people who purchased tickets for the film had no idea who Colonel Darby was, but they all knew and loved Brett Maverick and it was Brett Maverick they wanted to see.

In Philadelphia the fans tore Jim's hat, gloves, and scarf. They ripped buttons and shreds of fabric from his clothing. It was the same phenomenon associated with Frank Sinatra in the early forties and later with performers like Elvis Presley and Michael Jackson. There has never been any explanation for such behavior, which sometimes ends in great bodily harm.

Jim wasn't ready for his encounter with uncontrolled human masses. During the melee outside the theater following the world premiere, he was lost in the crowd for a few seconds, panicking the publicity people from Warner Brothers and the local police, who were there to protect him. He wondered if it was worth risking his life to come to Philadelphia.

For the film it was. The reviews throughout the country were good, with many raves and only a few unfavorable reactions. Critics began to dig up trivia items about James Garner. Assistant directors, script girls, and grips who had never become involved in a star's life were suddenly receiving calls from around the country. The media wanted every piece of information they could find about Jim. What kind of socks did he wear? Did he wear jockey or boxer shorts? These were just a few of the questions asked, and some were considerably more brazen. Oldtimers in the city of movie magic couldn't remember when there was such media interest in a star—and a television personality to boot.

Kay Proctor of the *Los Angeles Examiner* commented: "There's an interesting side angle to *Darby's Rangers*. On the strength of Garner's personal drawing power viewers can't help but get a good solid look at a number of shiny new players in the cast including Joan Elan, Edward Byrnes, Ve-

netia Stevenson, Peter Brown—a beautiful break for them."
And for Warner Brothers.

Dick Williams of the *Los Angeles Mirror News* also had
some observations to make: "James Garner, who was an unknown in a series of secondary pictures on the Warner lot
until the TV 'Maverick' series vaulted him into the big time,
has his first full-fledged starring role and he is excellent.
Garner is an ideal choice. Warners' have a real chance of
developing an important new young star in the Clark Gable,
John Wayne, Gary Cooper tradition if they give Garner the
right role in pictures and Lord knows we sure need one."

During an interview with Jerry Geghan of the *Philadelphia
Daily News*, Garner seemed to have his new celebrity status
under control. He said, "I enjoy it and it is a way of making a
good living but the acting bug never bit me." He described
his relationship with the movie studio as "good. I aim to keep
it that way. I don't want to be in and out in a year and a half.
There's no use getting hammy about things. They could drop
me and I'd be on my way to oblivion." He was asked about
the acting lessons he was reputed to have received from Uta
Hagen's husband in New York. "They didn't teach me anything I didn't have sense enough to know, so I quit." Did he
have ambitions, he was asked. "I'd like to be a retired mil-
lionaire."

How did he feel about having to go out and promote a film
right after his wife had given birth to their daughter? "My
wife is one of the most considerate people in the world. Fifteen days ago when we had the baby, Greta, I had just finished work on a picture at 6:40 P.M. She waited until 6:43
and rang me up and said, 'Now!'" He added, "This is a
strange business. When the picture went before the cameras
in April 1957 no one knew my name except my family.
Then came 'Maverick.'"

One questioner asked how he felt about Charlton Heston's not getting the picture lead. "Physically I'm better suited for the part. I have a picture taken of Colonel Darby just before he was killed. He was thirty-four and I look exactly like him. This is the first film that everything was thrown on my shoulders. When you find out that totals a million and a half dollars you realize you're not as strong as you thought you were."

The adulation continued in New York. The *Herald Tribune* said, "James Garner is fresh as a new mown lawn. . . ."

Jim returned to Hollywood to resume shooting "Maverick" with a bad case of laryngitis but without his wedding ring, which had been lost in the struggle to escape from his eager fans in Philadelphia. If there was any doubts about his status in Hollywood when he left to promote *Darby's Rangers*, those doubts had been erased by the time he returned. He was clearly a star, and his show, though not yet one of the top ten shows, was certainly well-accepted by the public and seemingly headed in the right direction.

Roy Huggins had a right to be particularly proud and satisfied. "Maverick" had been his baby from conception. Like most producers, however, Huggins did not choose merely to rest on his laurels. "It is foolish," he says, "to depend on last season's success—or even this season's. There is always tomorrow and one needs to prepare for that." Huggins was also aware of the lack of any off-camera relationship between Jack Kelly and Jim Garner. "I think I can explain that," he declares. "Garner was without question the real star of the show. Jack did not have in front of the camera the sense of humor he has in life. He's so lovable and funny and warm and great but you put him in front of the camera and something happens to Jack Kelly. He becomes more dramatic. He

did all the funny lines—overdid them. He never had Jim
Garner's genius. Jim Garner was Maverick. Kelly was his
brother."

Les Martinson directed many of the early segments of
"Maverick" and has some vivid memories of it. "Jim Garner
was just a natural. I'm sure maybe because the part was written so beautifully and beautifully defined. At the right time
someone else might have done it, but I can't think of another
person in the world where the shoe fit more beautifully than
with Jimmy Garner playing that part. His humor is difficult
to describe. It has an abstractness to it, an innate thing about
his personality. He was a fun-loving guy and his eyes were
very expressive.

"In those days of what might be properly called 'early television' the closeup was an intrusion. If you look back at those
shows there was an abundance of shots where the closeups
went right into the actor's face. It was very interesting to see
how you could see the inner amusement. Those little round
beady eyes of Jim's. It was a study the way they mirrored so
much of that quality. You could cut away from the actor and
play a lot of dialogue over Jim and he was always working.
The expressions and so forth. He was a marvelous listener
with great expression. Ross Martin and Mickey Rooney have
had and have, in Mickey's case, that same ability to act with
the facial expression. The actors who can play two whole
scenes just listening. Garner has that talent."

Martinson was eyewitness to Jim's way of dealing with the
pressures of stardom while on the set. "He was something
when he got angry, but he would never take it out on anyone
except himself. He would become frustrated. Sometimes he
would blow a line or two or three, or something of that
nature. He'd turn around and very quietly haul off and slam
his fist into the wall or a board. I used to caution him. 'Jim,'

I'd say, 'you're going to regret it when that arthritis starts creeping into your knuckles.'" Garner would merely grin.

Les Martinson understood Jim's need to get out his frustrations. He had his own frustrations. But if he was tolerant of Jim, Jim didn't always reciprocate. Huggins listened to Garner's complaints about his director.

"Jim used to come to me every two or three weeks and say, 'Roy, I will never work with that sonofabitch again,' talking about Les Martinson. I would tell him, 'Jim, we've tried other directors and they give us shit. Les knows what he's doing.'"

"'Yes,' Jim would respond, 'but the guy's crazy. He beats his head against the cameras and he's nuts and I can't stand him.'"

Roy countered, "You're not listening, Jim. We have tried other directors. The only other director who gives us good shows is Doug Heyes and he has other commitments right now. Don't ask me to take Les off because we need him."

Jim would hem and haw and finally drawl, "Well, all right, but he's still crazy."

Martinson remembers an incident of head-beating but sees it in a more humorous light. "There was one segment of 'Maverick' when one of the guest stars came in and I was working on take 17 and I didn't need the interruption. Also the production office was screaming and all of that. I just couldn't take any more for the day so I patiently told everybody, 'Let's take five.' I walked around in the back of the set and just gave my head a bump.

"When I came back in the next day, and I'm sure Garner was behind this bit of humor, there was a boom lined up and there was the whole crew side by side by height, from the tallest man all the way down the boom arm—resting their heads against the boom arm. When I walked onto the stage they all said in unison, 'Good morning, Leslie!' Well, I cracked up and whatever tensions I might have brought into the studio with me that morning evaporated in laughter."

It was the kind of incident that kept spirits high during difficult times. "In those days," Martinson declares, "we were just family. Oh, there were jokes. Everyone did that. I drove an old Jaguar—one of those old Mark Vs, I believe, and there was always a note on my car from the crew which said, 'We hope we won't have to bury you in this car.'

"It was very 'on' for me and we were all enjoying the success of the show. Every Sunday night we would sit in my living room to watch the show. My wife Connie [well known for her television show 'Connie Martinson Talks Books'], Jim Garner, Jack Kelly, and other members of the cast. I enjoyed all those 7:30 Sunday evening get-togethers where we gathered to watch and rehash what we'd done. Connie would serve a buffet and I used to say to her, 'These are the golden days, darling.'"

Connie would do a double take and say, "*These* are the golden days?" Everybody would laugh, no one harder than Jim.

"And they were in retrospect," Martinson feels. "When you're doing a show like 'Maverick,' it is special. I understand the people involved feel the same way about 'M*A*S*H' or 'Gunsmoke' when they look back from a different point of view."

There is no set of rules for achieving stardom and no way to explain why, when two actors are given equal billing in a series, one goes on to become a superstar and the other fades away. That's what happened on "Maverick." If background meant anything, Jack Kelly had the upper hand on Garner. On the Hollywood social ladder, Jack Kelly was a few rungs above Garner. "When I went over to Warner Brothers to do

'Maverick,'" he relates, "I was driving a current-year auto-mobile. Jim was driving an old, klutzy Oldsmobile. Another factor was, when I went into 'Maverick' as an unknown, I was certainly not unknown to Warner Brothers executives or to Hollywood. I had starred in a number of films as well as the television series. My career was well established. I also was receiving a considerably higher weekly salary at the time than Jim. I was able to ask for more because I wasn't bound by a contract. He was."

Jack was making more money, but Jim was getting all the publicity. "That didn't bother me," Kelly declares. "Of course there were questions in my mind but one must under-stand that I was doing a steady job and getting paid for it and whenever contract time or renewal time came around I hoped for a renewal because I wanted to continue earning a living. I wanted that paycheck."

While Warner Brothers continued to concentrate on Jim's television career, they were not unaware of the trend he had started: using television to promote films. Over the years few actors have managed to make the transition from motion pic-tures to television or the other way around. It is only very recently that major motion picture stars have appeared in sig-nificant numbers on the small screen. During the fifties most movie stars looked at television much the way the serious reader regarded comic books. They feared that television ex-posure would ruin their appeal with the movie-going public.

That didn't seem the case with Jim because Warner Broth-ers immediately set to work preparing another starring movie for him, to be filmed upon completion of the current "Maverick" season. In the meantime, he worked days and came home in the evenings to the family apartment in Stu-dio City, no more than ten minutes away from the Warner Brothers lot. Although Jim had an extended studio family, he still had his family at home, which was seeing less of him and to whom he owed some time and attention. He had a new baby daughter whom he had barely seen since she was born. Now he intended to spend some time getting to know her. Fortunately, neither he nor Lois cared much for night life so what time they did have together was spent at home enjoying family activities. Despite his new fame, he continued to live modestly in an upstairs, three-bedroom apartment, sharing the communal swimming pool with the occupants of nineteen other units in the building. Hardly the trappings one would expect of a television series star, but Garner was never interested in such things. Neither he nor Lois liked the idea of being in debt, and to buy a new home would have put them in an untenable position should Jim's series not be renewed, which was always a possibility.

When they rented the apartment, it was unfurnished. Furniture was bought piece by piece and was always paid for with cash. Jim swears that this had nothing to do the insecurity of an acting career: "I have never liked owing anybody for anything or being obligated." One of the reasons, perhaps, that the Garners didn't socialize with Jack Kelly was that they socialized more with the people who lived in their building than they did with the studio set. Lois did her own cooking, and they had small dinners to which they might invite the next-door neighbor or perhaps two couples. Bill Saxon, Jim's old high school classmate, and his wife were often at the Garners' for dinner. Jim preferred friends who had known him before he became successful. "I saw no reason to change friends," he said. "At least I know they liked me for just whatever I was, which had absolutely nothing to do with what people saw Sunday evenings in their living rooms."

Jim, also an excellent cook, sometimes relieved Lois in the kitchen, but not during the week. He was always worn out when he got home from the studio. His golf game suffered from the schedule he kept, but that was the only complaint he had. In those days Jim did not complain about the studio or executives or percentages. He was a contract player who was expected to do as he was told when he was told, and he was a good employee. On the surface he was the most relaxed man in the television and movie industries. His show was sweeping his time slot. He was recognized everywhere he went. People who worked with him shook their heads in amazement because he was, as one electrician commented, "as common as dirt. Not like a star at all." He once described his philosophy as "a good neighbor policy. I believe in the Golden Rule. It's a dandy."

In 1958 he was driving a 1956 Plymouth when he could have joined the Cadillac set. "I like it. It is a good serviceable car," he declared. "Why spend money on something pretentious to drive to and from the studio?" He also bought his clothes off the rack. "If they fit, what does it matter?" Will Rogers would have loved him.

Although he kept his personal and professional lives separate, he occasionally brought home the antagonisms of a bad day at work. On those occasions his family left him alone until he wound down and became his normal, easy-going self. Nothing gave him greater pleasure than getting down on the floor to play with Greta Scott Garner, who almost immediately became known as "Gigi." Born on January 4, 1958, just before Garner took off for his historic Philadelphia trip, she became the focal point of the entire family. She didn't belong to just Jim and Lois, but also to Kimberly, who was enthralled with the idea of having a baby sister. In the long run, this would prove to be economical. The Garners had their own baby-sitter—and one they trusted!

By early 1958 "Maverick" was being picked up by more

than eighty stations around the country. Although it was an ABC Network show, some independent stations purchased it, and not all of them aired it on Sunday nights. Independents did not have to conform as much to network policies and could place a show in the time slot they felt best suited their audiences. Consequently, in some areas the series was viewed in mid-week.

At that time Jim consented to a number of interviews but specifically requested that they deal with his career and "Maverick" and not with his private life. When an interview got too close for comfort to the personal realm, Jim either tried to change the subject or politely let the interviewer know that the interview was in jeopardy of being terminated. Interviewers got the message and returned to Jim's career.

Jim was very low-key in interviews, admitting that he was surprised by all the attention he was receiving. "I'm really flattered," he said, "but this is something that could have happened to anyone. I'm nobody special. It is like a political contest. The two front runners do each other in and the underdog wins." No one could deny that he had indeed entered the fray as the underdog. "If a family gets into an argument over whether to watch Ed Sullivan or Steve Allen, "Maverick" becomes the compromise. That's luck. Good luck for me, but still luck."

Garner always insisted, and still does, that he doesn't act. "I am just like John Wayne was. He never played anybody except John Wayne. I play Jim Garner—whatever that is."

Much of "whatever that is" involves self-confidence. His wife, Lois, swears she has never met anyone with the self-confidence of her husband. "He believes in himself. Nobody could destroy that confidence he has except himself. I might worry about something. He just shrugs his shoulders and tells me not to worry. In his mind everything will work out and so far it always has."

Interviewers get both the best and the worst of Jim during an interview. Blunt to the point of sounding insulting at times, he nonetheless never overstates his case. He says what is on his mind and lets the chips fall where they may. When he was battling the fan magazines, everyone sought him out for interviews—including the very publications he was attacking. They got one-liners around which they had to build their stories. Garner later would argue that this only proved his point: Some writers would say hello to him on the street or on a movie set and then write a long story intimating that he had given them a long interview. But when Jim really has something to say, he can be as long-winded as any politician running for local office.

After the initial success of "Maverick," Warner Brothers raised his weekly salary to $750. Garner accepted the raise gracefully and said, "Looks like I'll be around a while." He added, "A man has to make a living and he should do it by working at something he likes. I like what I'm doing. Life consists of making a living. If you're happy doing it, that's pretty much where it's at."

The year 1957 had been a whirlwind year for the Garner family. That Jim handled so much pressure with such grace is a tribute to his early life in Oklahoma, where he learned that because the morning is calm, it doesn't mean there won't be a tornado in the afternoon. By mid-1958 when he was ready to begin shooting his next film, *Up Periscope*, he had learned how to endure.

The original idea for *Up Periscope* was to shoot it on location in the Hawaiian Islands. The location was changed to the southern California coast, primarily to San Diego, with other location scenes shot in Santa Barbara. Tab Hunter was offered *Up Periscope* and turned it down. Jim also refused the film until the script was changed. The studio accomodated him by making the changes he requested. He was in an excellent position to bargain because of his success on "Maverick." Otherwise, he would probably have been suspended. Jack Warner was quick to discipline any actor who got too big for his britches.

Louella Parsons, a Garner fan from the beginning, gave him a slap on the wrist. In one of her columns she wrote: "This is no time to be backing out of pictures without a very good reason. Tab Hunter, who turned thumbs down on *Up Periscope*, could be making another mistake. He refused to do *Darby's Rangers*, which turned out to be a big motion picture success for James Garner and has started him off on what is a successful career in movies as well as TV. Now I am told that James Garner, whom everybody thinks highly of at Warners', is refusing *Up Periscope*. I can't say whether the boys or the studio is right because I don't know anything about the story, but things being what they are and studios making every effort to bring out good pictures I think these two young men would think before they bolted."

Shortly after the Parsons story appeared, Warner Brothers Studios announced that the Garner matter had been settled and that production would begin shortly on the picture. Parsons gleefully announced the signing of Edmund O'Brien to the cast of *Up Periscope*. It was obvious that she had been on the phone with Jack Warner. He must have been rapidly tiring of Hunter because Parsons added that "naturally he will not play in the role intended for Tab Hunter at one time. Eddie will play an important commander, an older man. He'll co-star with the one and only James Garner." This was also further evidence that Jack Warner wanted to get along with Jim.

According to some reports, Tony Curtis and Cary Grant were both considered for Jim's role in the film. This is probably not true since Warner Brothers wanted to push the hot property they had under contract. There would have been no reason for the studio to go off the lot when it had such a popular male lead which, as Garner was always quick to quip, "came cheaper."

The picture started shooting on July 8, 1958, on stage 3 at the Warner Brothers lot. Shortly thereafter the main company moved to San Diego for the submarine scenes. The picture was directed by Gordon Douglas, an efficient man who liked to bring in his films on schedule. On some days he worked his crew and actors until ten or eleven at night or even until after two in the morning. The picture was running four to five days behind schedule in San Diego and was six days behind when principal photography was completed.

The story line of *Up Periscope* was simple World War II fare involving the Pacific Theater of Operations. Garner played Lt. J. G. Ken Braden, a recent graduate from an underwater demolition school who is sent on a mission requiring him to sneak ashore a tiny, Japanese-held island to photograph the Japanese code. He is lured into the situation by a beautiful woman, played by Andrea Martin, with whom he falls in love and whom he must confront when he finds out he's been tricked. His antagonist is Commander Stevenson, played by Edmund O'Brien. What makes the picture unique is not only the involvement of the officers but the manner in which the director and cameraman utilize reactions from the crew. One member of the cast getting a major studio buildup was Frank Gifford, an MVP from the New

York Giants professional football team. Throughout the filming and afterward, the studio planted stories about Gifford and set up dozens of magazine interviews. No friction occurred between Gifford and Garner, although to some it seemed obvious that the studio was somewhat piqued with Jim's reluctance to do the picture and wanted to teach him a lesson by promoting someone who had a lesser role in the film. Gifford had a clause in his contract that permitted him to leave the picture in time for the 1958 NFL season, whether he was finished filming his part or not. None of this seems to have bothered Garner, who is an avid football fan and probably considered Gifford a bigger star than himself. Gifford had a small part in *Darby's Rangers* and had been given a better role in *Up Periscope* based on his performance in that picture.

The bulk of *Up Periscope* was filmed at sea aboard the submarine USS *Tilefish* at the San Diego Naval Base, but a special tank was installed at the studio for some of the underwater sequences while the tropical jungles were recreated on the back lot. The cooperation of the U.S. Navy was extended during the seven weeks of filming without bureaucratic problems.

The daily trips out of San Diego harbor on the *Tilefish* were the first outings at sea for Jim since he'd been in the Merchant Marine, and he had difficulty finding his sea legs. One day as he steadied himself on the deck of the submarine, which was rolling with the swells about three miles out of harbor, his deeply tanned complexion began to show traces of grayish green. He joked with the navy captain. "The least you guys could have done is spread a little straw and oats around. Might have made a dry lander feel a little more at home." Someone nearby suggested Jim might be suffering from a slight case of "mal de mer."

"Mal de mer, hell," Jim responded with a sickly grin. "I'm just plain seasick." And he was.

A local writer described Jim as "a big breeze, flippant sort with an airy approach." Jim would probably agree that his manner could be described as a bit cocky. It always had been. "There are actors," he said, "and there are personalities. I'm a personality. In pictures it is the personalities who make the money and last. Of course, if you're a personality who is an actor that's gravy for the long-range career. The big thing is likability. The public isn't half as interested in how well you act as they are in how much they like you on the screen. I stress the screen because I'm more interested in pictures than in TV simply because if you work, say, six weeks on a picture you make more money than if you work six weeks in TV. Frankly, I never expected 'Maverick' to turn out so big, especially with that competition. But I figure you might as well go for the best. Then, if you win out you've accomplished something. Of course, when we started we had no place to go but up. Now it is the other way around. All we've got going for us, though, is a good time slot, good production, and good writing. That's the secret sliced three ways. My own secret, if that's what it is, is that I flip through my lines trying to be as light and quiet as possible. In 'Maverick' the emphasis is on humor. I have no idea how long 'Maverick' will last. A couple of seasons, maybe more, but I expect to be in this business a long time afterward."

This commentary is significant for two reasons. First, the day would come when Jim would be highly critical of the production aspects of "Maverick," and second, he didn't know how prophetic he was being about the durability of the series.

He modified his stance about "Maverick" in another interview while in San Diego working on *Up Periscope*. "The scries is played by instinct. After more than fifty one-hour dramas I don't give a thought to characterization anymore. They just hand me a script and I go out and read the lines. But don't get me wrong. I love TV—especially the money. Show me a man who doesn't care about money and I'll show you a poor man."

The *Denver Post* acknowledged Jim's dual film personality, saying that he was "the first TV Western hero to make the transition to full stardom on the screen." Clint Eastwood, who got his start on "Maverick," also became a movie star, but Jim had made the transition first.

Each evening when Garner came ashore after a day's filming aboard the submarine, San Diego fans lined up to get his autograph, shake his hand, or simply get a glimpse of their new hero. He brought along his camera, having become quite a photographer, and took pictures himself. People loved his informality. He was obviously enjoying being the center of attraction but behaved more like someone at a family reunion than a star among fans. He was quite folksy and earthy. In her syndicated column Sheilah Graham took note of his new popularity. "James Garner is being mobbed by fans in San Diego. The present trouble he didn't have when he was making his acting debut there three years ago in the nonspeaking role of a navy lieutenant in the stage production of *The Caine Mutiny Court Martial*."

Garner waxed philosophical on this issue, which was totally unlike him. "It is important," he stated, "for an actor not to take himself too seriously. I am not interested in psychoanalysis or delving deeply into hidden facets of a character. In my opinion, to be overly intense or analytical robs acting of its naturalness."

Warner Brothers, anxious to capitalize in whatever manner they could on their new star, discovered that Jim had a good singing voice and encouraged him to make records. There were offers from several record companies, but Jim declined. There was nothing in his contract, he insisted, that said he "had to make records."

Some interesting trivia surrounded the filming of *Up Periscope*. For instance, the official record for the most people aboard a submarine at sea, in addition to the regular officers and men, was set during World War II when the USS *Pompanito* rescued seventy-three survivors in the Pacific. With sixty-six cast and crew members from Warner Brothers joining the regular *Tilefish* crew of eighty for two weeks to film location scenes, that record was nearly broken. The cast also had to learn that although listed officially as a ship, a submarine is called a boat by all navy men.

The motion picture people could not get used to the reduced space on the submarine and kept banging their heads on the low beams and bows of the submarine. Regular submarine personnel quickly become accustomed to the confined spaces during training—they duck automatically. The movie crew was used to wide open spaces and was pleased when this phase of production was finished.

During the filming of a torrid love scene between Jim and Andrea Martin, done on the beach, six different people were in charge of the personal appearance of the two stars. A makeup man applied face makeup to Andrea. (Jim never uses makeup.) The hairdresser touched up Andrea's hair after each take, a wardrobe man attended to Jim's clothes and a wardrobe woman to Andrea's. A special makeup woman applied special liquid coloring to Andrea's body because she played the scene in a two-piece bathing suit and needed to look completely tanned, and a special effects man sprayed the stars with water before each take to give the impression that they were just coming out of the surf.

Up Periscope was a "water" picture. Jim spent so much time underwater during the two-months' shooting that he dubbed his stand-in, Luis Delgado, a "swim-in." Working underwater was hazardous, and Jim had a scrape with serious injury or maybe even death. In one scene, he was swimming ashore in a skin diving suit and loaded with heavy equipment when a powerful wave grabbed him and flung him against the rocks, cutting off his air line. He didn't stop but held his breath, grit his teeth, and continued to swim while the crew stood by anxiously. When he surfaced upon completing the scene, someone asked him why he hadn't stopped. "What? And have to do the scene over again?" he asked.

The fact that Jim didn't know how to skin dive never occurred to anyone until the picture was in full production. He received an awful lot of on-the-job training. In one spectacular scene in which Jim blows up a wharf on the Japanese-held island, it took sixteen special effects men to prepare and set off the explosion and eight extra firemen to control the fire that broke out as a result. A near-inferno resulted, with fire spreading across the water rapidly. Jim may not have known how to skin dive but in this instance he certainly swam like a fish underwater to avoid being burned. He shrugged his shoulders. It was all part of the job. Not many of his fellow actors would agree with that.

Jim wasn't the only actor on the picture shooting risky scenes. His co-star, Carleton Carpenter, was required to do a scene that called for him to be strafed with machine-gun bullets while lying on deck of the submarine and then to be washed overboard when the submarine crash-dived. The scene was shot. Six small powder charges were strapped to Carpenter's body to simulate his body being riddled by machine-gun fire. Water from two large tanks then cascaded down to wash him overboard. But first he was slammed against the rails. Between the powder charges and the onrushing water he was black and blue by the time the film was done. His director was pleased. "It looked very real," he said.

A green man, in film lingo, is not a Martian. He is the person who takes care of the gardening needed for a film's backdrops. Stan Faulkner, the Warner Brothers green man, was called on to recreate a jungle for *Up Periscope*. In the scene in which Jim had to swim underwater after blowing up the wharf, he was supposed to come out of the water onto a tropical beach. An ideal site was selected near Santa Barbara, California. One thing was wrong—there was no tropical vegetation to make it resemble the South Pacific.

For Faulkner this was no problem. He made a large job look easy. With seven assistants and three truckloads of plants, trees, and grass, he arrived at the location site the day before shooting was to begin. After thirteen hours of arduous work, the green man and his crew of gardeners transformed the white, treeless beach into a Pacific paradise. They had, in addition to foliage, planted nine palm trees, each of which weighed over one thousand pounds and had to be planted in a minimum of four feet of sand. A large boom truck was called into service to accomplish this feat.

The following day the company arrived. The director and a crew of sixty production personnel filmed Jim outfitted in a skin diving suit with full pack. He swam ashore onto a tropical beach made luxuriant by the vegetation that Faulkner and his green men had supplied. As soon as the company finished shooting the scene, Faulkner moved in with his men, uprooted the trees and plants, and returned them to the studio, where they were replanted to be used at some other date on another film with a tropical setting.

Between scenes, when he could get away, Jim could be

found on a golf course. As one of Hollywood's finest amateurs he was invited to play in the Crosby International at Pebble Beach, California. He also played in pro-am tournaments in Florida, where his brother Jack operates a golf course.

Before embarking on a promotional tour for the opening of *Up Periscope*, Jim made a rare exception. He permitted the *Hollywood Mirror News*'s columnist Erskine Johnson to come into his apartment and interview him and Lois. Johnson gave the public a rare insight into the private James Garner.

"Jim's luggage," he wrote, "may have been packed for a personal appearance tour . . . but this was Saturday night at home in the San Fernando Valley with the four Garners. An apartment hardly big enough, I'd like to say, for all the happiness I found there." Jim made the trip worthwhile for Johnson. He fed Gigi her nightly formula, polished his golf clubs, and romped with his stepdaughter, Kimberly.

When Garner comes home from work, Johnson reported, "everyone jumps to attention." "When I'm not here," Garner said with a mischievous grin, "the whole place comes unglued."

Lois explained that her first marriage had been a big mistake, the only good thing coming from it being her daughter Kimberly, and she was happy that Kim now had a father in Jim. "I fell in love with Jim and married him because I knew he was in love with me."

Jim added, "You can know people for years and then suddenly realize you don't know them at all. I was lucky we had a short courtship. Lois didn't know about my temper until after we were married."

Wherever he went on the tour people wanted to talk about "Maverick" rather than *Up Periscope*. Whatever he said was a bonus for Warner Brothers. In San Antonio, speaking of his character in "Maverick," he said, "Anybody who is that cocky has to get shot." About the future of "Maverick," he commented, "I can't tell you that. I don't even know the future of television. I will tell you this, however. Whatever success I've had I owe to luck, timing—getting in at the right time and to producer Roy Huggins. Huggins supplies most of the ideas for the 'Maverick' series." This observation was important because in later years when Jim had soured on Huggins he made comments indicating that Huggins had had very little to do with the show.

In San Antonio Jim was asked why he had originally refused to do *Up Periscope* and what, exactly, had changed his mind. "It is a good movie. The first time they showed me the script, I said, 'No.' I could afford to. It was being produced by Warner Brothers and they do 'Maverick.' They couldn't suspend me. They changed the script. They changed the casting. I said, 'Yes. Now it will be a good movie.'"

He confessed that he was uncomfortable doing love scenes with Andrea Martin in the film. "Andrea was engaged to Ty Hardin, who was always hanging around and watching us shoot the picture. It was embarrassing, making ardent love to a girl when I knew her future husband was watching. I finally had to run him off the set, before 'Maverick' and 'Cheyenne' got into a pistol fight."

The reference to "Cheyenne" had much more significance for Jim than he realized. Earlier in the year Clint Walker, the star of "Cheyenne," sulking and angry with Warner Brothers because they wouldn't relax some of the more confining clauses in his contract, walked out on his series and contract. Jack Warner, not to be intimidated by an employee, replaced him with Ty Hardin. Walker had numerous complaints. He strongly resented having to give up fifty percent of his personal appearance money to Warner Brothers. He demanded higher pay for reruns; felt he should be able to make records for any company he chose, not just Warner Brothers (a requirement in Warner Brothers contracts); and generally did not want to be bound so tightly to his employer. The studio punished Walker by refusing to permit him to work anywhere.

When Ty Hardin replaced Walker on the show he created a new character called Bronco Layne, who became the lead in a spinoff series called "Bronco" when Walker, unable to work outside his contract, returned to "Cheyenne." Although Walker complained bitterly that he had been treated "worse than a caged animal," he performed to his trainer's specifications. It was not apparent at the time, but Walker had set the stage for a rebellion on the "Maverick" series that would have totally different results. James Garner watched the events with a scrutinizing eye.

The reviews of *Up Periscope* were mixed. Here are some of them. *Motion Picture Daily*: "Garner gives the same kind of pleasant, relaxed performance that has made him popular on TV and takes as easily to the uniform of a navy lieutenant as he does to his Western gambler's garb." *Motion Picture Exhibitor*: "The performances are average, as are direction and production. Garner, a prominent TV personality, might be an additional drawing card." *Variety*: "Garner as a good-looking young leading man shows a nice flare for comedy that hasn't been too evident previously and handles himself in all situations." *The Hollywood Reporter*: "James Garner has just the right combination of athletic prowess and intelligence in his personality to make the role credible. His mood is made less self-assured and therefore more jumpy when he learns the girl he has proposed to before sailing is really an agent for Navy Intelligence."

Before returning to Hollywood he gave a reporter one final

thought on "Maverick," which he seemed unable to escape. "I've never tried to analyze 'Maverick,'" he told Eleanor Hart of the *Miami Herald*, "but it is no Western. The situations are more modern with Western trappings. A horse instead of an auto. A single-action .45 instead of an automatic. I don't plan to make 'Maverick' all my life." He assured her that he would rather be called Jim than Brett and added, "I'm an actor and I do what I'm told. If I didn't play Brett, somebody else would."

Garner discussed his personal appearance tours and their value to his career: "One can never anticipate the public on personal appearance tours," he said. "I've barnstormed the country over the past couple of years and traveled more than 100,000 miles. On my last trip to Chicago extolling the virtues of Kaiser and 'Maverick,' very few of my fans realized that I had starred with Marlon Brando in *Sayonara*. There didn't seem to be any connection with the film and the TV show." His three trips to San Francisco, he stated, resulted in an "appreciable rise in fan mail," showing an increase in public acceptance of the show. "I love people, so the fourteen or fifteen hours a day I put in at press conferences and cocktail parties on tour, as well as radio and television shows, are all part of the game. It is a back-breaking pace, but the results are worth it."

James Garner was indeed a seasoned veteran of the wars of Hollywood. The naive young lad from Oklahoma with the all-American body had become a man who knew how to survive in the celluloid jungle of executive privilege and "star treatment." He would never be as easy to deal with in the future as he had been in the past.

VIII

A philosophical James Garner made a confession of sorts on the set of "Maverick" one day. Someone had commented that it appeared that Brett Maverick was simply an overgrown kid. Garner grinned. "It would be the right thing to say, I suppose, that I've outgrown or lived to regret my boyhood pranks, but I wouldn't be telling the truth. I'm not going to put down my self-indulgence during my teenage years, but . . . I'm not going to suggest that other kids take the same road I did.

"I goofed off a lot and everybody knows that's not the route to success. I got lucky and there's no doubt about it. If my kids try to do it the way I did there's going to be some real old-fashioned bottom-busting. Although it may seem easy to a youngster, there are no easy ways. You pay somebody, somewhere, for the shortcuts you take."

He had worked very hard as a youngster, but confessed readily that it "wasn't out of nobility. I worked because of need. I could overlook my natural prejudice against work because it was the only way I could obtain enough money legally to afford not to work. I just took jobs between loafing sessions. Anybody who knows me will tell you that I'd rather play than work. Would rather be on a golf course all day than in a hot, boring studio where I spend a great deal of time just waiting for a shot to be set up."

He doubted that teenagers of the late fifties were any worse than teenagers of his day. "I don't have any remorse. I won't even ignore the fact that I took a lot of advantage of people. Everything I did led up to where I am now, no matter how you look at it. So the things I did wrong must have been all right because I apparently learned from them. Here I am today, and I wouldn't have it any other way."

The more successful he became, the more Jim liked to reflect on the hard times of the past. So did Lois. "I remember," she said, "our beginnings. They were very meager. Our honeymoon lasted two days. We came back to set up housekeeping in a tiny apartment where our only furniture was a couple of chairs, a double bed, and a cot for Kimberly."

Garner was making $200 a week at the time. Kim had just returned from Children's Hospital and Lois spent most of her waking hours providing the child with physical therapy. "It didn't matter," she recalls. "We had no money, but we were wildly in love and that's all that mattered to either of us then. We also had our integrity—especially Jim, when it came to his work."

A man in need of money might have been tempted to accept any offer that was made to him, but when Jim's publicity representative at the studio came up with an idea that would put some extra money in his bank account—indirectly—he declined. *Look* was doing a big spread on stars and their culinary efforts. There was an opening for one more star and Jim could have that spot if he wanted it.

"I can't even cook," Garner said, hoping to get out of the offer.

"You don't have to cook. Just make believe. You'll be in

the company of some really big stars. It could do much for your career."

"There's another thing," Jim said, revealing something most stars would have been embarrassed to admit. "We don't even have the apartment finished. All we have are the bare necessities."

"Nothing to worry about," the publicist said. "I can provide all the furniture you need."

Jim's personal integrity came to the fore. "I can't fake something for the public. That would be totally dishonest. I'll just wait until I can legitimately do a story."

When looking back on those lean times, when he had stardom but little else, he has commented, "We thought money would solve all problems, but it never does."

Jim was now able to return to Norman, Oklahoma, as a native son who had become a success. Not as a football hero, which would have been his preference, but as a full-fledged star of both television and motion pictures. His homecoming was planned for weeks. Warner Brothers began feeding press releases into Oklahoma that would have an effect not only in Hollywood but all over the country. It would be what is now called "a media event." In June Jim by-lined an article that was picked up by the Associated Press and given prominent play in the Oklahoma newspapers, including his home town paper, the *Norman Transcript*. Garner tried to give a new perspective on the post–Civil War West, relying considerably on "Maverick." "I'm amazed," he wrote, "that most Western historians treated the post–Civil War period like a wake." He brushed aside the idea that the frontiersmen of that period were dour and without humor. "Our silent screen Western movies continued this mistaken premise." As a kid growing up, he recalled, he was given the idea that Tom Mix, William S. Hart, and Hoot Gibson were "nurtured on undistilled sour mash."

Again, he gave credit to his producer. "Roy Huggins," he said, "is a Phi Beta Kappa with enviable writing credits and considerable skill as a researcher. He doesn't go along with that premise. He saw 'Maverick,' and designed it as an adult Western with humor. I'm horribly miscast as Brett and Jack Kelly is a misfit as Bart if they were looking for performers to deliver the melancholy subtleties of psychological drama. We ain't the type."

Jim's popularity was further enhanced when he was shown to be "surprised" by Ralph Edwards on his highly rated show as the subject of a *This Is Your Life* segment in June. Family and friends recounted various incidents in his life, and at the end of the show the then governor of Oklahoma, Raymond Gary, made a special announcement. September 20, 1958, would officially be designated James Garner Day throughout the state of Oklahoma. Warner Brothers Studios would participate fully in making the event a grand one. Oklahoma State Fair officials, deciding that one honoree was not enough, declared that that day would also be designated as Cleveland County Day as well.

The event lasted a week and became as much a reunion of the Meeks and Bumgarners as anything else. There were formal and informal affairs, luncheons and dinners, and a grand reception. The Garner "banquet" had an overflow crowd of four hundred and the tickets (this was in the fifties, remember) were $2.50! Kim accompanied Jim and had the time of her life.

He introduced her quite proudly as "my daughter." Lois, just getting over a bout of pneumonia, remained in California. Mayor Fred Reynolds of Norman presented Jim with an engraved silver plaque naming him "Maverick Mayor of Norman." One Norman mother (who was unable to attend the banquet) wrote an anonymous letter to the *Norman Transcript*, humorously complaining that it wasn't fair that all the young marrieds with babies did not have enough money to go and see their favorite star. It would have been "a wonderful advance birthday present," she said, "but who could ask her husband to buy her a meal ticket with Maverick for her birthday?

"The crowning blow was to pick up the *Transcript* and find the policewomen clustered in his arms! All we get are parking tickets from hands he touched!"

Thanks to Jim's appearance at the Oklahoma State Fair, all previous opening-day records were broken. Sporting a bright red shirt with open collar (a Garner trademark), Jim strolled down Main Street in Norman unannounced. Within minutes there was a traffic jam the likes of which the small town had never seen before and has not seen since. What impressed young and old alike more than anything else was Jim's sincere interest in kids. He held an impromptu press conference for a newly formed fan club in Norman and fielded questions until there were no more.

Jim's surprise when he was asked by one young lady, "Do you know anyone famous?" turned to a grin. "Well," he drawled, "I know Ricky Nelson." The girls squealed. Another girl asked, "Is it true you were kicked out of Oklahoma University?" Jim roared with laughter. "Not exactly, but there a lot of people who were just as happy that I left." More squeals. When the meeting was finished one pretty blonde asked Garner, "May we kiss you?"

"Sure," he said. "Why not?" He was mobbed, disappearing into a sea of flying ponytails as he made a desperate attempt to reach his car.

On September 24 the City of Norman officially welcomed back "their boy" with a big banquet that resembled a Sunday picnic by the river. The proudest moment for Jim was the acknowledgment that both his grandmothers, Mrs. Lula Bumgarner and Mrs. Abby Meeks, were there to see their handsome grandson being honored by kinfolk and neighbors alike.

Jack Bagby of the *Norman Transcript* wrote the account of the welcoming-home supper. "It was far from a solemn affair," he wrote. "Too many people there were all too familiar with some of the antics of James Garner when he was growing up in Norman."

The master of ceremonies, Robert L. Bailey, allowed how nice it was that Jim had attended school in Norman, "now and then." Jim, attired in a conservative black business suit, white shirt, and dark tie, looked like a pillar of the community rather than the local Huck Finn but showed his rascally side by constantly interrupting Bailey as he rattled off a biography of the star. He groaned, grimaced, quipped, and shouted denials. When Bailey retold the story of Jim's birth at the old American Legion Hospital in 1928, adding, "A bank was robbed that day," Jim jumped to his feet and yelled, "I didn't do it!"

His brother Jack, then living in Florida, sent a telegram expressing regrets at not being able to attend the homecoming for Jim. He added in the telegram that he had just shot a 64 and a hole in one in golf. "He's lying," Jim yelled. "He never did that."

Bailey went on. "In most success stories, when the hero returns to his home town, everyone says, 'Glad to see you; I knew you'd make it.' When Jim came back everyone said, 'Glad to see you.'"

Jim jumped to his feet and waved his arms at the guests. "He's right," he bellowed. "Not a one of you said, 'I knew you'd make good!'"

The crowd roared at his antics. They loved him. But the evening turned serious when Jim was called upon to respond. Very humbly he took the microphone and thanked everyone for coming. He said, "I hope I can continue whatever I've done to bring honor to Norman." He added, "It's sure good to be home. All these honors and plaques, the all-around friendship—well, they make me kind of ashamed of some of the things I used to do." At that point he began to choke up and had difficulty getting out his final words. "And . . . well . . . you've all made me feel pretty good." He sat down and bowed his head to a standing ovation. It may have lacked the sophistication of a Hollywood testimonial, but it was an honest, heart-warming event that left everyone in the room feeling better.

Twenty-one Westerns were presented to the viewing public that fall—more than before or since. "Maverick" had brought the Western full circle. With its modern humor and concept, which could be adapted to other forms of situation comedy, it was only natural that "Maverick" would influence other types of programs. As a result, Westerns began a rapid decline.

"Maverick" was about to enter its second and most successful year. It was also the year when the show itself would begin to develop problems. The first episode for the second year, "The Day They Hanged Maverick," received considerable prepublicity. Jim discussed it at length while he was in Oklahoma but did not reveal the ending. Obviously, he said, Brett Maverick wasn't really going to be hanged. "You don't think we want to end the series at the beginning of the season, do you?" he asked. Doug Heyes directed that segment and Whitney Blake co-starred. The actors appearing in second-season episodes were top-rated and included John Vivyan, Efrem Zimbalist, Jr., Martin Landau, Charles Fredericks, Richard Long, John Litel, Regis Toomey, Diane Brewster, Reginald Owen, Ben Gage, Patricia Barry, Roger Moore, Abby Dalton, Edgar Buchanan, Clint Eastwood, Louise Fletcher, Robert Conrad, Jimmy Lydon, Connie Stevens, Buddy Ebsen, and Adam West. Some of them went on to superstardom, and many had their first real exposure on "Maverick." Agents did everything but stand on their heads to get clients on the show. Some would have done even more than that if they had thought it would have helped.

"Maverick" was special in a way that has escaped many commentators. The series was introduced at a time when the Western was beginning to lose popularity. It was different, which is what made it work, but there were just too many Westerns on television at the time and the public was saturated. It should have been apparent to forecasters that the Western was on its way out. "Maverick" may have been one of the new shows, but it had become "the Western" to watch. Other shows of the same genre suffered because there are only so many hours a week for the public to devote to television, and the public is fickle.

Les Martinson still had directorial duties on "Maverick" during the second year. Some of the show's greatest episodes came from what was called Roy Huggins's "repertoire company." That included Jim Garner and Jack Kelly before the cameras, of course, and Huggins, Doug Heyes, and Les Martinson behind it, together with writer Marion Hargrove.

"Roy set up certain guidelines for the writers. Marion Hargrove was one of those writers and I think I directed a dozen or so episodes written by him. Marion had a bead on 'Maverick.' Doug Heyes alternated between writing and directing. Doug and Marion, with the rules set down by Huggins, saw to the character and consistency of the character," Martinson stated.

Martinson directed a classic episode written by Roy Huggins. "It was called 'A Shady Deal at Sunny Acres,' and it was 'Maverick' at its very best. It was a marvelous caper and Jimmy spent most of the entire hour sitting on the front porch whittling."

In this episode Brett Maverick wins quite a bit of money. He goes to the bank after it has closed, sees a light on, and knocks on the window. The banker, played by John Dana, allows him to come in and make the deposit. The following morning when Brett goes into the bank to pick up his money, the banker pretends never to have met him before. It is clearly a swindle. Brett protests and soon townspeople are talking about how "this character Maverick is making a big ruckus about our banker."

Enter Jack Kelly as brother Bart. "I remember one scene," says Martinson, "where Jack takes the banker to dinner and John Dana leans over, the devil that he was in the episode, saying, 'After all, Bartley, if you can't trust your banker, whom can you trust?'"

Bart sits there nodding his head and smoking a big cigar. The banker has no idea that he is Brett's brother. Efrem Zimbalist, Jr., and Diane Brewster contributed much to the episode's success, but it was Jim Garner's show all the way.

Jack Kelly also had a high opinion of that episode and of James Garner's role in it. "The true essense of 'Maverick' was Garner in 'Shady Deal at Sunny Acres.' After he is taken by the crooked banker, then enters myself and members of what we called 'our road company,' which included Efrem Zimbalist, Leo Gordon, and Dick Long. Jim blew us all away sitting there on the front veranda of the hotel simply whittling and reacting. You saw the whole thing through his eyes and his facial expressions. That is real acting. It was lovable and fun."

One other episode is considered a classic and remembered by all who were involved in the show as well as by its fans. A takeoff on "Gunsmoke" called "Gun-Shy," it was directed by Les Martinson and written by Marion Hargrove. It was such an excellent spoof that the *New York Times* gave it a two-column review. It co-starred Ben Gage, better known as Esther Williams's one-time husband. Ben had been in show business a long time, having previously been a singing announcer for Canada Dry on the old Jack Benny show. Les had known Gage for many years.

"I cast Ben in the episode because I needed a behind as big as James Arness's. Ben played it beautifully. It was very funny. I had a marvelous opening shot where you see the takeoff on the opening of 'Gunsmoke.' Ben's big body moved in, the holster on the left side. I shot between his legs, did a shootout, and put a wide-angle lens on the scene. There was a big rear end, bigger than Arness's, and it turned out to be a hell of a spoof. We didn't mix oil with water. It was pure. Everybody played it straight and it turned out hysterical. Once again the Roy Huggins guidelines proved to be the right ones."

Of everything that happened to "Maverick" during its second year, the most devastating was Roy Huggin's decision to leave the show. "I left at the end of the second year because I had been carrying that show," he says without rancor. "I wrote every story except the ones that have Doug Heyes's name on them and I wrote those with Doug Heyes, and there was one that Marion Hargrove wrote by himself and my immediate comment was, 'By God, the guy's learned how to write a story.' I gave the stories to Marion. Not that Marion wasn't a good writer. He was a good writer. His books prove that. He must have written ten or so scripts in the two years he worked with me on 'Maverick,' and I always had to rewrite them because Marion's writing was always three feet off the ground. He was so busy being funny that you didn't believe him. Still being Private Hargrove.

"So I would rewrite them to get them to where people would believe the story and keep his humor because he had humor that worked on 'Maverick' when he wasn't too lofty. It was not unusual for him to get mad at me after one of those rewrite sessions; then it would go on the air and people would call him and say, 'Jesus, Marion, you're really back in form. God, that was good.' The following day he would call me up and say 'Roy, can we do another one?'" According to Huggins, it took a while for Hargrove to stop becoming angry with him, but he finally did.

Still, by the end of the second year, Roy Huggins was becoming weary of carrying so much of the load. "In actuality, there were fifty shows and the only ones I wasn't the full author of were the ones I wrote with Doug—and believe me, Doug was a true co-writer. Of course, Marion and Doug got full credit. Marion used to be so grateful he would haul in caches of Scotch for me because he was getting all the money. I had to tell him, 'Marion, for Christ's sake, will you stop it with the Scotch? I've got a closet full of Scotch!'"

Huggins says that the producer who replaced him didn't understand the show, couldn't rewrite as he had done, and couldn't come up with the proper stories. "He remained a producer for a few years and then vanished. I contend that no one could have done it anyway because there are very few people in the world who understand that kind of humor."

Cary Grant, a big fan of the "Maverick" series, wanted Huggins to leave television and write motion picture scripts for him. "I love Cary Grant and I would have enjoyed writing for him, but I wouldn't do it because I saw myself getting rich in television."

Some years later, after leaving Universal Studios, where he had been producing for some time, Huggins actually did begin to work on a motion picture script for Grant. In the middle of the project, however, Cary Grant decided not to make any more films. Huggins never finished the script.

Les Martinson directed another memorable episode of "Maverick" during the second year, memorable because by presenting an actor from a less successful series it demon-

strated what an actor can do when he is truly emjoying himself. "Colt 45," Wade Preston's series, wasn't doing so well.
"It was not considered a hit show," Martinson says, "and it
wasn't destined for a long run. Wade was the star and of
course Wade wasn't that totally involved and a series star
must be totally involved. He has to like what he's doing and
Wade was ambivalent about whether this business was for
him at that time, despite the fact that he had a unique opportunity that many actors would give their right arm for.

"Whatever it was, he wasn't that committed. Wade did
make waves at Warner Brothers [only one of many who
would have problems with the studio during that era]. He
wasn't happy with the material and he felt that the scripts
weren't right—the usual actor's complaints and many times
justifiably so. However, there was an episode on 'Maverick'
that year, 'The Saga of Waco Williams.' Wade was there to
do a guest stint as Waco Williams. He stepped out of his role
in 'Colt 45' to do it. In the opening scene Jim Garner [as
Brett] in a very funny, cowardly way inadvertently saves the
life of Waco Williams, who is a very famous gun, and now
Waco feels indebted to Jimmy and won't leave his side for the
ensuing hour, during which time he nearly gets him killed
about five or six times. Jim just wants this man, whose undy-
ing devotion has made him a clinger, to just leave him
alone. It was beautifully written and Wade received thousands of letters on that show about his ability as an actor. But
Wade's troubles with the studio continued and eventually he
left. The analogy is the difference between two actors and
their dedication. Jim's a big star and Wade now flies charter
planes, which was his real love in the first place."

Jim Garner felt that Wade Preston had not been treated
well at Warner Brothers and would later champion his cause
as a member of the Screen Actors Guild Board.

Jack Kelly believes that Wade Preston's cantankerousness

hurt him. "And he is cantankerous," he declares. "Jim, on the other hand, never took any training in how to be cantankerous and get away with it. I don't think he could. It is either an inbred, inborn, logical extension of one's personality, or they don't have it. Jim, in my [view] has never hurt anyone intentionally in his life. He has taken up the cudgel in some very obtuse causes, however."

With "Maverick" being shot exclusively at Warner Brothers funny incidents often occurred merely to break up the boredom. "We never went on location," Kelly continues. "I don't think one foot of film was shot on location with the exception of our library film. We just pulled out whatever resources the studio had. . . .

"But one day we were working back to back on the back lot of Warner Brothers. I mean the camera operators could have touched hankies in their hip pockets—that's how close back to back we were. There were four companies working at the same time. It got to be a panic with directors yelling 'action' and others calling out 'cut' with occasional overlapping sounds. It was hysterical." While waiting around for one of the other companies to complete a shot, Jim came over to Jack with an amused expression on his face.

"Come here," Jim said. "I want to show you something." The two men walked over to two fire hydrants that had hoses connected in case of fire. Kelly watched as Jim fooled around with the hoses for a minute. Jim said, "I'm getting the tool for this and we are gonna start spraying."

"I'm with you," Jack grinned. It was a very hot day in the San Fernando Valley. The temperature had been hovering around 100 degrees and everyone's wardrobe was drenched with sweat.

Jack continues the story. "We unrolled the two hoses and started spraying the whole goddamn area. All the uniforms were ruined. We had a two-hour brawl and the two of us were rolling on the ground we were so broke up. Meanwhile, the other stars are thoroughly pissed off because Jim and I are controlling the hoses. They weren't a party to it. The mayhem that occurred turned out to be one of those great morale builders on a day when morale was low. The camera crews were going bananas trying to protect their expensive Mitchell cameras, throwing whatever they could over the lenses to prevent them from being ruined. The extras were wrecks because they didn't have the guts or the privilege to get into the fray. They'd have been fired on the spot. But we were stars and had a field day usurping four different shows. It was a total brawl and Garner engineered the whole thing. Whatever complaints the directors or brass upstairs might have had were completely washed down the drain by the total efficiency of the shooting for the rest of the day. Shots were completed with less takes, actors stopped griping. It was the best possible thing that could have happened. Jim has a sense of knowing how to break tensions. No one who was involved that day will ever forget it. I'm sure a good many glasses and beer cans were raised in his praise that evening."

During the second year of "Maverick" it became obvious that the show could not be ignored when the Emmy nominations were announced, and indeed both it and Jim received nominations. At the time it seemed almost impossible for Jim to be beaten out as best actor in a continuing dramatic series. Huggins had already made his decision to move on because of the unbelievable hours he was putting into producing this first-class product. "Believe me," he says, "it was a twelve-hour-a-day job or more because I would come home and work at night after being at the studio all day long. My family hardly ever saw me. It was too much."

According to Roy, on the night before the Emmy Awards, Jim phoned him at home and the following conversation took place.

"Roy, listen," he began, "I just wanted to let you know when I get up there to get the Emmy I'm going to give a lot of credit to Les Martinson. I just wanted you to know. I feel we owe a lot to Les. I'm gonna give a lot of credit to him."

"Jim, if you get up there and you want to give all the credit to Les, that's your privilege."

And that was the end of the conversation. Roy went to the awards the following evening intending to give credit to everybody if he won for the show, knowing that Jim intended to give credit to Les Martinson, the director.

"The only problem with that," Roy relates, "is that Jim didn't win—I did, for the show itself. When they made the announcement, I got up and started down the aisle and there were people all over the place in loud stage whispers saying, 'No speeches! No speeches! We're running out of time.' Three other people said the same thing as I came on the stage to accept the award. Another guy was holding up a sign indicating that I should not make a speech.

"When I arrived at the podium, Jack Benny was at the microphone and he hadn't seen the signs. I don't think he was overjoyed since 'Maverick' had knocked him out of the box with the 'Gun-Shy' episode, which was opposite his 'Gaslight.' Jack and I had a personal bet about that particular night and I won. We destroyed him. He had no audience at all. We got the big ratings."

When Huggins arrived at the podium, Benny, not having seen any of the "no speeches" signs, refused to give Huggins the statue.

"I was wondering," Roy laughs, "what in the hell do I do to let him know they're running out of time and there's no time for speeches and horseplay? He finally did give me the Emmy and all I said to the audience was, 'Thank you very much.' Then I left the stage. I had a prepared speech in my pocket, ready to deliver, in which I gave credit to Marion

Hargrove, Douglas Heyes, Les Martinson, Jim Garner, and Jack Kelly—in that order. But I never got to make the speech. When I came back down the aisle my eyes met Jim's. There was disbelief and wonder in his and I never had a chance to explain what happened.

"Jim and I had never been close personal friends, never really spoke much except in connection with the show, but he and I didn't speak after that for quite a long time. I don't think he took it personally, though. He may have wondered why I didn't give a thank you speech including him and the others. I explained to the others. The minute I got up the next morning I called Doug Heyes and Les Martinson and told them what happened. I never bothered to tell Jim Garner because by that time I'd had a chance to think about the phone call I'd had from him the night before the awards and the whole thing was ridiculous. That's like giving the credit for *Time* magazine to the printer. Les Martinson did a pretty good job as a director and I fought with Jim to keep Les on. However, the director doesn't invent the characters and he doesn't write the script and he doesn't produce the show. Les never tried to rewrite any scripts. He directed."

Television has producers, writers, directors, and actors— and politics. Both Roy Huggins and James Garner understood the politics, and a cooling-off period between the two would have to take place before the relationship was to resume.

IX

It had been some time since Jim had made a movie. With "Maverick" already nominated for an Emmy, Warner Brothers capitalized on the television publicity and cast him in *Cash McCall* opposite Natalie Wood, who was returning to her home studio after a long suspension. Under the terms of her Warner Brothers contract she had been forbidden to work as an entertainer while suspended.

The film was tailor-made for Garner. Cash McCall is a boy wonder of modern finance—a casual, charming man in his early thirties. He has made and lost several fortunes by buying and selling shaky business empires, an activity he carries out behind a screen of anonymity. He is now comfortably ensconced in an elegantly appointed penthouse in Philadelphia's swank Ivanhoe Hotel, keeps a converted B-26 as his private plane, and indulges his various caprices to the tune of $250,000 a year just for pocket money.

Natalie Wood plays the daughter of a character named Grant Austen, played by Dean Jagger. Austen is in bad shape financially, so he sells his business to McCall for $10 million. Thus the stage is set for the characters played by Natalie and Jim to meet.

Jack L. Warner liked to be kept abreast of his employees'

activities. He especially wanted to know about any illness, whether it occurred on the set or led to a failure to report to work. The picture had started on schedule on April 10. Garner reported for work at 4:10 in the afternoon. Usually, his days on this film were long and arduous, often starting as early as six in the morning and ending late at night.

This exhausting schedule took its toll. On May 18 Jim reported to work early in the morning with a sore throat. He worked until noon, when his voice began to go and he felt so bad that he was sent home and advised to see his physician, Dr. Ewing Seligman. Dr. Seligman advised him to rest his voice for a few days. The studio accepted this dictum, and the company, under director Joseph Pevney, continued to work around him for three days.

Jim returned to the set, and shooting continued normally until mid-June, when he reported for work one afternoon complaining of severe stomach cramps. His illness resulted in a flurry of memos between the set and Jack L. Warners's executive offices. The assistant director drove Jim in a company car to Dr. Carl Karp, another of Jim's personal physicians. After examining him Dr. Karp called in another doctor for consultation. Afterward Karp advised the studio representative that there was the possibility of appendicitis, which could have necessitated surgery. He arranged to have Jim admitted to Cedars of Lebanon Hospital in Hollywood, creating a flurry of rumors among the gossip columnists, which usually occurs when a star is hospitalized.

After an overnight observation revealed no further complications, Jim was released from the hospital and sent home to rest. Still without pain, he spoke with the studio representatives, assuring them that in two days he would be on the early-morning plane to Monterey for location shooting. Everyone breathed a little easier. The company had shut down because Jim was needed in virtually every scene left to film.

As a precaution, the assistant director told Warner, "We will travel to the location at Monterey tomorrow morning to work with Natalie Wood and a double for Garner. If he is able to travel to the location on Thursday they will complete the sequence that day and return on Thursday night. In the event he cannot work, the sequence will be shot with a double and process plates for the dialogue to be shot whenever he is able to resume." Jim was able to work, and the picture was completed on schedule on Monday, June 29.

The postproduction phase posed numerous problems, including the shooting of publicity photographs, which required both Jim and Natalie to be free at a time when the photo studio was available. Mort Lichter was in charge of the photo studio at the time. It took some doing, and tempers flared, but the shooting was finally accomplished. This problem was nothing new. The still photo studio is in great demand—always.

A big event occurred in the Garners' life during the filming of *Cash McCall*. They moved out of their apartment into a new home in Belair, a choice area on the west side of Los Angeles, near Sunset Boulevard. It had been purchased from Quincy Jones, who had designed and built the home some ten years earlier and had agreed to help the Garners do a complete restoration, including authentic Scandinavian furniture.

Mort Lichter sent a memo to Bill Hendricks, head of publicity at Warner Brothers, which read in part: "*House Beautiful* magazine has covered things like this in the past and the Garners are very anxious to have a layout done on their home. Mr. Jones has worked with *House Beautiful* on a similar layout for the Gary Coopers and tells us that Helen Hathaway in New York, editor of *House Beautiful*, flips over layouts involving movie stars. Would it be possible to suggest . . . that our New York office explore this with Miss Hathaway? Garner plans to begin work on his house early in July so if *House Beautiful* is interested they would want to be in on the first steps of this restoration."

House Beautiful was not interested in being in on the first steps or any other steps of the restoration. Katherine Murray, West Coast editor of *House Beautiful*, advised the studio that the magazine wasn't interested in "before and after" restoration pieces; it only did a house after it was completed and then only if it felt it was "worthwhile." The only exception was if *House Beautiful* did the interior decorating and it wasn't interested in decorating Mr. Garner's house.

The studio publicity department suggested to Jim that they could try *House Beautiful* later, but he wasn't interested in that. There was some talk of pursuing other magazines, but nothing happened.

Natalie Wood's return to Warner Brothers from her suspension received most of the media coverage. Natalie was a superstar and always good for interviews that were sure to be provocative. She didn't fail the writers, nor they their readers. All the frustrations she'd held in during her suspension seemed to come out. In one such interview she said, "The whole routine about submerging your personality in a role is a lot of bunk. You have to bring your personality to every part you play. Some of these people are so tense they can't talk. Then there is the other extreme, the people who think that fur-covered cars mean glamour. The vulgarizing of the idea of glamour has hurt Hollywood as much as the nose-picking method fringe group who never got closer to the Actors' Studio than Sunset Boulevard." Later she let loose a bombshell. "One thing we could do without, however, is fan magazines." Jim loved her for that.

Natalie's barb received immediate attention from Muriel Babcock, then vice-president and editorial director of Ideal Publishing Corporation, which at that time published some important fan magazines, including *Movie Life, Movie Star Parade,* and *TV Star Parade.* In a bristling letter to Bill Hendricks of Warner Brothers, she said, "You and I know how much Natalie Wood's career owes to the buildup the fan magazines have given her with cover stories and pictures and particularly the buildup from the Ideal magazines. We did a job for her as part of the role Mr. Cotton our publisher believes fan magazines should play in the motion picture industry." She advised him that she was also writing a letter to Harry Brand, head of Twentieth Century Fox publicity, criticizing Natalie's husband, Robert Wagner, for similar remarks.

Many of these interviews had been done while Natalie was still on suspension but did not appear until after her return to the studio. There were uncomfortable feelings all the way around. An interview with John Wilcock in *Star Weekly Magazine* revealed how frustrating the suspension had been for her. "She is so determined, in fact, to be able to pick and choose that in return for Warners' allowing her to accept outside roles she has offered to extend her contract for four years in addition to the four it still has to run," he said.

Stars of the era, including James Garner and Natalie Wood, did owe a lot to fan magazines. Either individually or through publicity representatives or their studios, they all solicited stories in fan magazines. They were, as Muriel Babcock of Ideal pointed out, part of the star system and the making of stars. Even today, actors on their way up use tabloids and fan magazines to help their careers along, but once they become "big," many of them no longer even speak to the writers who helped bring them to stardom. Gossip columnist Sheilah Graham accused the fan magazines of being "self-appointed arbiters of moviedom's morals." Gossip columnists were always criticizing the fan magazines while writing columns for them—Sheilah Graham included.

Despite all the mudslinging that summer, Warner Brothers got its picture made, pacified the fan magazines by setting up interviews with more cooperative stars, and went on with the business of making pictures.

Interestingly enough, on the day Jim went before the cameras to start his work on *Cash McCall*, he observed the second anniversary of his original appearance as Brett Maverick. His co-star, Jack Kelly, was brought in by Warner Brothers for a photo session to celebrate the event. Fan magazines received a generous supply of the still photos for publication.

Jim was often quoted by the columnists because of his witty comments. To one writer, he explained a major difference between making television movies and theatrical films: "In TV when I court a gal, I maybe take her to a dance, squeeze in a little smooching, and possibly a few other things. That's all in the space of at most a couple of hours' shooting time. In *Cash McCall* we've already spent three days working on one of our big love scenes and so far I still haven't gotten around to even kissing Natalie."

Natalie did, however, spend a great deal of her time kissing her French poodle, Chi Chi. As a result, the poodle received an equal amount of coverage in the fan magazines. As a welcome-home present from Jack L. Warner, Natalie took over the most lavishly appointed dressing room in Hollywood, which had previously belonged to Joan Crawford. Joan sent her a congratulatory message, saying, "It was right after I moved in that I got an Oscar for *Mildred Pierce* and I just hope the dressing room is as lucky for you as it was for me."

Jim proved during this picture that he himself was not seeking "the star treatment." He was free to play at any of the many excellent private golf clubs in and around the city, where he could have been photographed in the Hollywood fashion. But before becoming a star, he had played golf on the public greens in Los Angeles's sprawling Griffith Park. He continued to play there, explaining, "All my old golfing friends hang out there and that's where I feel most at home."

Everyone on the set of *Cash McCall* loved Jim. He was always cooperative, always willing to listen, and didn't interfere with the director or the scriptwriters. Director Joe Pevney, a former actor himself, sang Jim's praises. "He takes his work seriously, but never himself. He's a born clown like Red Skelton or Sid Caesar. He can do extemporaneous take-offs on almost any personality you can name, complete with facial grimaces and manner of walking. I've never seen anything like him."

Robert Wagner was so in love with Natalie Wood that he was always on the set, but that didn't seem to bother Jim as much as it had when Ty Hardin came to visit Andrea Martin on the set of *Up Periscope*. It is possible that Wagner, having been in the business for such a long time, appeared less intimidating to Jim than did Hardin, a young man just starting.

Bob and Natalie had just acquired their fourth boat, a forty-eight-footer that they boarded on weekends for trips to Emerald Cove on Catalina Island (where Natalie would, many years later, meet an untimely death). To surprise Wagner, she found time away from *Cash McCall* to pass the rigid FCC test that would allow her to operate the ship-to-shore radio on their next trip out. In addition, the Wagners had just purchased a new home, and as a gag, Frank Sinatra had given them their first house gift—a hundred-pound sack of coarse salt in order for them to "sustain the salinity of the salt pool."

Jim had some outside activities, too. He appeared on the Bing Crosby television show and did a vocal duo with Bing. Said Jim of his own singing, "I like to sing and I can sing as loud as anybody but the professional quality of the singing is something else again." Here he exhibits the ability he has always had to make himself the butt of a joke—the hallmark of the classic comedian.

He also revealed his sense of humor when giving out advice about how to pick up a girl. "Well," he said, "you do what I do. When you're trying to obtain the attention of a beautiful doll and every other approach has failed, the thing to do is take the tack she least expects. Feign complete indifference. It's an attitude that very few women can bring themselves to understand—that it is possible for the male animal to be oblivious to their charms and graces. There's always the danger, however," he cautioned, "that the girl will simply ignore you entirely and never give you another chance to make amends. But," he grins, "that's an outside risk well worth the effort."

Marion Hargrove wrote *Cash McCall* but, announced that he would not be writing anything else for "Maverick." "I love 'Maverick,'" he said, "but the satire on 'Gunsmoke' laid an ostrich egg." He had the same comment on Jack Benny's takeoff on *Gaslight*. "There is a vast difference," he added, "between satire and comedy." This observation totally contradicted the feelings of the actors, the director, and the producer.

Garner lost twelve pounds to do *Cash McCall* and never looked better than he did in the finished film. A picture that boasted a top-rated television star and Natalie Wood's first film appearance since *Marjorie Morningstar* over a year before was sure to be a box office success. Warner Brothers was looking forward to a big promotion tour.

All was not well on the Warners' lot, however. Charles Denton let slip an item in the *Los Angeles Examiner* when he reported that "the Waddies are getting powerful restless out on the Warner Brothers spread. Scouts report that the outfit's top TV hands held a mass powwow recently to list their beefs, largest of which are short money, long hours, and rare residuals. Jim Garner isn't exactly enthusiastic about starring in a big budget feature like *Cash McCall* for the same weekly loot he gets for 'Maverick.'"

The story had been leaked by the Screen Actors Guild in preparation for a bigger story was yet to come. The problems between Warner Brothers and James Garner were not abating. Jim felt he was underpaid, that the working rules were like sweat-shop conditions, and that he was too restricted from outside work by the contract between him and his studio.

The Screen Actors Guild, with Ronald Reagan as its president, appointed Jim to its prestigious Board of Governors at about the same time trouble was beginning to stir within the ranks at Warner Brothers. Jim was now in an excellent position to do something about the unfair treatment he felt actors were receiving at his studio. He now had access to files, work records, and studio negotiations with the big screen union that represented the bulk of working actors in films and television. A fellow vice-president on the Board was an old friend and fellow actor, Jimmy Lydon, now an important man behind the cameras as well as in front but who continued to be thought of as "that kid who made the Henry Aldrich movies."

Prior to Jim's promotional tour for *Cash McCall*, a meeting was called to investigate actors' complaints at Warner Brothers. Jimmy Lydon, who organized the meeting, reconstructs it:

"Garner, like numerous others who were under contract at Warner Brothers, had what seemed to be some serious accusations against their employer. There were far too many abrogations of contract, according to the reports we were receiving at the Screen Actors Guild. This was prior to Garner's lawsuit against Warner Brothers. We in the guild had heard rumors that many actors and actresses were being harshly treated as far as their working hours, payment scale, penalties, and all that sort of stuff, which was of tremendous interest to the guild. We were in business to protect the actor from such illegal activities. So I called a secret meeting of all the Warner Brothers contract players in my house. The meeting was set for about 8:30 one evening. The turnout was tremendous, even more than I anticipated.

"All of these young people came and began to list their grievances with the studio, which I wrote down on a yellow legal pad. It was obvious to me that Warner Brothers would have to be called to account by the guild and I intended to do just that."

Lydon remembers something about James Garner that night that is indicative of the care and concern he has for others, especially his family. "We worked quite late—I don't think the meeting broke up until after one in the morning. But at eleven o'clock Garner, who had been quite vocal about the situation, came up to me and said, 'Jim, may I use your phone a moment?'

"I said, 'Of course' and we went into the other room and he called his wife to let her know where he was, which she already knew of course, but he wanted to reassure her. I overheard him when he said, 'I'm still at Jim's house. We have a lot more things to discuss and I wanted you to know that I'll be home in another hour or two. I didn't want you to worry. I love you.' That was the conversation, but I was deeply impressed by this man who, in the heat of a debate on union business, would take time out—perhaps even lose his train of thought—to let his family know he was okay and not to worry. Very few people in any business really have that kind of concern or even think about such niceties. It was thoughtful that he had told his wife where he was going, what the meeting was about, and that he would be home at a certain hour. It was even more considerate that he would let her know the schedule had been extended. I saw it as another mark of a very decent human being."

During the debate that night, Garner neatly laid out his complaints against the studio. They included the injustice of being put into a major motion picture while drawing the salary of a television series actor. He was appalled to discover that the $500-a-week salary he had been raised to wasn't an honest salary at all. The salary was $285. Warner Brothers had cleverly hidden the fact that $215 of that $500 was "an advance against residuals." In other words, he was starring in major motion pictures as a major star for $285 a week. Contract players, he argued, "simply do not get residuals at Warner Brothers. They pull every trick in the book to avoid payment to their actors. Even our personal appearance money is paid to the studio."

He still tells the story of events leading up to his appearance on "The Pat Boone Show." A contingent of Warner Brothers "cowboys" were to appear in the show, including Clint Walker, Ty Hardin, Peter Brown, Jack Kelly, James Garner, and several others who were on the studio's ABC Network television shows. Jim was offered $7,500 for participating. It sounded fine. The money was right, it was good exposure, and the studio wanted him to do it. The studio wanted something else, which Jim refused to give them. "They wanted my entire $7,500. That's the way they did it. If you did a personal appearance they took your money and paid you your regular salary. That's bullshit! That was a lot of money to me, and I could use it."

The others caved in and appeared for $500 each, with Warner Brothers receiving the rest of their payment from Pat Boone, but Jim balked. Jack Warner was furious. Furious or not, however, without Jim, the contingent of "cowboys" would be somewhat lackluster. So even though Warner detested giving in to actors, Jim got the best of him. For his appearance Jim received $2,500 in cash and a brand new Corvette "with everything on it." Jack Warner's revenge against James Garner would come soon, but it would prove more costly to the studio than any personal satisfaction he might gain from "teaching that sonofabitch a lesson."

Lydon, who would later become a producer under Jack Warner at the big Burbank studio, returned to his office at the Screen Actors Guild the following morning with the list of complaints amassed the night before during the meeting at his house. "It was a terrible situation," he states. "I intended to write Warners' a letter but changed my mind and got them on the telephone. I talked to their business affairs man, identifying myself as a vice-president of the Screen Actors Guild. I said, 'We are going to send over three representatives from the Screen Actors Guild and we want to see your books on television for the last three years regarding actors.'

"He asked, 'What's the matter?'

"'We want to see your books,' I told him. 'We want all of the books opened to us on every one of your shows.'

"He didn't sound too happy about the whole thing, but he asked, 'When are you coming?'

"'Nine A.M. Monday morning. Nine A.M.'

"He hesitated and finally mumbled, 'Very well.' He and his superiors all knew that they had to show us everything. There was no way to stop us from investigating their activities. It was part of the basic agreement between the Screen Actors Guild and all the signatories, of which Warner Brothers was one."

When Lydon's committee of representatives from the Guild returned from Warner Brothers, they brought a list of complaints that filled ten legal-sized pages. One actress, for instance, was eight months pregnant. She was required to start work at six-thirty in the morning and didn't finish until one o'clock the following morning with only one meal break and three or four meal penalties, which as Lydon explains, "was staggering. They hadn't let her go off the set and she was eight months pregnant and putting in a nineteen-hour day. That is practically slavery. Further, they never paid any of the meal penalties involved.

"The president of the Guild was away in New York, so I wrote a letter to the studio, under my signature, addressed to Mr. Warner personally. I notified him that if these fines and penalties were not paid within two weeks, and if any of these things ever occurred again we would refuse the actors the right to enter Warner Brothers. In other words, we would put Warner Brothers out of business. We couldn't say it in those words, but we could tell him that we would not allow our members to work at his studio—which would have the same effect. A studio can't hold out long without actors."

Warner Brothers paid all penalties and formally apologized to the Guild. Many people would say that Jack Warner was a cold-hearted man, but this has proved untrue. Lydon thought he would never work at Warner Brothers again, but he spent a long time there after the Guild action. Roger

Moore, one of the young actors who attended the protest meeting, went on to become one of the co-stars of "Maverick" after Jim departed. Warner most likely blamed Jim more than anyone else for the Guild's action. Jim's reluctance to do *Up Periscope* without script changes still rankled. Although Bill Orr was head of television production, his father-in-law headed the entire operation and had a long memory. If he was sometimes benevolent, he could certainly be vindictive if he felt justified. He had spies everywhere, even at the "secret" meeting, so he got some rather accurate first-hand information, including Jim's statement that "what's right is right. Let's go get them."

Hollywood had always had its inner circle of powerful men who ran things, but they didn't always get along. Jack Warner never got along with Harry Cohn at Columbia, nor with Louis B. Mayer or Darryl F. Zanuck when Zanuck was a producer for him at Warner Brothers (Zanuck eventually left to form Twentieth Century Fox). But certain "business" rules were observed by all the moguls. For instance, if Columbia Pictures had a problem with an actor or an actress—if they were asking for too much money, for instance—Cohn would call that person into his office and threaten him or her with cancellation of contract. This meant the end of that person's career, because Cohn would then get on the phone and talk to the heads of Warner Brothers, Paramount, Metro-Goldwyn-Mayer, and Twentieth Century Fox and would say, "So and so is no longer employable at my studio." As a result, no studio would touch that actor. Though it could not be proved that these exchanges actually occurred, they were accepted as fact. This is the situation that the Screen Actors Guild faced. The studio system had not yet been broken and if the moguls' power was not as great as it had been in the thirties and forties, it was still enough to cancel a career. Jimmy Lydon's experiences at Warners' are important because they show what kind of a man James Garner would be up against when he challenged Jack Warner.

Moguls make mistakes just like anyone else. Warner was the first to admit his. He had turned down Marilyn Monroe, Clark Gable, and Mario Lanza and allowed David O. Selznick to obtain the film rights to *Gone with the Wind* when it was Warner's for the asking. Bette Davis never forgave him for that error in judgment because had the picture been done at Warner Brothers (and Warner wanted it—he just didn't want the cost involved) it would have co-starred Bette Davis and Errol Flynn. So when William Conrad and Jimmy Lydon were under contract at his studio as producers Warner didn't put them through too rigid a chain of command. They were allowed to come directly to him with their ideas. Within a couple of days, he would be back to them by memo, saying either, "Yes, go ahead with this with the following suggestions," or "No, I don't like this." Sometimes there would be nothing more than a little card attached to the top of a memo from the producers that said, "No, you can't make this."

Costs were calculated from the initial go-ahead and included every last pen and paper clip. The budget was restrictive. In one particular instance it was $75,000. Jim Lydon and Bill Conrad came up with a screenplay by Rod Serling. They were ecstatic when they sent the screenplay to Warner. A couple of days later he sent it back with a simple comment: "No, I don't want to make this." They wouldn't let up. They took turns approaching Warner from different angles. One day it was Conrad's time to make the pitch. "Mr. Warner," he said, "I think this would make a lot of money."

Warner grinned and said, "So I made a mistake. I've made lots of mistakes in my life. So now let's go enjoy lunch."

Warner had two families at the studio. There was the family of actors, technicians, and office workers and there was the executive family, which was known as "Mr. Warner's inner family." There has been much written about Jack Warner's fights with his stable of superstars: Bette Davis, Olivia de Havilland, Errol Flynn, James Garner. He never fought with them directly. He had others do that, and they were well paid for their onerous duties.

Lydon, who knew him well, always referred to him as "Mr. Warner" and knows exactly how the inner family worked because he became part of it. "Mr. Warner's studio was a feudal estate and he ran it like a feudal estate. Some of it was very funny and amusing, like when you became part of the inner family, and started to have lunch in the private dining room, which wasn't even near the studio commisary. It was completely across the lot on Barham Boulevard. Mr. Warner had his own chef and maître d', who now owns a big restaurant in Hollywood called Emilio's. Emilio Barrone was our maître d'. We had our own kitchen and everything. So, after a certain period of time you would get the call as I did—after a number of years working for him. Mr. Warner never had a female secretary. He had two men. Bill Schaeffer and Tommy Murphy.

"One day I got a call from Bill Schaeffer and he said, 'Jim, Mr. Warner would like you to have lunch today in the private dining room.' That meant I was accepted as a member of the inner family. You weren't just invited to have lunch in the private dining room—you *had* to have lunch in the private dining room."

Warner had certain rules that were strictly adhered to. A man was required to wear a shirt, tie, and jacket, and there were to be absolutely no business discussions during the lunch hour. When someone became a member of the inner family he could expect certain things to happen. First of all, $20 a week was deducted from his paycheck for those lunches whether he could make it or not. "Twenty dollars a week," Lydon said. "You couldn't have purchased such food for one hundred dollars a week. It was fabulous. Also, Mr. Warner didn't allow drinking. No alcohol except at Christmas Eve luncheon, and then you were allowed two drinks, if you drank. But never a third. The napery, the silver, were all of the finest."

Warner did everything in his own time and way. Lydon had been a member of the private dining room for months. He was now a producer, but he kept his membership in the Screen Actors Guild. He still used it occasionally to do voice-overs and for the insurance benefits to his wife and children. "It was kind of an automatic thing," he says, "and having your picture in the Academy Directory went with that. I never even thought about it anymore."

One day Warner entered the private dining room, and as he walked along the long table—he always sat at the head of the table and nobody sat at the foot—he stopped and spoke to each friend there. When he reached Jimmy Lydon, Jim said, "Good afternoon, Mr. Warner."

He stopped and said, "Kid, you work for me?"

"Yes, I do, Mr. Warner."

"What do you do?"

Lydon said, "I'm a producer." Warner knew that, of course.

He leaned over close to Jimmy and quietly said, "Take your picture out of the Players' Directory," then kept right on walking toward his seat at the end of the table. He didn't think studio executives should be listed in the Players' Directory.

Despite his proprietary air, Warner had a good sense of

humor. Conrad, Lydon, and Warner often went together to see the Los Angeles Dodgers play baseball in Chavez Ravine. They had seats in the first row on the first-base side and used the top of the dugout as a table for their dinner. One afternoon they were driving down to the ballpark, with Warner behind the wheel. Bill Conrad sat in the back seat—he was so huge he needed a lot of room—and Jimmy Lydon rode in the jump seat. Warner looked up in the rear view mirror at Conrad and said, "Bill, I was driving to work this morning and I must have heard two commercials with your voice. You still doing that sort of thing?"

Bill said, "Sure, Mr. Warner."

Warner said, "Look. You work for me and I pay you enough money. I pay you lots of money. I want you to cut out all that crap."

"Mr. Warner," Bill said, "do you have any idea what I make doing voiceovers in a year?"

"Well, no, but it couldn't be that much."

"Mr. Warner," he explained, "when I do those voiceovers I do them at night and on Saturdays and Sundays and they do not interfere with my working for you and I make upward of two hundred thousand dollars a year for doing that."

"My God," Warner replied, "can you get me a job?"

Warner was also a compassionate man. He headed up dozens of charity drives and also gave generously to them. One year he invited the United Jewish Appeal to hold its annual luncheon in one of the studio's private dining rooms. It was a lovely affair, and lots of speeches were made. At each place there was a little placard to be filled out designating the amount of your donation. One producer took the card back to his office, filled it out, and attached a check for $100. Two weeks later his intercom to Warner's office buzzed and he picked up the phone. "Yes, Mr. Warner?"

"You're a Catholic, aren't you, kid?"

"Yes, sir. Why?"

"Well, you signed a card I have in front of me for a pledge to the UJA for one hundred dollars. You know, you don't have to do that."

"I know I don't, but I enjoyed the lunch and I wanted to do it."

Warner said, "Well, okay. I just wanted to know." He did not want to pressure *anybody* in "his family" and he didn't want anybody else doing so either. For every detractor there was someone who would call Warner a gentleman; many loved him. Jimmy Lydon was one of those people. Jimmy also had great respect and admiration for James Garner.

Still, Jack Warner viewed the world from a position of strength and endurance. He also had his millions to support that position. Warner's adeptness in dealing with adversaries is brilliantly exhibited by the way he handled his sale of the Warner Brothers studio to the Seven Arts group. Before selling, he was down to only two producers under contract. Nobody understood what was going on and he wouldn't tell anybody. He demanded blind loyalty and for the most part received it.

Films were being canceled or put on hold. "Make no commitments," he told his producers. "Trust me." One director had been contracted to direct a picture that was already committed.

The producer advised Warner of the situation and the director's contract. Warner said, "Call his agent and cancel the contract."

"Mr. Warner, I don't want to do that because the man will sue you. He has a legitimate contract."

Warner said, "What do you think I've got a staff of lawyers up here for? That's all they do all day long, all year long.

They'll take that director to court and they'll keep him in court for two years and finally it'll be so damned expensive for that man he'll settle for twenty-five cents on the dollar. Call the agent and do as I say."

The producer delayed phoning the agent for a couple of days. Finally he received another call from Warner. "Did you call the agent?"

"No sir, not yet."

"Don't call him," Warner said. "I don't own the studio anymore. And let me teach you a lesson, kid. That's the only reason I am paying the man off. Otherwise I'd keep him in court for as many years as necessary." That is the awful truth about the film industry. Studios have always done what was expedient if they could get away with it legally, and in that instance everything Warner intended to do would have been legal, if not necessarily moral.

Warner demanded loyalty. If an actor opposed him, he considered that action disloyal, and no matter how long he had known the employee or how much he liked him, he dealt with disloyalty with the swiftness of a tiger pouncing on its prey. When he was selling the studios he called in all his managers, one at a time, and said, "I have a two-year contract here with no options, no raise in pay. Sign it." Many of these people had contracts coming up for renegotiation in the next year or so or had options to be handled within a few months, but they all did Warner's bidding and signed where he indicated. All but one. Hoyt Bowers, head of the casting office, resisted. Hoyt had been a Warner Brothers employee since he was a kid messenger on the lot and had worked his way up the ladder to the head of casting.

Bowers said, "Wait a minute, Mr. Warner. I've got an option coming up in two months with a very substantial raise. I want to think about this a minute."

"Hoyt," he said, "sign the contract."

"No, sir. I want to take it back to my office and read it and think about it."

Warner very calmly nodded. "Hoyt, you do that."

Bowers picked up the unsigned contract and walked across the lot to his office. By the time he got there his intercom was buzzing. He picked up the phone and said, "Yes, Chief?"

Warner said, "Hoyt, be off the lot at six o'clock tonight. You're fired!"

What Warner was trying to do was to protect his family from the new owners by locking the buyers of the studio into a two-year deal with each of his key personnel. Hoyt Bowers was the only one who questioned Warner's judgment, and he was fired on the spot.

The stage was now set for some heavy fireworks between Garner and Warner—and Warner Brothers Studios—within a few weeks. For the time being it was business as usual.

Handsome young James Garner made his first appearances before the camera as a sportswear model for Jantzen. *Jantzen Company of Portland, Oregon*

An early publicity photo of Garner taken circa 1954 while he was still a supporting player. *American Film Institute*

James Garner and Edward Ashley in *Darby's Rangers*, a 1957 movie that later aired on "The CBS Late Movie." *CBS-TV*

James Garner with Mike Connors and Karen Steele in an early segment of "Maverick."

Jim performed dangerous stunt work as a Navy frogman in *Up Periscope* (1958). *Larry Edmunds*

After a year's suspension by the studio, Natalie Wood returned to Warner Brothers to co-star with James Garner in *Cash McCall* (1959). *Kenneth Norris Collection*

LEFT: Lois and James Garner enjoy a rare night out at the Moulin Rouge in Hollywood at the peak of his popularity as the star of the ABC-TV series "Maverick" (March 1959). *The Cleveland Press*

RIGHT: Fellow actors Robert Sterling and Jim Backus join "Maverick" star Garner in a 1960 celebrity golf tournament. *Lester Nehamkin/Jack Scagnetti*

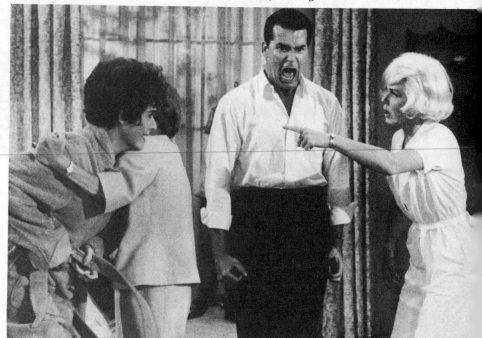

Polly Bergen and Doris Day both claim to be the legitimate wife of James Garner in *Move Over, Darling* (1963). *Kenneth Norris Collection*

Doris Day and James Garner in *The Thrill of It All* (1963). *Doug McClelland Collection*

Kim Novak talks things over with James Garner in *Boys' Night Out* (1962). *Kenneth Norris Collection*

Lee Remick and James Garner in *The Wheeler Dealers* (1963). *Kenneth Norris Collection*

Day and Garner share a romantic mood in *The Thrill of It All*. *Universal Pictures Company, Inc.*

James Coburn gets a mouthful of advice from an irate James Garner in *The Americanization of Emily* (1964). *Kenneth Norris Collection*

Julie Andrews and James Garner listen to Joyce Grenfell in a scene from *The Americanization of Emily*. *Larry Edmunds*

Garner and Angie Dickinson in *The Art of Love* (1965). *Doug McClelland Collection*

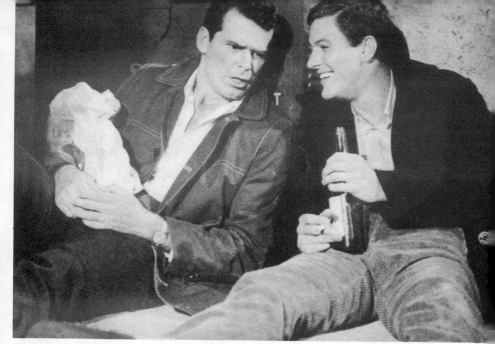

Garner and Dick Van Dyke share a friendly bottle in *The Art of Love*. *Kenneth Norris Collection*

James Garner and Eva Marie Saint face interrogation by Nazis in *36 Hours* (1965). *Kenneth Norris Collection*

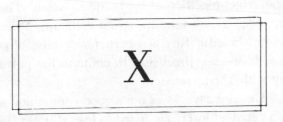

X

Cash McCall had its premiere at a theater in a town where Garner was extremely popular. It opened at the Stanley Theater in Philadelphia on December 30, 1959. The reviews were generally good but not necessarily glowing. *Variety*, which was not too enthralled, said, "Still, for audiences willing to accept a surface story with some romantic shenanigans, the picture will have attraction. Garner deserves better and so does Miss Wood. They are both intelligent actors capable of handling more incisive material."

Down the street, *Variety*'s competitor, the *Hollywood Reporter*, said, "Garner is surprisingly believable in this sort of role." *Limelight* commented, "James Garner does a bang-up job . . ." and the *Motion Picture Herald* said, "Whatever it is that makes a top-money-making star—James Garner has it. . . ."

Though Howard Thompson of the *New York Times* sniped, "Very fortunately, indeed, Warners' *Cash McCall* and its hero, James Garner, both have a sense of humor," Sidney Skolsky with the *Hollywood Citizen News* put things in proper perspective: "It's doing business and that's the important thing."

Jim, a disgruntled star, continued to grind out episodes of

"Maverick" without the guidance and ideas of Roy Huggins. During that year, however, he began to see Roy socially. Most of Roy's friends, like Jim's, were not part of the Hollywood crowd, but there were some exceptions. Huggins hosted poker get-togethers at his home in Belair. The participants included David Janssen, Andy Williams, Pete Rugulo, and Henry Mancini (Roy was particularly fond of people in the music business). Jim began to come to the poker games, probably with David Janssen.

"Jim," Huggins says, "was not a good companion in poker. He was a very bad loser. He hated to lose at poker, would get furious and leave the game, go out and walk around in the streets. So I stopped inviting Garner to the poker games. It is no secret that losing drives him crazy. At golf he used to throw his clubs. If people are honest with you, they'll tell you it makes him a little bit sick to lose at anything."

After the poker games were no longer open to him, Jim once again drifted away from Roy and the two rarely saw each other.

The quality of "Maverick" was not as good the third year as it had been previously. Jack Kelly and James Garner were still Bart and Brett, but the stories weren't as good. The crispness that had originally characterized the show seemed somewhat diminished. Writers have written, misleadingly, that "Maverick" didn't start to decline until *after* Jim Garner left the show. Huggins says that is erroneous. "That ain't so," he says. "Ain't so at all. Garner was still in it in its third year and it went into the sink. It went into the toilet. It fell out of the top ten and out of the top twenty and by the time that third year was over its national ranking was about thirty-sixth. It lost its audience. Garner was still there. Kelly was still there. It continued on and continued to decline. By the halfway point in the fifth year it fell below fifty and was mercifully cancelled."

Huggins stresses the significance of Jim's still being the star when the show started to decline. "The reason I say that," he explains, "is because it has meaning. It means that James Garner must be given the kind of material he knows how to do. He is not a star without his material. His whole support group left at the same time. I left. Marion Hargrove left. Doug Heyes left. The three of us left together. They weren't going to stick around without me, because they knew what would happen. Marion couldn't come up with a story and Doug was being kept at it by me, by my sitting down with him and working out stories. Both of them were very hot after the second year of 'Maverick' and were interested in going on to other things. Each went on to very brief screen careers [as screenwriters] . . .They were both highly talented people and deserving of good assignments. Marion wrote the screenplay for *The Music Man*. There was a difference in the two, however, that is important. Marion had his reputation based upon a very rich contribution he made to 'Maverick.' Doug, however, has always been an excellent television writer. He went on to write and direct 'Captains and Kings,' one of the best mini-series ever made."

In Hollywood rumors of strikes always abound, so there was little concern when the trade papers began to hint that both the Writers Guild of America and the Screen Actors Guild might strike if their current demands were not met by the producers, which meant the studios. Ronald Reagan had for several years been president of the Screen Actors Guild but finally stepped down. He stayed on the Board of Directors but became less active in Guild affairs. In 1959 the Guild was having great problems with the studios because of long-standing arguments over the profits being received by the studios on the sale of post–1948 movies. The television industry was paying large sums for the use of films that had already completed first runs on the big screen, but the actors who had performed in these pictures weren't getting anything. The studios were making huge profits. They did not want to part with their windfall.

Howard Keel, the current president of the Guild, was leaving to do a play in New York and would not be available for the negotiations that lay ahead for a new contract with the producers. The Guild needed to find someone dynamic who could maintain enthusiasm for the strike if it materialized. John Dales, the executive secretary of the Guild, called Reagan and asked him if he would return as president. The nominating committee had already decided he was the one person who could hold together the giant union during a strike. Reagan, already eyeing California's governorship, decided to confer with his MCA agent, Lew Wasserman, to see if it would "damage my career" before giving an answer. Wasserman assured him that it would be all right, and Ronald Reagan once again assumed the presidency of the Guild.

The Writers Guild preempted the Screen Actors Guild and struck in mid-January. Like the actors, they wanted to be recompensed for the post–1948 movie sales to television. It was the first strike in the union's twenty-seven-year existence and the studios were stunned. The strike had one odd aspect: Many members of the Writers Guild were also directors and producers and continued working in that capacity, although some did their writing on the set and got away with it. Some people believe that it was during this strike that the directors gained ascendancy in the film industry because not too long after the strike was settled, directors began to infringe on the writers by rewriting their material right on the sets.

The strike was not devastating to the studios, although seven major and forty-six smaller independent producing companies were affected by it. TV producers had stockpiled scripts in anticipation of a strike, and had more than enough scripts to finish out the season. Production was booming because the studios feared something worse—a strike by the Screen Actors Guild. There was no way to stockpile actors.

When the writers walked out, Warner Brothers, at the insistence of Jack Warner, suspended James Garner and Jack Kelly on the grounds that the studio "had run out of scripts." It created one of the biggest uproars in the history of Hollywood. With the "Maverick" ratings declining, the studio saw an opportunity to "legitimately" punish its outspoken star by putting him out of work for several months. Jim couldn't work without the studio's permission.

Jim responded by announcing that Warner Brothers had breached his contract when they stopped his paychecks and that he was now a free agent. Warner Brothers then filed suit against both actors to determine "the validity of the contract" they had with the studio. Sympathy was with the actors, but tradition favored the studio. Over the years several players had challenged the movie moguls, and most had lost. Giants like Bette Davis had challenged Jack L. Warner and had their careers put in limbo for long periods of time. But Olivia de Havilland had beaten Warner in court. She broke a long-standing contract clause that entitled studios to keep their players for life if they so chose. With the Screen Actors Guild behind her, she contended that contracts should be limited to no more than seven years, with no additional time because of suspensions. Although the courts decided for Olivia—and Jack Warner thought afterward that the decision was probably good for the entire industry—Warner Brothers would no doubt have won had the Guild not joined forces with the star.

Regarding James Garner, Warner Brothers committed a crucial error in judgment. The studio's legal department had advised Warner that a clause in Jim's contract allowed the studio to lay him off. Its contention was that Jim was employed to perform in "Maverick" and that if the series was shut down, then so was the actor. Of course, this contention was contradicted by Warners' actions: starring Jim in motion pictures at the same time that "Maverick" was running without giving him a separate film contract.

Jim didn't fool around. He employed Martin Gang, a prestigious film lawyer from a prestigious law firm in Beverly Hills, to bring suit against the studio for breach of contract. If sustained by the courts, the suit would make him a free agent. Suddenly Jim was not only out at Warner Brothers but facing the possibility that he would never work again as an actor in Hollywood.

Jim was angry, so it didn't matter to him if he never made another picture or television series. "I've been on my own since I was thirteen years old," he declared, "and I know I have to fight my own battles. It's true that I enjoy acting, but it isn't my whole life. I'd like to continue doing what I'm doing, but not for those people." He believed that Warner Brothers wanted it two ways: They wanted to be right when they were right and they wanted to win through manipulation when they were wrong.

Whether or not he was serious about not wanting to work at Warners' is conjecture. Despite his protestations, he was smart enough to know that even though the series was on a decline it was still the most recognizable show on television and he was the most recognizable star. No career actor wants to walk out on something that prestigious. If, as he suspected

they might, Warner Brothers offered to shake hands and rewrite him a more lucrative contract, everybody would win.

Warner Brothers had no such intentions. The studio saw
Jim's winning as the destruction of its power. Control over
contract players was what sustained the Warner Broth
ers–ABC coalition, which produced over a dozen highly
rated television shows.

It was a repeat of history: the Warner Brothers studio challenged by a disgruntled actor and the Screen Actors Guild.
Additionally, Jim was a powerful vice-president of the Guild.
"Warner Brothers," he said, "thinks I'm the ringleader of the
revolt against their slave labor tactics. I don't know about
being the leader, but I'm certainly against their tactics. Actors
have dignity as well as financial needs." Jim entered the fray
against Warner Brothers with an ulcer that he blamed on his
working conditions and ill-treatment by the studio.

As an unemployed and unemployable actor Jim had to
look outside Hollywood for employment. Oddly enough,
even though no other studio in town would touch him for
almost a year, producers Ben Segal and Burton Bonoff offered him the lead in a summer stock production of *John
Loves Mary* opposite Barbara Lord. One condition was im-
posed. Jim would have to put up an indemnity bond to protect the producers in the event that Warner Brothers
triumphed in their countersuit and called upon them to turn
over Jim's salary at some later date.

It was a breath of fresh air for Jim. The case was not set for
trial until fall and he had not looked forward to an entire
summer of loafing around and feeling miserable. He had always worked and needed to keep busy as much from habit as
from desire.

Prior to leaving with *John Loves Mary* on the straw hat
circuit, Jim kept some television commitments that had been

160   • *Raymond Strait* •

set prior to his layoff and had to be honored by Warner Brothers. He appeared on the popular "Dinah Shore Show," a Bob Hope special, and a number of exhibition golf tournaments that were televised. On "Celebrity Golf," he fired an exciting low score to tie veteran Sam Snead, which caused him to quip, "I might even take up pro golfing." He wasn't serious, of course, but he did have a high amateur standing.

Jim had started on the stage without lines. He was now back on the stage in a show that had originated on Broadway. Norman Krasna's *John Loves Mary* opened in New York in February 1947 and brought fame to its stars, William Prince, Nina Foch, and Tom Ewell; Ewell went on to a highly successful career in movies and television. The play ran a full year on Broadway. The hilarity of *John Loves Mary* lies in the complications that result when John, who loves Mary, decides to do a favor for his army buddy, Fred, who has arrived home from Europe before him. The favor means that John must marry Fred's girl Lily—an English lass—so that he can bring her into the United States as a war bride and then divorce her so that she can marry Fred. In the meantime Fred, a forgetful type, has married someone else without notifying either John or Mary. John, then is stuck with Lily whether he wants to be or not. And John still loves Mary. How John manages to get out of this bind is the crux of the show, which delighted fans across the country. This enchanting comedy was perfectly suited to Jim's sense of humor. The reviews throughout the tour were without exception raves.

Jim had a great time; being in the play gave him the moral support he needed for his upcoming court battle. Mavor Moore, theater critic for the *Toronto Telegram*, spoke for the other reviewers in his terse but accurate summation of Jim's performance: "Star James Garner as Seargant John is extremely amusing in his put-upon way. I would say that he is by far the most energetic and theatre-wise film type I have seen on the stage in a long while, except that this left-handed compliment does him less than justice. He is at home in this league, too."

As to the Screen Actors Guild strike, Universal Pictures was the first to break ranks. It agreed to pay the writers two percent of any post–1948 film sales to television, following a forty percent deduction for distribution costs. The same studio then entered into a separate negotiation with the Screen Actors Guild, which was the more important of the two striking unions. Although Spyros Skouras, head of Fox, had said that the strikes were "a fight to the finish," Universal's capitulation opened the floodgates and within a short period of time all the producers in the industry had capitulated. The strikes ended, and everybody went back to work as if nothing had happened. Everybody except James Garner.

Jack Kelly had originally joined forces with Jim, but as time went on he changed his mind. He opted for economics. "A lot of us," he explains, "were brought up in a much different familial environment than Jim was. Some of us want to be actors and we have the dedication to it and we start taking on immediately the trappings that we know stars must have and so as a result, we are polluted already before we even get to the first job. My decision to say, 'Hey, I want to go back to Warner Brothers,' was a symbol of that pollution. The guy on television who says, 'To hell with this. I want out of television. I don't like what I'm doing'—ever notice how they don't say that about picking up lucrative paychecks? Another symbol of the pollution. I was involved in what I wanted to have in terms of security. Mr. Warner understood my needs and my ambitions. When he offered me a fifty-two-week paycheck out of fifty-two weeks a year I said to myself, 'Hey man, I'm made.' Normally that would be a forty-week deal—if you were lucky. So I got twelve extra weeks. Plus, they promised me an extra picture a year and all of the bullshit, which didn't cost them anything extra. A major studio is in a position to make concessions that don't cost anything because they go with the package in the first place. So my attitude, in essence, was fuck Jim Garner. I'm in it for number one."

Warner played Kelly against Garner, hoping to weaken Jim's case by splitting it in half.

"Whatever Mr. Warner's theories or applications were," says Kelly, "they worked as far as I was concerned. But I went to Jim and told him. I left Jack L. Warner's office and even before I left the studio, I went to a telephone and called Garner and told him I wanted a private conversation with him. He said, 'Sure, Jack. I'll be here at home.' We lived close. He was in Belair and I was at Sunset and Sepulveda. I was within walking distance to his house. I went over to see him and it was the only time I was ever in his house. He appeared totally amicable to me. I would give him every license to despise me. We had started out in a joint suit against Warner Brothers and I left him hanging. Sold out for the buck. No question about it. It momentarily weakened his posture, but I figured that was his problem—not mine. I was looking out for me. I was a merchant. I don't know if Jim ever held that against me, but if he did he never showed me. I have worked with him five or six times, many times since then, and he has never changed one bit. All he said to me that night was, 'I understand.' And I believe he did. He always did look out for the other guy."

Toward the end of his tour with *John Loves Mary*, Jim took time out to visit Ponca City, Oklahoma, where he participated in the sixty-seventh-anniversary celebration of the opening of the Cherokee Strip on September 16. He was having a great time, appearing in the rodeo on Friday and serving as Grand Marshal in the morning parade on Saturday. Relatives attended by the dozen; it was like a family reunion—and there is nothing in the world more important to Jim than family. Having witnessed the crassness and materialism of Hollywood, he has been especially careful to preserve and protect his family and family love. His plea for privacy is sincere: When he does let someone come into his private life, he lets them in all the way, but he only does that with someone he trusts. He is loyal to friends, no matter what the situation. When he appeared on "This Is Your Life" he was surprised by the appearance of an old pal who told of being busted by the cops on a speeding charge and jailed. Jim needled him on the show for being "a common crook." But his friend countered by explaining Jim's part in the event: "He kids me about that, but he doesn't tell you that he hocked his overcoat to go my bail." It was a true story, and Jim seemed at a loss for words—almost embarrassed. He cares for others, even if his generosity is often hidden by design.

A bitter court battle awaited Jim when he returned to Los Angeles. He and Warner Brothers had fought quite a fight in the newspapers before the actual court hearing. Jim testified in his own behalf. To the surprise of almost everyone, Jack L. Warner took the witness stand to defend his studio's position. It was an unusual action for a movie studio head, but Warner felt very strongly about the studio's position. Of course, executives at other studios were praying for a Warner Brothers victory. But it wasn't in the cards. An actor, backed by the Screen Actors Guild, triumphed for the second time against Warner Brothers when in December a Los Angeles Superior Court ruled in favor of James Garner. Jim would never work at Warner Brothers again as long as Jack L. Warner headed the studio. Warner couldn't control the entire film industry or dictate to the courts, but he could certainly rule over his own house.

Garner savored his victory, considering it a victory not only for himself but also for all the other actors who were locked into punitive contracts. From the time of his layoff to the settlement of the suit, he talked very little of his own position. When he appeared on talk shows (where it was hoped that he would let slip some tidbit not yet revealed) he spoke mostly of the plight of others. He protested Wade Preston's situation at Warner Brothers as an example of the wrongs perpetrated by the studio, saying, "Here's this kid working his butt off, making three or four hundred dollars a week with nothing up the road anywhere. This kid has worked hard, and for what? He got nothing because Warner Brothers gives nothing!"

Roy Huggins paid particular attention to the case. "Jim," he says, "always put himself out for other people. He's helped many—not always so public as with Wade, but just as sincere."

Demonstrating how he felt the system discriminated against series actors, Jim pointed out that he had made more money during those eight weeks of summer stock than he had in three years on "Maverick." "Hell," he said, "I lost money on "Maverick." In three years I earned ninety thoudand dollars on the show and it cost me a hundred thousand dollars in costs and lawyers to get out of it."

Jim's was a victory for all actors. What he had accomplished would give a billion-dollar boost to the financial situation of the actor in years to come. It was a landmark decision upheld by the appeals court. James Garner's long struggle was over.

Huggins says, "It was the biggest break that any actor ever

got because he was free to pick and choose whatever he wanted to do thereafter—and he was a proven box office attraction, so producers from other studios were anxious for his services." But it was no immediate windfall. The appeals court did not hand down its decision until November 1961— a year later. During the interim producers were hesitant to make offers for fear that the original ruling would be overturned.

Jim has always been lucky, and this situation was no exception. "Maverick" was beginning its decline when he was laid off but was still high enough in the ratings to be renewed the following season. But it was headed into disaster, and Jim got out just in time. The show ran for four and a half years. Jim left before the end of the third season, but all shows for that season had been completed and work on the fall schedule was proceeding by that time. That was one of the reasons Jim was so upset with the studio. They could well have afforded to wait a while before starting to shoot the series again and could have used him in other areas, such as guest stints on other shows or movies.

Jack Kelly remained on "Maverick" and was joined by Roger Moore, who later proved himself in the James Bond movies. But Jim was "Maverick," with the creative talents that made him work as "Maverick": Roy Huggins, Douglas Heyes, Marion Hargrove, and Les Martinson. With Jim's departure the entire inner workings of the show had been removed. The show was now like a clock with only a dial. What was essential was missing.

XI

Garner had been suspended on March 2, 1960. He sued Warners' and shortly thereafter they countersued, and the matter dragged on until December of that year. The trial was conducted in the courtroom of Superior Court Judge Arnold Praeger. The judge, in finding for James Garner, held that Warner Brothers had indeed breached the employment contract and that Garner was free from any obligation to the studio under that particular contract. Warner Brothers immediately appealed.

After the decision was rendered, there was a discussion in Judge Praeger's chambers regarding Jim's attorneys' request for a permanent injunction restraining Warner Brothers from sending letters or otherwise interfering with Jim's relations with prospective employers. Judge Praeger hesitated to honor the request, stating that such an injunction was not necessary since Jim was in a position to apply to the court for relief should Warner Brothers take any steps to interfere with his livelihood, and this courtesy of the court allowed Jim to look for employment in the motion picture or television industry without much fear of Warner Brothers' interfering.

The Mirisch Company was preparing a major motion picture in connection with United Artists and had James Garner in mind for the male lead. The film, *The Children's Hour*, had an extensive history. Originally written by Lillian Hellman as a three-act play and copyrighted in April 1934, it was later published by Knopf in November of that year. On August 8, 1935, Lillian Hellman Kober, Herman Shumlin, and The Children's Hour, Inc., assigned the motion picture rights to Samuel Goldwyn "forever." On June 23, 1936, Samuel Goldwyn assigned the copyright to Samuel Goldwyn, Inc. That year, with William Wyler directing, Goldwyn made a motion picture from the play. The film, retitled *These Three*, starred Miriam Hopkins, Merle Oberon, and Joel McCrea.

As originally written the play concerned the scandal surrounding a possible lesbian relationship between two unmarried women who operate a private, all-girls school. Due to the Motion Picture Association of America ban on any deviant sex themes, *These Three* involved not a relationship between two women but an illicit affair between a man and woman.

On December 4, 1942, Samuel Goldwyn, Inc., assigned the copyright of the picture to Samuel Goldwyn. This was followed by an agreement dated March 10, 1943, in which Samuel Goldwyn, Inc., assigned "all rights in the agreement with Lillian Hellman Kober and The Children's Hour, Inc. (dated August 8, 1935) back to Samuel Goldwyn, with respect to the motion picture rights and the radio and television rights to the play." On April 23, 1946, Samuel Goldwyn assigned all these rights to Frances Howard Goldwyn, including the copyright for the film. On March 17, 1953, Frances Howard Goldwyn assigned all her rights to the play and film to Howard Pictures, Inc. Sometime thereafter the legal title was disentangled, allowing Samuel Goldwyn to sell the film rights to The Mirisch Company for $350,000.

The original *These Three*, which was rejected by the Hays Office (MPAA) when first presented for approval, was re-edited and retitled to meet the objections of that office and was also stripped of its lesbian theme. Critics referred to it as "a transmutation of the play."

Two members of the first film adaptation of the play were involved in the second effort: William Wyler and Miriam Hopkins. The 1961 production was a major motion picture. Wyler was hired both to produce and direct the film. His salary was $200,000, with escalation clauses assuring him close to half a million dollars. The first star signed was Audrey Hepburn, whose salary was $500,000 plus percentages. Robert Wyler, William Wyler's son, was hired as a consultant and associate producer for $100,000, half of which was borne by his father. William Wyler's compensation was computed on what was known as "the Billy Wilder Formula." Wilder always received 17½ percent of the first $1 million gross after the break-point of a film's receipts and 20 percent of the gross thereafter. Only someone of the caliber of Wilder could demand such a lucrative arrangement.

James Garner and Shirley MacLaine both worked in the film as a part of a multiple-picture deal. In MacLaine's case the deal involved films that have endured as audience favorites: *Two for the Seesaw, The Children's Hour, Roman Candle,* and *Irma La Douce.* She received $350,000 plus percentages. She was one of the hottest stars in Hollywood at the time, as was Audrey Hepburn.

Jim's compensation was revealed as being "as good as that of anyone else involved in the picture." Jim has always been reticent about his finances, but his income has usually been $1 million a year or more. To invest that kind of money in a player the producers needed assurance that there would be no repercussions from the Garner–Warner Brothers litigation.

Jim's law firm assured The Mirisch Company and United Artists that there was little if any possibility that Warner Brothers would win a reversal of Judge Praeger's decision on appeal. A memo from the producers' own legal counsel supported that contention. In a lengthy legal opinion the studio lawyers concluded, "We are of the opinion that the employment of James Garner by The Mirisch Company in *The Children's Hour* is a good risk from a legal standpoint." The doors of Hollywood were officially reopened to the handsome leading man, and most of the studios in town were attempting to secure his services as an actor.

It could have worked the other way, however. At one point, while the picture was still in the planning stages and had the working title *The Infamous*, there were serious discussions as to whether an insurance company would cover the picture with Jim as the star because of his litigation with Warner Brothers. Wyler wanted Jim and only Jim for the part and that, in effect, was the pivot upon which Jim Garner's career turned. Had Wyler wavered, Jim might not have worked again for a very long time—certainly not until the appeals were completed.

The Children's Hour was one of the most unusual films that Jim had ever made—different from anything he has done before or since, except perhaps *Victor/Victoria*. The picture was not submitted to the MPAA for approval by its producer-director, William Wyler. He had inside knowledge that the Johnston Office was about to reverse itself on the sexual deviation clause and permit films to deal with the subject, providing the film was given the proper rating.

The film was completed on September 1, 1961, and premiered in Los Angeles on December 20 of that same year. Critics were vicious in their assessment of the film. One reviewer prated, "The dialogue oriented drama is often too wordy for the film medium; and occasionally, its dramatics are too heavy-handed. At times the story strains the viewer's credulity." Other important reviews followed immediately.

Bosley Crowther, *New York Times:* "It is hard to believe that Lilliam Hellman's famous stage play, *The Children's Hour,* could have aged into such a cultural antique in the course of three decades as it looks in the new film version . . . but here it is, fidgeting and fuming, like some dotty old doll in bombazine with her mouth sagging open in shocked amazement at the belatedly whispered hint that a couple of female schoolteachers could be attached to each other in an 'unnatural love.' . . . More incredible is its assumption of human credulity."

Time: The film, they said, "was directed at the assumption [that] the perceptive level of the audience is that of a roomful of producers' relatives." They were kinder to Shirley Mac-Laine who, they said, "gives the best performance of her career."

Newsweek: "Few things are so frustrating as the movie that takes a purposeful whack at a serious theme and just doesn't quite connect head-on."

In the *New Yorker* the queen of New York critics, Pauline Kael, said that Wyler "carries on" as if he had only just learned about lesbianism and was feeling distinctly let down by human nature. She accused the picture of being "such a portentous lugubrious dirge (that seems to be part of the funeral of Hollywood moviemaking) that I developed a rather perverse sympathy for the rich old lady villainess. . . ."

Even Lillian Hellman detested the new version, complaining that Wyler had clung to old mores and failed to update the story. Wyler, in defense of his blunder, weakly rebutted that he had so much respect for Hellman's writing that he had hesitated to make changes. The Mirisch brothers dismissed the failure as "one of those things. Sometimes you win, sometimes you lose."

Critics, for the most part, had kind words for Miriam Hopkins and Fay Bainter (who played the role of the misinformed, cold, and sexless grandmother who made an issue of her granddaughter's slanderous lies, thereby ruining the lives of two teachers). But they were so preoccupied with the numerous women in the film that they almost completely ignored Jim in the role of Audrey Hepburn's doctor boyfriend. From his point of view it may have been just as well. It was his first major motion picture bomb.

The biggest advantage for Jim was being able to work in films again. He signed a four-picture deal with The Mirisch Company, of which *The Children's Hour* was the first to be completed. At the same time, he had many other offers from major studios. Thus, following the courtroom battle with Jack L. Warner, Jim's career moved into high gear.

Jim's home life was also happy, although there were rumors that the Garners' marriage began to suffer once he emerged as a major star. If there was any tension at all in the Garner household, it was because Lois did not like the demands made upon her husband—demands that kept him away from his family. Jim had become a workaholic, sure that every picture would be his last and that he would then have no source of income to support his family. He still has that "actor's insecurity." Gigi and Kim were growing up and the demands placed on Lois by her two energetic daughters heightened her frustration with "going it alone" at home. As a result, tempers may sometimes have flared, but the marriage remained intact. Lois still loved her husband deeply, and, more importantly, in a town where the gossip columnists generally know who's quarreling before they really are, she never aired her difficulties in the press.

Jim had been reasonably cooperative with the press on his way up. Even during his squabble with Warner Brothers he had given reporters and writers interviews to press his case, candidly expressing his feelings about Warner Brothers, which he referred to as "Warners' penitentiary." But then the press began not only to pry into but actually to fabricate stories about his family life. Stories from his past were dug up, some factual but most exaggeration or innuendo. For instance, it was reported that his father and stepmother Wilma did their share of drinking and even made home-brew. What is left out is the fact that in those days—it was the Depression and prohibition was still in force—rich and poor alike made their own. Once Jim became a star, the Hollywood scribes began creating fantasies about his life, and he resented the lies. Thus, he promptly closed the door to them and began what is now known as "Jim Garner's annual interview." He never understood why he was being attacked by those with whom he had been so open. Jim has a long memory and a fierce temper. As a result, at times he still finds himself doing battle when someone ill-advisedly trespasses too far into his privacy.

This was the situation when he began working on *Boys' Night Out* at M-G-M in October 1961. He threw himself into the picture, determined to not make another picture with a bleak premise.

Boys' Night Out was a Kim Novak film. Everybody else was supporting cast. The picture focused on Novak as a provocative blonde, the femme fatale in the lives of four attractive but frustrated Connecticut suburbanites looking for escape from the doldrums of everyday life as they commute back and forth from their Manhattan offices to home life an hour away.

Marion Hargrove, who had written a number of "Maverick" scripts, had taken the premise from a story by Marvin Worth and Ruth McDevitt. The screenplay, based on Hargrove's adaptation, was written by Ira Wallach. Michael Gordon directed the Martin Ransohoff production. Numerous writers were involved in the project; fifteen completed scripts were turned in before the final working script was accepted. Besides Jim, the original male leads included Gig Young, Tony Randall, and Howard Morris. Young was later replaced by Howard Duff, making his first motion picture in several years. He had been preoccupied with television, starring opposite his wife, Ida Lupino, in the mystery series "Mr. Adams and Eve." The supporting cast included Jessie Royce Landis (superb as Jim's worldly wise mother), Zsa Zsa Gabor, William Bendix, Jim Backus, Fred Clark, Larry Keating, and Ruth McDevitt.

The wives of the errant gentlemen were portrayed by Janet Blair, Patti Page, and Anne Jeffreys. Suspicious of their spouses' activities on their night out, the women became jealous. That's when the fun really began. Jim, playing the only single man in the group, romped through the farce with all the gusto of a soldier on leave.

Making the film was an uplifting experience for Jim, providing him with the type of humorous role to which he properly belonged. A major reviewer gave the story and winning critique in one line: "Bachelors. Suburbanites. Students. Detectives. Sex Research. Imposture. Jealousy. Infidelity. Marriage. New York City. Connecticut."

The making and distribution of the film was not without its unusual aspects. The apartment, erected on stage 25 at M-G-M Studios, which in the story was rented by the "boys" for their frolics with Kim Novak, was meant to startle and startle it did. Designed by art directors George W. Davis and Hans Peters together with set decorators Henry Grace and

Jerry Wunderlich, the "pad" attracted dozens of spectators who wanted to view the riot of stunning color, brilliant and imaginative decor, and wild apartment furnishings. The set was valued by the producer at $100,000. Most of the picture was shot at M-G-M and at various location sites around Los Angeles with preproduction background shots done in New York City.

Making films with James Garner was always fun. His sense of humor, which had broken up sets and left everybody rolling in a dusty Western street on the back lot of Warner Brothers when he was making "Maverick," became a trademark. Anyone involved in a James Garner picture anticipated his humor, and he never let them down. On *Boys' Night Out* he had great fun with Tony Randall. The two of them clowned around constantly.

Jim did not like doing homework. He was known to go off in the corner alone for a short time to rehearse and then to walk onto a set with his lines down pat. Consequently he loved teasing other members of the cast about their lines. Standing behind the camera one day with Tony Randall (Randall was waiting for a closeup to be readied), Jim and Tony kept up an agitated repartee. Just before Randall moved in front of the camera for his closeup he was the victim of Jim's one-upmanship—Garner always gets the last word. Tony promptly blew his lines, and Jim broke up. Randall cried out, "No fair! I know what happened. You got the last line!" With that, the entire set went into convulsive laughter.

During another interlude, Jim crept up on Tony Randall, who was in the makeup artist's chair being powdered and painted for the cameras. Jim approached him humbly, bowed as if to royalty, and loudly announced, "Aha! the king of comedy!"

Randall quickly countered, "I'll bet you don't know where that started, do you?"

Jim thought he'd invented it on the spur of the moment.

"Not true," Randall purred with all the comedic superiority he could muster. "It began one night when I was a guest on 'The Jack Paar Show.' I wasn't the only guest on that night. Among the others was a trained dog. Now this dog was endowed with high intellect according to his trainer. In order to prove the dog's intelligence, the trainer showed the animal a microphone and said, 'Now go find one.' The dog romped across the stage and returned with a microphone. The dog's owner then asked the animal to find the lady in the audience wearing a plaid suit. Again the dog leaped into the audience and stopped before a woman in plaid. Paar then turned and said to the dog, 'Now, who is the king of comedy?' The dog turned and stared right at me." Randall had gotten even with Garner for always getting the last word.

Not *all* was fun and games. Behind the scenes, away from the actors, a couple of sticky situations arose during the filming of the picture (and shortly thereafter) on the executive level. Although Jim was in no way involved, these situations are worthy of mention if only because they illuminate how jealously the film animal guards his position. Martin Ransohoff, the picture's producer, received the following memo from Ray Klune at M-G-M, dated October 18, 1961:

Dear Marty:

I have just learned that you are holding discussions with a commercial firm to supply you certain wardrobe for your picture for some of the male members of your cast which might involve giving them a screen credit. I must advise you that giving commercial screen credits is

*contrary to our established policy and therefore request
that you do not make any commitment to do so.*

Five days later Ransohoff responded that it was "unfortunate that I was unaware of your screen credits policy for tie-in
deals re pictures produced here at Metro."

A more serious squabble developed between M-G-M and
Joseph E. Levine over screen credits. Upon being informed
that Levine was advertising the film as "Presented by" Joseph
E. Levine, M-G-M fired off a telegram to Levine informing
him, "This picture was neither produced nor financed by
Embassy Pictures [Levine's company] or Joseph E. Levine. It
was produced by Kimco-Filmways and financed by M-G-M.
Additionally, it is being released and presented to the public
by M-G-M." Levine responded by announcing that he would
"take whatever action necessary to protect our credits" and
wouldn't tolerate being left uncredited.

The matter was settled, as most Hollywood squabbles are,
and the picture was finally released as "Metro-Goldwyn-
Mayer and Joseph E. Levine present."

The Rosenberg-Coryell Agency was handling Jim at this
time, his personal representative being Meta Rosenberg.
Meta's handling of Jim was impressive. She made excellent
deals on his behalf. She made enemies because she always
seemed to get more for Jim than the producers had intended
to give. One producer grumbled, "Garner will distract you
with charm while Meta picks your corporate pocket." But
whatever Meta did, it was always legal and always in the best
interest of her client. Most Holywood agents worth their salt
make enemies.

In less than a year, following *Boys' Night Out*, Garner had
completed four more pictures: *The Thrill of It All* for Ross
Hunter, *The Great Escape* under the Mirisch–United Artists

deal, *The Wheeler Dealers* at M-G-M, and *Move Over, Darling* for Marty Melcher (Doris Day's husband) at Twentieth Century Fox. The failure of *The Children's Hour* had caused Jim to reassess his talent, future, and choice of films. When he was under contract, Warner Brothers had chosen his vehicles for him. One of the gambles in being a free agent was deciding which offer to accept and which to turn down. In retrospect, Jim admits that that was a problem. "I knew I didn't have the experience to carry a movie by myself," he said. He therefore aimed to put himself in film situations where "I couldn't be held responsible for keeping people out of the theater." He preferred "being a plus factor" without having to bear the full blame if a picture failed. *The Children's Hour* and *Boys' Night Out* both reflect his decision to be surrounded by proven star talent.

He began to read scripts seriously before accepting a role. In an interview for *Seventeen* with Edwin Miller he explained his position. "I want to know who the director is, who else is involved, . . . and then I make up my mind whether or not to take it. This is a very insecure business. The public is fickle. You can be on top one year and disappear two or three years later."

Feeling insecure, Jim started to spread his income around, investing outside the motion picture and television industry. He would later discover that entertainment is not the only insecure industry and that money can be lost through friends, however well intentioned.

After his skirmish with Warner Brothers, Jim continued criticizing the film hierarchy and has done so throughout his career. He takes issue with the idea that movies are "a creative art form." The writer, he says, starts out with a creation but it becomes diluted by actors, directors, technicians, and so forth. "Something gets lost along the way." By the time all these people have contributed their particular expertise to a film, the creation has been transformed into "something to entertain."

Critics, he has always declared, do not take him seriously. "They see me as a personality," he complains. "I'm just somebody from television who moved over to movies. No matter how much money my films make, despite the reviews, they don't accept me as a serious actor." Actors have bigger egos than most people. "Of course it hurts when someone writes that you're never going to be an actor."

The media have always missed the point with James Garner. In a sense, even he misses the point. He is not so much an actor as a humorist in the mold of Will Rogers—if not in his private life, most certainly in his film portrayals.

Boys' Night Out gave Jim the opportunity to delineate the frustrations of a bachelor surrounded by married couples. His next picture, *The Thrill of It All*, permitted him to delineate the perplexity felt by a married man whose wife enjoys celebrity while he takes a back seat. Jim played a gynecologist with a nice, middle-class clientele who is considered a pillar of his community. Through a fluke his wife, played by Doris Day, becomes a celebrity via a television soap commercial. The high jinks that follow involve everything from housewives, psychiatrists, and swimming pools to expensive imported automobiles—plus loads of hokey, good-humored comedy. As the *New York Times* said, the picture was "loaded with good, clean American laughs." Jim had a ball making the picture, and columnists immediately began a campaign to set up Garner and Day as a new romantic team like Rock Hudson and Day. That helped sell the film and created interest in seeing the two act together again.

Hollywood didn't understand Jim any more then than it does now. He didn't march to its beat. He walked out of television when he was one of the top draws on the small screen into what most considered a highly uncertain career in motion pictures. He stumbled a couple of times but learned from his mistakes, vowing never to take the same route again. His experience with television had left deep resentment. Television stardom, he avowed, was a "thin, meaningless thing" with no more substance than "a soufflé." Television was illusionary: "Try trading what you have in a market with real values, not freaks. Try motion pictures." The list, he pointed out, of television superstars who have tried movies and have failed to achieve success was a long one. He compared television values to an inflated popover. "Put your fork into a popover and see what you have—there's almost nothing there. It's all air."

Questioned about the failure of *The Children's Hour*, he shrugged. "That wasn't my picture and I wasn't trying to make a big splash on my own. I wanted to be surrounded by top talent in the motion picture business. I had Audrey Hepburn as a love interest, there was Shirley MacLaine and William Wyler. They're the best and that's what I wanted to be involved with. Nothing but the best."

He wasn't the least bit perturbed that Rock Hudson had turned down *The Thrill of It All*. "It doesn't matter who turns a role down," he argued. "What's important is how the actor performs who *gets* the part. That's what people remember."

Thus, his working with first-class people was by design. His hiring a personal publicist was also done carefully, with career considerations in mind. Jim became very selective about interviews. Fan magazines were definitely out; he did not want interviews to appear in select-audience publications. He aimed for publications with a larger audience, those that did not appeal simply to adolescent fans. It was at this time that he made a confession: His real complaint about the fan magazines had to do with an article that appeared that hurt Lois's feelings. From that time on, he said, all fan magazines were alike in his mind. They were to be avoided at all costs. People loved him for it. It reminded them of Harry Truman's threatening to punch *Washington Post* critic Paul Hume in the nose for criticizing his daughter Margaret's voice. It was homespun Americana at its best.

Jim's views on politics, religion, and human rights have been carefully kept from public view, but there are indications that he has strong emotions about these highly personal issues. Although he has privately disagreed with certain black civil rights leaders, his public stance has been supportive. When everyone in Hollywood was seeking publicity for having "been to Selma," "been to Birmingham," and elsewhere in the civil rights fight of the early sixties, Jim very unpretentiously joined the more than hundred thousand people who gathered before the Washington Monument to listen to and support Martin Luther King, Jr. It was somebody else's show and he was a loyal spectator. Most people in Hollywood who really care enough to be interested in his politics assume that he is a Democrat. He *did* meet his wife at a fund-raiser for Adlai Stevenson, the Democratic candidate for president in 1956; and the March on Washington boasted more Democrats than Republicans. But Jim keeps his own counsel.

He had made enemies in the film capital. His detractors criticized him behind his back, but rarely did anyone criticize Jim or his family to his face (nor would they now). He would most likely flatten them. Disgruntled co-workers or technicians occasionally bad-mouthed him but were generally not taken seriously. He was accused by a few of being superficial, hypocritical, and for "having an ego larger than any Roman emperor's." He shrugged off such negative comments. "That's their problem," he would say. "I have enough trouble just taking care of my own life. I don't need hassles."

Jim embodied the "good ole boy" image. His adversaries may have complained that this "hokey" image would end his career in short order, but what they failed to realize was that Jim was more representative of what America was, or at least thought it was, than was the more sophisticated and polished actor. If Doris Day was the national symbol for the all-American girl, then Jim was her male counterpart—somewhere between a steelworker and a Saturday afternoon football hero. They were also representative of better, calmer times. America was being invaded by a new culture: the sixties brought with it an antiestablishment generation prepared to drop out and turn on. Jim's appeal was to the defenders of the American tradition of mom, flag, baseball, and apple pie. Those standards were to be greatly challenged in the coming years, and James Garner is to be greatly admired for weathering the sixties while evoking a fifties morality in his films. It was no easy task, but Jim was no easy taskmaster.

XII

In January 1962, the California State Supreme Court refused to hear the Warner Brothers appeal from the District Court of Appeals, ruling in favor of James Garner, and Jack L. Warner decided not to try further appeals. The matter was settled once and for all. It didn't matter much to Jim. He was confident that the ruckus was behind him, and he had many commitments on his film agenda, as motion pictures were his priority now. He was through with television.

During the filming of *Boys' Night Out* he was the subject of many articles and interviews. John Whitcomb of *Cosmopolitan* asked him if he was out of the saddle for good. Jim grinned in true Brett Maverick style, drawling, "You couldn't get me back with a crane. All the time I was under contract to Warner Brothers I felt like a side of beef hung up in a refrigerator and from time to time they'd slice off a piece of me and bring it out on display. I escaped by reading the fine print of my contract. I also got my golf handicap down from seven to one during the year I was prevented from working."

He was doing his best to stay away from roles that did not fit his image of being a nice, humorous fellow. "My agents get offers for me all the time to play heavies. I rely on their judgment. They don't want me killing anybody on film."

When Jim went home to his family he left his work behind

him. He also left the press outside his big iron gates. Even the tabloids were unable to come up with gossip about his private life. He has never been so lucky outside his home, however. When he signed to make *The Great Escape*, eyebrows were raised. One of his co stars was to be Steve McQueen, known to be highly opinionated, brusk, and extremely volatile on occasion. A Steve McQueen picture was all McQueen. He was difficult to work with, and his disagreements with directors were well known.

James Garner was known as a man easy to get along with on the set. Yet his manipulations behind the scenes generally had a profound effect on the final product. He had not come so far and been so successful without knowing what was right and what was wrong and correcting the wrongs along the way. He might be a "good ol' boy," but he was, as a friend said of him, "no dumb hick."

The Great Escape, produced by Mirisch Corporation– Alpha Corporation, was shot on location in Germany. It was the story of a group of British and American officers in World War II who were captured and imprisoned in a Nazi stalag. Jim played a prisoner in charge of digging up supplies for his fellow inmates while McQueen played a character always in trouble and usually in solitary confinement. The movie involves the prisoners' attempts to tunnel their way out of the camp to freedom.

Director John Sturges wanted to shoot the film in the United States. Paul Brickhill, who wrote the book from which the film was made, adamantly opposed such a location, arguing that it would "lessen British Commonwealth gross." After much argument and badgering, it was decided to shoot the film in Germany, with a largely British cast.

William R. Burnett, the author of such famous adventure sagas as *High Sierra*, *Captain Lightfoot*, and *The Asphalt Jungle*, was brought in to write the screenplay. The proposed budget of $2.6 million included $750,000 for a cast of stars that, in addition to Garner and McQueen, included Richard Attenborough, Donald Pleasance, Charles Bronson, and James Coburn. World-famous stunt motorcyclist Bud Ekins (whose San Fernando Valley motorcycle shop catered to many film stars) was flown from Los Angeles to Germany to perform in the film for several of the stars.

Star egos influenced the language of the contracts. On April 27, 1962, Marvin Mirisch issued a memorandum to another executive at United Artists in which he stated, "Based on our tentative shooting schedule . . . we expect that we will go into overtime to the extent of two weeks with James Garner due to the fact that we are wasting four and a half weeks of his twelve-week commitment. . . . We have been able to secure an agreement with Garner to the effect that should we go overtime to the extent of two weeks he will defer the overtime compensation for the period. Afterward we will have to pay him his full overtime. . . . He has been cooperative to at least this extent."

Steve McQueen's contract was more demanding. His own production company was to receive $100,000 for a minimum nine weeks. He was to receive first-class round-trip air transportation for his wife, two children, and their nurse plus $750 per week in living expenses. His screen and paid advertising credits called for his name to lead the entire cast and to appear above the title in type not smaller than the type size of the film's title. He was to be excluded from paying foreign taxes. If John Sturges was not available to direct the picture, then McQueen's company had the right to approve a substitute director. McQueen was also not a "dumb hick" when it came to his contracts.

John Sturges, recalling his directing chores on this film, said, "I was thinking about Jim Garner and it is hard to come up with anything particularly colorful. He is a bright, likable, uncomplicated, and talented guy. Not much you can say about him except that he is a terrific fellow. He's an awfully good actor and I admire him as a person."

Also on the picture were James Coburn and Charles Bronson, known to be individualists and opinionated. "I didn't have much trouble with them," Sturges said. "Bronson and Coburn as well as McQueen worked for me in *The Magnificent Seven*, so I knew their personalities pretty well. They knew each other, too. McQueen and Garner got on quite well because they had so many common interests. Both were interested in cars and racing and that sort of thing. Later on I think they did a racing film together.

"I think one of the reasons everything went so well on the picture was that we were all away from family and friends. We just wanted to get the picture done and go home." All except McQueen.

Steve McQueen had rented a chalet and had a chauffeured limousine transport him back and forth from the chalet to the set. He rarely mingled with the others away from the set. Phil Scuer of the *Los Angeles Times*, covering the film on location for his newspaper, found McQueen to be just as intense off the screen as on. He had been promised an in-depth interview with the recalcitrant actor. "We had no sooner shaken hands," he said, "when Steve turned to the unit publicist and commanded, 'Get in the car and follow me to my chalet and I'll give Phil his interview.'"

Seuer recalled "We got into the car and followed Steve to his chalet, but out in the rolling Bavarian farm country with the Alps on the horizon my interview wasn't much but the view was." McQueen spent most of the interview time patting himself on the back because he was "free as an angel" in terms of his contract. Yes, he and Jim did have a lot in common.

Away from the set, Jim managed to become embroiled in

one of the many public skirmishes for which he has become famous. Jim at times likes to refer to himself as "Crusader Rabbit." (Crusader Rabbit is a sort of mythical part-time hero who hits and runs—all in favor of the underdog.) In this case it was almost an international incident.

The filming of *The Great Escape* took place during the early stages of youth uprisings throughout the Western world, and in Munich there was almost daily conflict between local police and what they referred to as "beatniks." On a Saturday night, with filming shut down for the weekend, Jim Garner and British actor John Leyton were out walking for the evening, taking in the sights. There are several versions of what happened then—two or three at the time and one related by Garner to *TV Guide* nine years later. A wire service report from Munich date-lined June 26, 1962, carried the following version:

> *James Garner claims that he was shoved and pushed by police in the weekend rioting in the Bohemian Quarter of Schwabing. Garner, from Los Angeles, is making a picture here. He said he was walking in Schwabing Saturday night when the police stopped him. "I found myself in the middle of a crowd. Suddenly a group of police stopped me. I told them I was American but they pushed me to one side and grabbed my wallet which was sticking out of the back pocket of my slacks. My passport and about $400 were in it and [a policeman] was just about to throw it in the gutter when I snatched it out of his hands."*
>
> *He said he was later stopped again along with two American soldiers from AFN (Armed Forces Network) who were in uniform. "Five or six policemen began pushing me around and swinging at me with lead-weighted rubber clubs and one of them hit my arm." He finally*

escaped. The police earlier had reported the arrest of two
hundred persons —three Americans—but they did not
identify them in a past midnight battle with a crowd
described as "Beatniks" and "Teddy Boys."

The following day the United States Deputy Counsel in
Munich issued a statement indicating that U.S. State Department employees were beaten in a series of riots between be-
tniks and police in Munich's Bohemian district. "There have
been a series of at least seven riots recently in Munich's
Greenwich Village," Owen Zurhellen, the American official, stated. "Members of the counsular staff had been clob-
bered two nights ago. They were not leading officials so we
do not want to release any names before we have completed
our investigation." Jim's name was not mentioned in the
statement. The State Department preferred to keep a low pro-
file in the matter. Jim, however, had plenty to say. "I was
pushed and shoved about and the cops went at me with a
blackjack," the strapping former football player told the press.
"This couldn't have happened in the United States."

In his second meeting with the press Jim said the policeman was "trying to throw my wallet in the gutter but
when I told him I was an American citizen he finally returned it to me."

Yet another interview with Garner had him saying, "We
had gone down for a cup of coffee. All of a sudden everybody
starts running at us. We start running, too. Then you think,
if you've done nothing wrong, why run? A policeman
grabbed my wallet, passport and all, and threw it in the gutter. I grabbed it up. The police were hitting people with
clubs. It is something you don't believe until you see it."

During the interview with *TV Guide* in 1971, in a story
written by Al Stump, Garner's remembrances were quite different than at the time of the incident. Jim declared that he

was on his way to the airport, walking on the Leopoldstrasse, when he came upon two thousand student demonstrators battling police and losing. Jim immediately became involved. He claims that he was shouting at the crowd to "Stop this! Move back! Stop now, you terrorists!"

According to Jim, everyone quieted down, not knowing which side of the fracas he was on. He then approached a "large police sergeant" with "a broad, ingratiating smile. Then—boom! The officer never saw the explosive right-hand punch which connected with his chin and flattened him in the street."

According to Jim, "The guy was down longer than Max Schmeling against Louis." It was nothing, he claimed. "The kids needed help, so I stopped in. You should have heard the cheers for Crusader Rabbit." He says he quickly disappeared into the crowd, out of modesty.

Each account is interesting, and which is the most believable might depend on an individual's opinion of Garner himself.

In Munich he also spoke of the differences between television and movies. "When a TV series dies," he declared, "whoever is in it dies with it. The actor has become associated with the type and it reflects on him individually. At least I think I can overcome, one or two even bad films because they are released over a much longer period of time. TV eats up quite a bit of talent, as you know. If you could make a comparable splash in movies it would last a lot longer time."

Garner was probably right in his assumption that a few bad pictures could be overcome, because *The Great Escape* was shot down by most of the important critics. Bosley Crowther's review was scathing. "Nobody," he penned, "is going to con me . . . into believing that the spirit of defiance of any prisoner-of-war camp anywhere was as arrogant, romantic and Rover Boyish as it is made to appear in this film. . . . I find it artificial. . . . Steve McQueen, surly and sophomoric . . . James Garner, silken and mysterious, light-fingeredly lifting crucial tools from trucks without a single guard's noticing the pilfering—in a maximum-security prison yet! . . . It is callow and obvious play-acting. . . . The whole picture is that way . . . all two hours and fifty minutes of it."

One dissenter saw it differently. "What is unique," wrote Carl F. Mack, "is the sense of camaraderie expressed through various characters in the film. There is a feeling of community enveloping the prison camp which is not found in such films as *The Bridge on the River Kwai* . . . *Stalag 17* . . . or *King Rat*. . . . James Garner as the 'scavenger' is perfectly suited to the role of the wheeler-dealer."

Jim seemed not to worry about critics. "I just do my job," he said. "Others have to do theirs as they see fit." His attitude was that as long as somebody was willing to pay for his services as an actor, he was available. He had no real worries. He was actively sought out for starring roles by major producers.

Nothing seemed to worry or stop Jim. There was one temporary slowdown in 1962 when he picked up chickenpox from his daughter Gigi, but he afterward went on to complete four films for release in 1963—twice he would have four films in release in a year. It was a phenomenal production record seldom equaled since the demise of the studio system, which often had contract players making several films at the same time. He felt that two of the four films he made that year were especially good: *The Wheeler Dealers*, which he made with Lee Remick, and *Move Over, Darling*, his second picture with Doris Day. He rates both actresses highly. While filming a romantic scene with Doris Day he did manage to crack a couple of her ribs, but it was merely his way of "putting my all into my work." Doris was quite impressed with his concern and quickly forgave him. They did not become a romantic comedy team in the Doris Day–Rock Hudson mold, but the film was well received.

It was on the set of *Move Over, Darling* that he uttered his now famous (and often quoted) line, "I've never made a mistake in my life. What d'you think of that for a statement?" He wasn't serious, of course, but he knew the quote would be picked up around the world wherever television and film fans read entertainment and gossip columns. While working on this same picture he discussed further his reticence to do interviews. "I'm not a great windbag. In fact, being interviewed makes me feel funny. I absolutely hate publicity. I'd rather go play a round of golf than sit down for publicity stills. I see no comfort in going to a premiere of one of my films, knowing that the press is all around me. I'd rather dig a ditch than do an interview. I think I should be entitled to hate something. I should hate something, so I do. I hate phony stories!" Especially phony stories written about him. Jim Garner is one who believes that an actor owes nothing to his public except his performance. It was the philosophy of the late Steve McQueen, a close buddy of Jim's, as well as his film idol, Marlon Brando. Other friends, like Henry Fonda and Dennis Weaver, have not shared his concern with absolute privacy, having often permitted writers and photographers to come into their private lives for stories and films. Fonda once discussed the subject of privacy. "I have nothing to hide in my private life, so why not talk about it? For Christ's sakes, the world knows more about my kids than I do!"

The Wheeler Dealers was produced by Martin Ransohoff for Filmways in Metrocolor and Panavision. Arthur Hiller, a mild-mannered, gentlemanly director, presided over the filming. In addition to Jim the cast included Lee Remick, Phil Harris, Chill Wills, Louis Nye, John Astin, and Jim Backus. It was a return to comedy for Garner—a genre that he always has preferred. The plot was simple and conning—

very much in the Garner area of expertise. Although some of the comedy was contrived and predictable, it was brought off well by a cast who seemed to be having a romp doing it. The reviews were good, and Jim was highly praised as one of film-dom's better romantic comedy leads—of which there was a dire shortage during the mid-sixties. Jim was one of few actors not making "message" pictures, though such films were not excluded from his future.

While Jim cavorted across the screen with beautiful leading ladies, Lois was committed full time to bringing up the children—plus taking care of her husband's needs when he was able to spend time in Los Angeles. He managed to have more time at home during the filming of *Move Over, Darling*, which was shot on location in Los Angeles. The film was produced by Doris Day's husband, Martin Melcher, for Twentieth Century Fox distribution. Michael Gordon directed from Hal Kanter's hilarious screenplay. The picture boasted a top-notch cast, including Polly Bergen, Chuck Connors, Thelma Ritter, Fred Clark, Don Knotts, Elliott Reid, Edgar Buchanan, John Astin, Pat Harrington, Jr., and Eddie Quillan.

The picture was a remake of a late 1930s picture called *My Favorite Wife*, starring Cary Grant, Irene Dunne, and Gail Patrick. The story concerned the return of a missing wife, thought to have been killed in an accident five years earlier, after the husband has remarried. Although contrived, the comedy prevailed over the obvious conclusion.

As usual, Jim frolicked away from the cameras as well as before them. One could hardly believe he was really earning his keep, since he seemed to be having such a good time. One afternoon while filming a scene on location at a car wash near the Fox Studios, Garner noticed a couple of kids playing one-on-one basketball nearby. During a break in the shooting he casually approached them and asked if he could shoot a few baskets with them. The two teenagers, George Goodspeed and Sam Hyman, were somewhat awed as they handed the ball over to Jim. As members of the cast and crew joined the two boys watching Garner shoot baskets, he worked up a healthy sweat and was greeted with applause when he tossed the basketball back to the boys. Goodspeed remarked that Garner was one swell guy but added, "I think he could use a little work on his hook shot."

The relaxed and casual star talked freely to writers while making this picture. "Me," he revealed to Don Alpert of the *Los Angeles Times*, "I'm funny. I may be wrong, but let me be wrong. Don't let anybody else do it for me. If I fail, I'll do it myself." He declared that he hoped he would be quoted properly, even if "I show my ignorance," further stating that he would "rather be honest than right" and admitting that he had just made a stupid statement.

He delineated his current likes and dislikes, particularly the latter. "I enjoy interviews if I have something to say, but I don't like having stories made up about me. I hate fan magazines. They're my pet peeve." It was not the first nor the last time that he would castigate fan magazines, which at one time were the main means of communication between Hollywood and moviegoers the world over.

Jim had iron-clad opinions on what was popular with the moviegoing public and where he should be at any given time. He had been making one film right after another since leaving Warner Brothers and saw no reason to change that pattern. He was satisfied with his career. "It just so happens," he said, "that the best things now coming out of writers are comedies." He allowed that many writers were still doing what he called, "sickies" but felt that entertainment comedies or action dramas are best. "You're kind of stuck with what's available," he said. "For quite some time I've been looking all over town for a good Western or action picture but haven't found one." Not too long before he had vowed never to do another saddle-bound film.

He attacked television as a starless industry. "I would have hated to die with Maverick, he proclaimed. "It would have made it more difficult to find a job. I'm going to make a lot of enemies saying this, but it is true. I've always thought a star had to have a lasting quality. That doesn't happen in television. In TV if you have good ratings you're a star. Nobody has been on long enough to prove it. I've classed the name of *star* with movies. You can take that program off the air and within one year you won't remember the name of the actors. There are people doing commercials today who, years ago, were stars on television." As to his own classification as a star on "Maverick" he commented, "I never felt like a star. When I was in television, I was filmed as much as Clark Gable was in his entire motion picture career. My show was at one time the most popular series in television, but none of that was as lasting as one of Clark Gable's pictures. Television is so fleeting."

Discussing his home life in relationship to work he explained why he didn't like to take scripts home to study. "I can't concentrate on a scene when my daughter wants to play or if my wife wants to talk about something."

He told Peer Oppenheimer during an interview that he didn't mind giving up his lunchtime to do interviews. "I think it has been good therapy for me. I've learned a lot about myself from interviews." Again, he attacked fan magazines, even citing experiences as a youngster as a reason for his distaste of them. "I was like any other kid, picking up fan magazines and reading through them. I thought they were in bad taste, even then. All those phony shots of some actor and his girl friend on a shopping spree somewhere in Los Angeles."

Though he didn't like them, he catered to the fan magazines at the outset of his career. "It is true," he admitted readily, "that I got sucked in with those interviews. It is sort of automatic and it's in print before you realize what's happening." When he saw the way his words had been "editorialized," he was outraged. "I literally got sick at my stomach to see what had been written about me. It embarrassed me to think that people I knew would read it and maybe even believe I'd said the crap that was printed in those bad excuses for magazines." He declined, as had many actors before him, to sue the perpetrators. He simply did not wish to give them added exposure.

Asked why he did not mingle more with the movie crowd, he said, "Lois and I go out maybe a couple of times a month—sometimes not at all. What I hate most," he grinned, "is having to dress up. That reminds me of punching a time clock. It is not that I don't like people. I love people and being with them. The same as I enjoy working with people—just as long as it doesn't require a lot of work on my part. I don't like to work away from the studio. I won't so much as pick up a leaf anymore. I hire people who earn *their* living doing that sort of thing."

He also revealed a bit of his private philosophy, stating that he didn't create "money-making" schemes for his daughters. "I hated working as a kid and I am not going to make my kids earn money by doing chores. I expect them to keep their rooms clean, but as a matter of good manners—not that they should get paid for it."

Though Jim was circumspect about his private life, and especially about his early years, since he didn't want anyone in his past to be badly portrayed in the press, even after his marriage to Lois Clarke he submitted (through Warner Brothers) to photographs and interviews that involved his home and private family life. Once some Hollywood writers—most of whom are honest and report accurately about the city in which they make their living—began to distort facts and fabricate stories to suit their own ends, however, Jim began resisting the press. So whenever he said anything concerning his private life, it was newsy and informative and worth repeating. He always hoped that his words would not be twisted out of context. Those writers who have not done so have usually found him available for an interview. There are only a few writers he trusts.

In fairness, however, there are writers who do not believe that Jim has always leveled with them, stating that he has created a story and gives it out repeatedly, year after year. His former producer, Roy Huggins, says, "Garner says he only gives one interview a year. I understand why. He only has one and he gives it once a year—the same one."

By the end of summer in 1963 Jim was a very tired, workworn actor. He was working incessantly, one film right after the other, having completed six or seven pictures in two years, and was at the crossroads of his career. He had made thirteen pictures, none of which, with the exception of *The Children's Hour*, were anything more than purely entertaining. There were no lasting messages or statements. Although he had disdained message pictures, he knew the mood of the times. There was, for instance, the Vietnam War, an unpopular war that half the population almost violently opposed as a useless and unwarranted endeavor that was depriving America of its most precious commodity—its youth.

Jim had carefully chosen the route he took when making war pictures. *Darby's Rangers* and *The Great Escape* were not message films. Antiwar films were just beginning to challenge the heavily traditional John Wayne brand of patriotism. Most of them focused on dissatisfied youth, the drug culture, arguments against the draft. The Hollywood establishment had not dared, as yet, to produce a picture that would show war to be in opposition to the American heritage.

Such a film was on the horizon. Such a film would star the humorist, the front-porch whittler who would rather fish than work, the man not to be taken seriously: James Garner. Considering its nature, Jim was the least likely actor to play the lead in a film like *The Americanization of Emily*. Seemingly, he would be the last one to accept such a role, not only because of its antiwar theme but because it was a location picture. Rumors that his family life was unhappy continued circulating. He has stated privately on numerous occasions that such stories did not bother him because he knew they were not true. Nobody in his family—neither his wife nor his daughters—had ever told anyone that there was discord in their family. Yet he had spent a long time away from his home and family over the past few years.

His decision to accept the lead in *The Americanization of Emily* was due partly to the changing times. Yet to accept it was to risk being considered a little too far to the left by the bulk of his foot-stompin', blood-and-guts, down home, good ole boy fans. But, as Jim has so often stated, "I have gambled in my career. I gambled when I left Warner Brothers. People said I was through and would never work again—but look where I am. I didn't get here by playing it safe. And I haven't done badly, have I?"

Indeed he hasn't.

XIII

The Americanization of Emily had a history of controversy long before a single frame of film was shot. The first script sent to the Motion Picture Association of America's code office as far back as 1960 drew immediate criticism and statements of caution. In a letter to Robert Vogel at M-G-M Geoffrey Shurlock said, "But above all there is a question is our mind whether the portrayal of U.S. Army personnel in this film is not of such a derogatory nature as to present a serious problem of industry policy. This means we feel this film over and above any specific code problems may bring down serious complaint should the organized industry appear to be sponsoring it by issuing its seal of approval." The usual code language was discussed, but the focal point of Shurlock's communication was the antiwar theme of the picture.

The Americanization of Emily was originally a book written by William Bradford Huie and published in New York in 1959. The protagonist is a character named Charlie Madison, a lieutenant commander in the U.S. Navy and aide to an eccentric rear admiral by the name of Jessup. The setting is wartime London as D-Day approaches. Lieutenant Commander Madison is by nature a coward who believes cowardice to be virtuous in that it helps to prevent war. He falls in love with Emily Barham, his British driver from the local motor pool, who has every reason to feel both reverence for heroes and bitterness after having lost both her husband and brother in the war. Admiral Jessup is determined that the first man to die on Omaha Beach will be a sailor. He feels the army has had too much glory and the navy too little. At gunpoint Madison becomes that first man—a sailor—to hit the beach on D-Day. Tripping on a land mine and not found following the explosion, he is assumed to be dead. There is extensive commentary in the newspapers, which makes him a hero—but he is not a dead one. He had escaped death but sustained an injury that in the finale makes him a hero—the one thing he had never wanted to have happen.

As seen by the MPAA, the problem with the novel, as well as the screenplay later written by the great Paddy Chayefsky, was the cowardice of an American serviceman. Cowards had always been ushered out of the service, given dishonorable discharges or shot. World War II had been a victory—the last American victory in war—in the mind of the American filmgoer. Korea had left many Americans embittered because the peace appeared to be a truce rather than a victory. Such people believed in the military adage that "there is no substitute for victory." According to the motion picture industry and its governing association, to have an American coward become a hero on film could result in a devastating backlash at the box office. And not only for this film; possibly a boycott of films might ensue.

The book had sold well, but reading and viewing are totally different forms of entertainment. What one reads, one does not always like to see on the screen. Such was the fear of many who would have liked to have made the picture but hesitated.

Metro-Goldwyn-Mayer was a conservative studio. Its reputation had been built on solid family fare—musicals, humor, human interest, and throughout the forties and even into the fifties, war hero themes. Nonetheless, the Culver City film giant purchased film rights to the book and set about obtaining a script, assigning a producer, finding a director, and signing up stars.

The star and director finally chosen were not the studio's first choice, but director William Wyler and actor William Holden were ultimately unavailable because of contractual difficulties. Martin Ransohoff had been chosen by M-G-M as producer. The film had been expected to start rolling sometime during the summer of 1963, but by mid-July of that year Ransohoff confirmed postponement to approximately September 15 for the start of principal photography. By the end of July an interoffice memo at M-G-M declared that "New York does realize that with Willie Wyler on the picture the shooting schedule will be longer and we did this thus lengthening the schedule by approximately two weeks."

Wyler's financial demands were exhorbitant. He asked $400,000 to direct the film plus escalation percentages that could run into perhaps millions. Additionally, he requested $1,250 per week living expenses on location away from Los Angeles, a car and chauffeur, and reimbursement for a minimum of two trips to Europe to be made by him in connection with publicizing the film.

That was just the beginning. He further asked that round-trip transportation expenses be paid for members of his family who traveled from Los Angeles and back to visit him on location. His son, Robert, was to be employed as Wyler's assistant for $25,000. He expected to have certain control over the final print in that he wanted the right to make three cuts following three previews—only the final cut was to be left to the producer. He wanted the production credits to indicate that he was co-producer.

William Holden had similar demands. He requested $750,000 during the production of the picture against 10 percent of the gross. That demand was later modified.

The restructured agreement included the following requests:

1. $200,000 to be paid during the production to Holden's production company, Helvia Productions, S.A.;

2. $400,000 payable to William Holden directly at the rate of $50,000 per year commencing January 1, 1965;

3. 15 percent of the net profits after the picture had grossed $4 million; 10 percent of the net profits after the picture had grossed $5 million.

It was projected that if Wyler were chosen as director, the budget would be $2.8 million. That figure would increase, however, if Elizabeth Shephard, tentatively selected to play the female lead, should be passed over for a more expensive actress, which did indeed happen.

The battle between William Holden and the studio was gigantic. It mostly centered around Holden's having approval of the director if Wyler was unable to perform for whatever reason. Holden approved the following directors: William Wyler, Blake Edwards, David Lean, Joseph Mankiewicz, Howard Hawks, Richard Quine, George Seaton, and John Sturges.

For one reason or another, most of these directors were either not available or, depending on whose communiqués one believes, not wanted for the job or refused to accept it. In a lengthy wire to M-G-M Holden's representatives declared, "It is our intention, of course, to cooperate in this manner as we have repeatedly done and with which you are familiar in line with our original agreement and understanding that selection of any director and co-star or co-stars would be mutually agreed to by the parties and then only a director of the highest caliber be engaged. In response to other conditions stated in your wire concerning selection of director we must disagree and reject them . . . and how can you expect a director to blindly accept an unfinished script and not discuss the story with you and the writer?"

At this point Paddy Chayefsky had written 120 pages, an incomplete script that M-G-M did not wish to send on to Holden. It preferred to wait until Chayefsky had completed a first draft of the script, and thus a completion date couldn't be established.

Then there was the argument about the salary offered to the as-yet-to-be-named director. Holden argued that he could not understand or accept the formula offered by the studio, "as you already have offered in prior negotiations with directors for this picture salaries most substantially higher than that paid them for last pictures." In the meantime Ransohoff sent a wire to Charles K. Feldman at Famous Artists that emphatically stated his position and Filmways': the studio "under no circumstances" would relinquish its "right of decision as producer with respect to any production matters and this particularly relates to the choice of director, terms of his employment, amount of compensation to be paid to him and all other elements."

This sort of bickering went on for weeks. Meanwhile, although still negotiating with Holden for the lead, M-G-M was already considering Jim, although it is uncertain whether it was originally considering him for the lead. On September 5, 1963, Martin Ransohof declared in an interoffice memo that the "addition of Garner to cast of *Emily* increases budget to $3.155 million."

Jim may not have been aware of all the bickering. His

status at this point was that of actor signed, role not clear, and shooting date uncertain. It gave him a chance to play golf and spend time with his family. He needed the rest and an opportunity to be close to home for the first time in almost two years.

Ransohoff made an immediate check into the availability of the directors Charles Feldman of Famous Artists had suggested to be certain his position was correct. The William Morris Agency advised him that David Lean, Blake Edwards, and John Sturges each had other commitments that prevented their meeting the starting date set for the picture. A script had been submitted to Joseph Mankiewicz. He, too, was unavailable. Irving Lazar, agent for Richard Quine, reported that his client was unavailable as he was in the middle of making *Sex and the Single Girl* at Warner Brothers. Howard Hawks declared that he considered himself primarily a producer-director and would not undertake directorial assignments alone. George Seaton had a contract with Perlberg-Seaton and was "unable to take directorial assignments on pictures where Perlberg is not the producer."

Wyler, by this time, had been rejected as director for reasons, Ransohoff said in his communication to Famous Artists, "well known to you." Those reasons were apparently Wyler's contractual demands, but once he was off the picture there was no reason to discuss them further. The important thing was to find a director for a film that was almost ready to be made.

For the first time Ransohoff confronted Famous Artists directly about the directorial matter. He wrote to them: "Your submission of a list of names as possible directors . . . was a patently useless procedure on your part since you are well aware that all of these persons are unavailable. It appears to us that the only motivation for you to send us such a list was your desire to avoid your contract with us. . . . You know that we have already committed large sums of money constructing sets and in other production work. This entire envestment is in jeopardy and great damages could result if we do not obtain the services of a director immediately." Ransohoff went on to discuss previous exchanges between the two parties that had merely brought the matter to an impasse. It looked as though the picture might not be made at all.

Ransohoff referred to another possible director. "As a matter of fact," he wrote, "until the date of your telegram the only director you would even consider approving was Blake Edwards. I had two meetings with him for the purpose of making a deal with him for this picture but his terms and conditions were so onerous as to be unacceptable to Filmways and M-G-M. He insisted on the right to recast the leading female role and to approve the ending and have changes in the script to accommodate the ending he would approve. Furthermore, we have been advised by his agents that he is unavailable to direct this picture and as a matter of fact was not available during the times we were talking to him."

Had the gossip columnists known what was going on behind the scenes on this film, there would have been banner headlines. Fortunately for the executives trying to put together the package, they did not.

Ransohoff gave Famous Artists a deadline of noon PDT on Monday September 23 to come up with an available director. Otherwise he intended to "endeavor immediately to obtain a satisfactory agreeement with an available director of our choice." For the first time the name of Arthur Hiller was mentioned as a possibility. Hiller had directed James Garner in *The Wheeler Dealers*.

Hiller himself has clarified Jim's being signed while Holden was still in contention for the male lead. "Garner," he says, "was signed to play the James Coburn role before Bill Holden backed out of the deal." This was the second time Jim had been up for the second male lead and ended up with the lead (the first time being in *Darby's Rangers*). Being second seemed to become Jim; he was always there when the number one man left the scene.

When Hiller was signed to direct the picture, the screenplay had been completed by Paddy Chayefsky. "I read the screenplay," Hiller explains, "while I was working with Marty Ransohoff on *Wheeler Dealers*. However, at that time they felt I wasn't ready for *Emily*. I was so mad for that script. It was the only picture that I had pursued and I pursued Marty Ransohoff through, I think, fourteen directors that were being considered—not all of whom he made offers to. I think I was number fourteen they spoke to. I think they turned down a lot of directors and a number said no, because they felt the film was too anti-American. It wasn't even that. It was the antiglorification of war. Garner has a couple of speeches where he says you have to defend your home when somebody attacks. You have to take steps, but don't glorify war. Don't name streets after the heros. Don't build statues. Don't make war seem such a heroic thing. That's basically what Paddy was saying. That we not glorify war."

The critics were always chiding Paddy Chayefsky for his antiwar positions, which Hiller found interesting. "It was interesting because I remember some of those critics making their points and I suggested to them that Paddy had been in the service in the Southeast during the war and that I had been in the Canadian Air Force in the European Theater. It wasn't as if we were pacifists. We were not a bunch of left-wingers. We had been there and knew what we were talking about."

Holden, of course, wasn't satisfied with Arthur Hiller and

backed out of the picture. Jim took his place immediately. Garner's demands were not nearly so outrageous as Holden's. The salaries of the principals on the picture were as follows:

James Coburn	$2500 per week, 10 weeks guaranteed.
Melvyn Douglas	$5000 per week, 10 weeks guaranteed.
Julie Andrews	$12,500 per week, 10 weeks guaranteed.
Arthur Hiller	$2500 per week, 20 weeks guaranteed.
James Garner	$22,500 per week, 10 weeks guaranteed.

Even though Jim was the highest paid actor in the film, his salary was about half what would have been paid to William Holden.

The London office of M-G-M was standing by waiting to find out who the cast and director were going to be. Ray Klune of M-G-M in Culver City wired his London offices on September 26 that Arthur Hiller was directing and would arrive in London on September 28th at 4:30 P.M. on BOAC Flight 592.

The following day another wire went out to London: "James Garner will replace Holden in lead. James Coburn 99 percent set as Cummings. Will take care of wardrobe. Hiller will direct. Ritz Hotel okay with him. Re Garner Work Permit: American citizen born April 7, 1928, Norman, Oklahoma."

It was finally set. *The Americanization of Emily* would soon start principal photography. The ridiculous arguments with the MPAA went on right up until the picture was released. A Mr. Dougherty from the MPAA met with Martin Ransohoff, Arthur Hiller, and Paddy Chayefsky, resulting in the following memo from R. Vogel of M-G-M:

> . . . *Dougherty underlines reasons the unacceptability basis of which is the fact that the boy and girl are attracted to each other physically the moment they meet and start a sex affair at that moment [referring to the characters portrayed by Garner and Andrews]. Their relationship continues though it changes to a romantic one later on. The affair continues with reasonable success throughout and there is not the slightest indication of its being immoral. We found that Chayefsky had in the interim been doing some rewriting which included a number of very forceful speeches by both the boy and the girl which very adequately supplied the missing voice for morality. There remained the affair itself. It was agreed that the relationship between the boy and the girl could be straightened out by changing the nature of their first private meeting when Madison enters his room after the card party and finds Emily waiting on his bed and they start caresses which will doubtlessly lead to a sex affair interrupted only by the arrival of Jessup. This will be changed so that Emily has come to Madison's quarters out of curiosity. His personality has titillated her and she is interested in trying to find out what makes him tick. The meeting begins to develop into a romantic, not sexual one, when it is interrupted. Aside from this it was agreed that (a) Chayefsky will eliminate those "hells" and "damns" which are not dramatically essential and (b) the three sequences wherein Madison discovers Kennedy in bed with "nameless broads" will be keyed to develop their humor and the fact that the girls are "pre-*

*sumably" naked and that Madison ignores them com-
pletely. The emphasis will not be on actually seeing the
girls nude.*

The memo to end all memos on the subject of censorship
was delivered to Ray Klune from Robert Vogel at the Irving
Thalberg Building on the Metro lot in Culver City. It was
dated October 8, 1963:

*I asked Dougherty to assume that the following hypo-
thetical question must doubtless be asked: "Mr. Dougherty, this is Paddy Chayefsky speaking. Wherein does
our love affair differ from the one in* Irma La Douce
*other than in the fact that our people are always fully
clothed whereas the boy and girl in* Irma *are almost always unclothed and in bed?" The question was not answered then or at any subsequent time. It obviously
affected Dougherty strongly and his approach to the
problem at the meeting.*

James Garner, his publicity agent Jim Mahoney, Arthur
Hiller, James Coburn, and Melvyn Douglas all arrived
within a two-day period early in the second week of October
for location shooting in London. Jim registered at the May-
fair Hotel, ready to go to work. The London shooting was
expected (although nothing *expected* on this film had ever
transpired) to begin on October 14 in London and last for
about two weeks, with the balance of the film being shot at
the studio in Culver City, commencing on approximately
November 4.

Once filming actually started it appeared that the MPAA
was standing behind the cameraman. Almost from the outset
of shooting the memos objecting to suggestive lines began

flying fast and furiously. On October 22, 1963, the MPAA asked that the following expressions be omitted from the completed product:

> "To these resolute *pimps, procurers and lush menschen*
>   *this film is gratefully dedicate.*"
> Emily's line "I couldn't say no to them, could I?"
> General Johnson squeezing Sheila's thigh.
> Emily's line "Oh, Lord, I hope I don't get pregnant."
> Madison's line "Oh, Lord, I hope you get pregnant."

Robert Vogel wrote to Martin Ransohoff on October 23, 1963, regarding the ongoing censorship battles with the MPAA and Geoffrey Shurlock in particular:

> *Our New York attack on Dougherty of the Code Office
> must have been more brutal than we realized. He has
> had one gall bladder, one appendix, and other items re-
> moved since then. As a result Geoffrey Shurlock has now
> read the new script. . . . He's emphatic about the naked
> broads. He objects to the scenes both because they show
> an officer of the armed forces who apparently devotes all
> of his time to hitting the hay and also to the nudity
> element. He says that if he is to approve the presumably
> naked women they'll have to stay under the covers and
> not be hopping about. The audience is to catch no
> glimpse of them. He thinks scenes would carry some com-
> edy effect if they wore provocative nighties. As to the two
> lines about being pregnant he says everybody knows, of
> course, that the boy and girl haven't devoted all their
> time to having gone to see movies but these two lines pin
> down the sexual relationship much too definitely. I think
> we're going to have to get together with him.*

James Garner very much approved the watchdog actions of the MPAA. Throughout his career he has argued in favor of clean, wholesome films that may suggest but not show sexual situations. He has turned down many scripts because they were either too violent or too sexually explicit. He values his image among fans, friends, family, and community as "an average American with average American values." He is not ashamed of that nor does he consider himself out of step. "It is," he has said, "the smut peddlers who are out of step."

The film progressed with the actors in harmony and the budget ever-increasing. It cost the studio $55,000 to settle the William Wyler contract. William Holden's settlement was a considerably higher $150,000. Incidental expenses paid out of the location budget in London included the following:

10-12-63 *Flowers for Julie Andrews from Marty Ran-*
          sohoff
10-14-63 *Flowers for Julie Andrews from Jim Garner*
10-17-63 *Drinks with Jim Bacon [columnist] and his*
          wife
10-18-63 *Phone call from Jean Seberg in Paris for Ran-*
          sohoff
10-20-63 *Phone call to Jean Seberg from Ransohoff.*

The budget was Martin Ransohoff's problem. Arthur Hiller had other problems. A major one was simulating the American invasion at Omaha Beach in France on D-Day. The United States military establishment was very unhappy with the antiwar theme of the picture and was consequently withholding cooperation in the shooting of the picture.

"They were terrible," says Hiller. "Wouldn't loan us anything. I remember we had no cooperation from them, for instance, when we wanted to borrow landing craft for the invasion scenes. They had always loaned equipment for the gung ho war movies, but not for us. We had to go find an old landing craft. They simply refused to help us in any way—all because it was an antimilitary picture." That one landing craft saw a lot of action in the shooting of *Emily*.

Hiller has nothing but praise for his stars. "James Garner was terrific to work with. I found him unchanged from *Wheeler Dealers*, our first picture together, to *The Americanization of Emily*. I've analyzed both films and what comes through is this basically really nice, caring person, which is not always true in actors I've worked with. That personality shines through. In fact that caring leads me to recall a specific scene in *Emily*. It was the tea party sequence, which, in a sense, expressed the whole philosophy of the picture. When we were working on that scene, I just couldn't get what I wanted at first. Couldn't get the performance right from Jim, so I finally said, 'Let's just leave this scene and go on to something else.'

"We did that and I met with him later on the weekend and we discussed the scene. He was very attentive, as I recall. I explained to him what it was and what the problem was with it.

"'Jim,' I explained, 'you care so much about the picture and are so dedicated to Paddy's words and have such belief in them that you are playing every line as if it is the best line in the movie.' Indeed, we all cared about Paddy's words and it was easy to see every line from such a brilliant screenplay as great, but an actor cannot peak on every line. So I cautioned him. 'What you have to do,' I said, 'is play the character. If you play every line as the best line, you're playing at one level.'

"He looked at me very sincerely and quite simply responded, 'Oh.'

"The following day we did the scene again. It was just marvelous. There had not been a lot of give and take and becauses and whys and why nots in our conversation. He accepted and understood my explanation of the scene and did it just as I had suggested. Garner has a powerful sense of perception."

His performance in *The Americanization of Emily* was the coming of age as a star for James Garner. It was a film that required him to be more than a tough guy or a romantic lead. He had to be a person.

"That was the strength of that character," declared Hiller. "That he was real and charming, and it is hard when you are playing an antihero to make the character appealing. That was his great strength—that he could play an antihero and you still just loved him. It is easy to love heroes who choose these wonderful things, but to love a man who says, 'I don't want to be the first dead man on Omaha Beach'—that is something else."

There was a moment on the beach in the picture that Hiller believes displays a realism that most actors never achieve in a film. "When we landed—the D-Day landing scene—if you watch the film, you will see that when Garner is shot—when you think, indeed, he is the first dead man on Omaha Beach, that he gets shot and hits the ground—you will notice a little death jump when he fell. We were taking all kinds of precautions to keep anyone from being actually injured. I had spent the previous weekend with all the special effects men laying out exactly where the charges should go to be sure everybody was safe and sound. We ran through and everything was fine. But when we shot the scene and Jim was shot and fell, the canteen can on his belt got between him and the ground and he fell on it, cracking a rib. The crack of the rib caused him to do that little jump. We left it in the film because it looked so authentic."

The scene was shot as far away from Omaha Beach as possible—at Hollywood by the Sea at Oxnard, California, with weather less than optimum. "It was bad," Hiller recalls, "but not terrible weather. All the better to simulate the other side of the English Channel."

Jim got along well with the cast and crew on location. As Hiller remembers, "He certainly was with everybody. I would call him a very social person on the set. I don't know if he went with the others to dinner and things like that but he was quite friendly with Julie Andrews and Jimmy Coburn. We all had a good time. I'm sure that looking back on the experience, Garner would say it was his favorite film. I look back and say it is my favorite movie and Jim Coburn still says it was his favorite. It made a star of Coburn."

James Garner tends to understate his ability as an actor, causing Hiller to comment: "I think from a director's point of view, you can either let an actor treat a role as if he is not making an effort or you can make him do what he is capable of doing. That's a challenge to a director. I had that experience with Jim Garner. I could see from working with him on *The Wheeler Dealers*—I could see the actor there. I knew what was in him and I was determined I was going to get that out of him. The minute you show him you care about his acting, and that you believe in him, he believes in himself and gives the performance he is capable of. No matter what he says, Garner is no walk-through actor.

"You have to give him a feeling of his own importance. Tell him how good he is. He doesn't realize how good he is. But if you bolster his confidence in himself then you get all that good stuff out of him."

Hiller believes that the child in every actor has to be

stroked and made to feel important. "On the set that is true. They're children on the set. I don't think that's necessarily true away from the set, however. But on the set you must treat them as children. My wife has said to me, 'You treat those actors better than you treat your kids.'

"I say, 'No, no, my dear. I treat them the same as I treat my kids. I slap them on the wrist, pat them on the back. Sure.'"

During the making of *The Americanization of Emily* Melvyn Douglas became ill. When the picture was finally completed and previewed, some of the preview cards were not as kind to Douglas and his performance as Hiller thinks they should have been.

"It was the under-twenty-five audience which gave him less than perfect marks. I don't think they understood the role he played. Douglas was not only a marvelous actor in a marvelous part, he was a trouper without peer. I don't recall what his illness was, but I know he was in the hospital and when he got out we were night shooting and he came to work at two in the morning and worked all night. I recall this particular scene. It was at the airport and he was just leaving London, I believe. He forgot a relationship in the scene and I went over to him and commented to him about it. He said, 'I'm terribly sorry. You're absolutely right. I apologize.'

"I said, 'No, no don't apologize. It's the first time I've been able to direct you in this picture.'"

With tears of laughter in his eyes, Hiller remembers Jim Garner in the beach scene. "This is a scene I always discuss when I do seminars—a scene from *Emily* that sets the tone for the picture: the D-Day landing on Omaha Beach, beginning aboard the landing craft as it approaches the shore and carried through until Garner is shot on the beach. He's there in the water and Jim Coburn is with him. He has seen all the explosions on the beach, blown out of the landing craft, and looks at Omaha Beach and the devastation that's going on and he turns his back to it and starts toward the landing craft again. Coburn says, 'The beach is that way. The beach is that way.'

"Jim says, 'I know which way the beach is!' It was a devastatingly telling line about men and their emotions—their real emotions. Nobody wants to die in a war. But that one line makes you laugh and it is the tone of the picture in the sense that you're laughing and suddenly you grab yourself and ask, 'Why am I laughing?' Because you know in thirty seconds this man is going to be the first man killed on Omaha Beach. He did survive, but it hits you right away what war is all about. Coburn, of course, played the gung ho type.

"James Garner was probably the perfect choice for that role. He delivers lines, when you have faith in him, that hit home. An excellent actor."

Audience reception of the picture was generally good. Jim's reviews were excellent and the film established him once and for all as a serious dramatic actor.

XIV

When the new year broke Jim was back in Hollywood with his family, *The Americanization of Emily* still being completed (he had finished his shooting on the picture), and business to be taken care of. With so many pictures back to back he had hardly had time to tend to personal matters. He did a lot of catching up, even taking time to become a director of the newly formed Silverlake National Bank, which he had purchased with eight other investors. Its office at 1824 Sunset Boulevard opened right after Labor Day 1964. Television and other celebrity types showed up for the event. Also, Jim and Doris Day were honored by the Sixty-first Annual California Federation of Women's Clubs Conventions and named best actress and actor for their performances in *The Thrill of It All*, which had been released in 1963.

By April he was back in the saddle, although not literally. He began filming *36 Hours*. Once again, the picture was to be filmed on location, but this time Jim had more than an actor's interest in what happened with the film. His own fledgling company, Cherokee Productions, was co-producing the picture with William Perlberg and George Seaton, with Seaton directing.

The new film was another World War II prisoner-of-war

thriller in which Jim plays an army intelligence officer abducted by the Germans just prior to the D-Day landings at Normandy—almost a reversal of *Emily*. The picture had everything wanted by the fans of wartime adventures: Nazis, psychiatrists, escapes, S.S. interrogations, amnesia, suicides, D-Day, U.S. Intelligence, and the Gestapo.

Shot on location in Portugal, Germany, and Yosemite National Park, *36 Hours* was an excellent beginning for Jim's Cherokee Productions. He had put together talented people both in front of and behind the cameras. The cast, in addition to himself in the lead, included Rod Taylor, Eva Marie Saint, Werner Peters, and other excellent character actors. Bill Tuttle from M-G-M did the makeup, with Sydney Guilaroff supervising, and the theme music was composed by award-winning composer-conductor Dimitri Tiomkin. It was a first-class production. Garner invested time and money in the picture with the hopes that it would produce handsome profits. Unlike his contemporaries, he did not demand ever higher salaries to make a film. As he said, over and again, he worked cheaper. In this instance he was doing so for himself. His salary was $225,000, with ten weeks guaranteed. As producer of the picture he stood to make many times that amount if the film did well—and it obviously did since it is often shown on commercial television, occasionally in prime time. Eva Marie Saint and Rod Taylor received $50,000 each for their work on the picture. It was Jim, however, who profited handsomely in the long run. Little wonder that he still resented his treatment at Warner Brothers.

Jim was used only a few days in Lisbon as mostly second-unit filming was done there. He utilized his behind-the-scenes expertise, however, to manage indirectly every facet of the film. Following the filming in Germany the picture was completed in Yosemite, with a few background road shots filmed at remote Lake Arrowhead locations about one hundred miles from Los Angeles.

Once the principal photography was completed Jim ran into difficulties with the use of German newsreels. Transit Films of Germany, an organization with a complete file of German news film of World War II, claimed title to "all German newsreels prior to May 8, 1945," which coincided with the Allied occupation of Germany. Hitler, they said, had endowed them with the copyright of such materials. Nevertheless, Perlberg–Seaton–Cherokee Productions managed to get the proper clearances to complete the picture with authentic inserts of wartime Germany's news clips.

It seemed, however, that James Garner would never completely satisfy everybody. The preview cards from the Warfield Theater in San Francisco, where the picture received a sneak preview on August 10, 1964, favored Rod Taylor though Jim came in for a share of the plaudits. At the Paramount Theater in Oakland the following night, the comments were more restrained but were "conservatively approving."

Though one critic deemed it to be "like a boring endurance film that just wears on and on," it has endured as a crowd pleaser for twenty years. Jim's willingness not to "make the big killing" but to continue to amass credits and comfortable bank accounts paid off. He was satisfied with his co-production. It didn't matter much to him what the critics had to say. All he cared about was entertaining the people who paid their money to see him up on the big screen.

Having taken on the additional obligation of producing films, Jim again attracted the attention of the media, but he continued to evade their efforts to pry into his personal life. He did have one interesting confrontation in public, however.

It occurred in July and involved Los Angeles City Councilman Karl Rundberg.

During a fiery hearing in City Council chambers over park and wildlife facilities that were to be part of a very controversial master plan for the nearby Santa Monica Mountains, Jim clashed head-on with the equally adamant councilman. A group of over a dozen residents gathered in the councilman's office for a hearing on how much of the mountain area would be set aside for development and how much would be retained as park land. Steve McQueen and Eva Marie Saint were there with Jim. Both Garner and McQueen were angrily vocal but it was Jim who edged away from the group and engaged in a one-on-one shouting match with Rundberg that came close to physical violence. Six-foot-three Garner and six-foot-six Rundberg stood nose to nose, Garner jabbing his forefinger for emphasis:

Garner: Do you represent the Eleventh District? (The mountain area in dispute was partially within that district.)
Rundberg: I certainly do.
Garner: You do not represent the district. You are interested in certain developments proposed there.
Rundberg: (whirling around in his chair, voice raised) You're a liar! (his face white in anger) I will not be intimidated by you or anyone else!
Garner: (moving in closer) I am not a liar and I am bigger than you.
Rundberg: In height, weight, or stature? (Rundberg jumped up from his chair, moving in on Garner.)
Garner: (still jabbing his forefinger) Remember, we are the people.
Rundberg: (shouting) You're an actor!

The shouting match continued until wiser citizens prevailed upon the two to desist before blows were exchanged. Steve McQueen's encounter with Rundberg was polite in comparison.

The matter simmered down and several years later the Los Angeles City Fathers were still debating the fate of the Santa Monica Mountains. Rundberg was gone and Jim was busy with other problems. The affair does indicate, however, that even though Jim doesn't like to tip his hand about his political beliefs, he will speak up if he feels the people are not being treated fairly. In this instance some thought he was concerned mainly with the interests of the wealthy residents (of which he was one) who did not want housing to interfere with their view and privacy.

The Americanization of Emily was released in the late fall, and Jim went on a tour to promote the picture. He had apprehensions about public reception of the antiwar film. "I hope this one comes off," he told reporters. "It is a hell of an actor's part. So well written. Most antiwar movies are preachy or sentimental or noble. This one is not."

Tours revealed Jim's feelings not only about the picture he was promoting but about acting, his life, and the world in general. Always outspoken and spontaneous, he often said outrageous things without hesitation.

Asked if he preferred drama or comedy, he said, "I'd rather do the story itself. If you can, try to balance the career with versatility for wider audience appeal, I'm trying." He referred to the comedies he'd made with Lee Remick and Doris Day. "Those did well."

When the conversation turned to his private life, again he brushed it aside. "I'm very particular about my private life. We live in Belair, though they don't like to claim us because we are at the very edge of it."

Questioned about his previous statement that he had never made a mistake, he responded, "That's a novel question and I mean it. I have worked hard and success didn't come in a flash." He recalled guesting on "The Steve Allen Show" with phone-in questions. A woman called in and asked him how long it took for him to become "an overnight success."

"I told her ten years," he laughed. "Mistakes? Well, I'm a free lance. Nobody owns a penny of me now. I have a wife, kids, my work, I'm healthy and happy. I've made mistakes. Yes, oh, yes." Then, grinning, he adds, "Apparently they were the right ones." Few could deny that.

During an interview with *Weekly Variety*, a trade paper, he explained why he objected to most interviews and why he didn't care for promotion junkets.

"Mainly," he griped, "interviewers are more interested in things you'd only tell your family or doctor. I don't like that. If I hit twenty cities on a promotion tour, business in those twenty cities will probably be increased by the attendant ballyhoo, but I'm a lousy interview. I just don't talk about the things they want me to. I'll discuss the film business or anything else for that matter, but that's not what they ask me. No matter how many times I say my private life is my own and I intend to keep it that way there are always a couple of writers or interviewers who will ask the forbidden question."

The media had had every opportunity in the world to see an angry James Garner on the golf courses around the country. "I used to be the Tommy Bolt of the amateurs," he grinned while competing in a Pro-Am Golf Tournament in Palm Desert, California, early in 1965. "I'm the only guy who threw a club after a practice swing." He confessed that even on the golf course he has an aversion to the sound of film cameras. "The whir of one of those old 1903 cameras sets my teeth to grinding. You're on the backswing and there

it is." At that time he belonged to nine different golf clubs—
as many as any Hollywood actor then or now. On the circuit
he played with the stars of golf—Palmer, Nicklaus, Snead—
and knew them all on a first-name basis. He was, by his own
admission, far more comfortable on the greens soaking up
sunshine than under the hot lights of a movie sound stage.

Standing around at the Pro-Am Tournament waiting to tee
off, Jim exchanged banter with the press as well as the other
golfers. He seemed to be having a great time. Asked if he
would have preferred a career in golfing, he winked devilishly
and said, "Maybe." Then he added, "But don't tell Nicklaus." He recounted an incident on the seventeenth hole at
the Bing Crosby Invitational at Pebble Beach. "There we
were. Nicklaus shanked his tee shot. I asked him, 'What goes
here?' Then I stepped up and I bombed it, too—right on
national television. Not the best credentials, but generally
speaking I play better with the pros. I don't feel the pressure
as much and the galleries don't bother me. The galleries respect the pro. When an amateur makes a bad shot they laugh
at him. That's embarrassing."

On a more serious note he revealed his method of playing
with the pros. "The James Garner manual on golfing says
that you have to have a certain temperament to stand up to
the sight of a pot-bellied duffer wedging a divot right over the
ball. I actually saw that once. It shakes the pros up if you
don't observe the etiquette of the game. For instance, picking
up when you're hopelessly out of a hole or making sure not
to step in the line of his ball on the putting greens." Dave
Marr, he confessed, "made me stand over the ball to keep
from swaying, which was one of my bad habits. Bob Rosburg
helped me with my chipping and putting."

After the promotion tour for *The Americanization of Emily*, Jim said, "I haven't made a picture in five months even

though two of my pictures are now in release. I need to get back to work. I'm just about golfed out."

His director and co-producer on *36 Hours* talked about working with Jim and what he thought of his talent and potential. "Any producer," said George Seaton, "would like to make a picture starring Jim. He is what a pep pill takes when it's tired. He is one of the industry's fastest-growing box office attractions." He pointed out that Jim's name on the marquee of a theater "spells dollars and financial success for a film."

Jim had certainly proved to skeptics that he was a sound businessman as well as an "almost pro" golfer and a movie star. In little more than a dozen years he had gone from pumping gas for less than a hundred dollars a week to earning over a million dollars a year. He had an active role in the Silverlake National Bank, and was expanding into other areas in the business world.

Seaton added, in his evaluation of Garner, that "Jim Garner is that rarity among actors—one who cannot be typed. He is the perfect leading man and proved it by playing so expertly against such diverse talent as Doris Day, Audrey Hepburn, Shirley MacLaine, and Eva Marie Saint. Watch him as the serious American officer in *36 Hours*, a role that demands depth of feeling and emotional sensitivity. Combine these traits with Jim's great vitality and physical attraction and he's going to be hard to stop from becoming one of our great screen stars."

Jim embarked on another period of frenzied activity, which found him completing five pictures in less than a year. Four of them were released in 1966 and one in 1965. They were *Mister Buddwing*, *The Art of Love*, *A Man Could Get Killed*, *Duel at Diablo*, and *Grand Prix*.

Production started on *Mr. Buddwing* in New York on February 22, 1965. It was a DDD–Cherokee Production and was

distributed by M-G-M. Delbert Mann, a seasoned professional, directed the film. His assistant director, Erich Von
Stroheim, Jr., was the son of the famous silent-film director,
who was also an internationally known film heavy and whose
greatest role was probably as Gloria Swanson's faithful chauffeur and companion in *Sunset Boulevard*.

The film was taken from a book by the same name, which
had been written by Evan Hunter and published by Simon
and Schuster the previous year. Jim had fallen in love with
the story and wanted to turn it into a picture. M-G-M owned
the movie rights to the book, having paid over $200,000 to
obtain them. The book had been so recently published that
there was not as yet a paperback edition on the market. Jim
had very specific ideas about the use of his name and picture
in connection with any movie-connected paperback of the
book. He granted the right to use his name in any paperback
advertisements as long as the names of all principals in the
movie appeared also. Jim's agent notified the producers that
"under no circumstances may Garner's likeness be used on
the cover or anywhere in the book—whether by way of a
drawing or an actual still photograph.

Jim was particularly delighted to learn that the book had
been purchased out from under Jack L. Warner, his old
nemesis. Warner was set to make a bid on the project the
following week, but M-G-M beat him to it. M-G-M had several reasons for wanting to purchase this particular book, and
they had nothing to do with James Garner. An interoffice
memo at the studio, dated April 27, 1964, was issued after a
reading of the galley proofs from the book's publisher:

1. *In view of extraordinary theatrical potential—must
be a major picture in every way.*

2. *Two hours ten minutes to two hours twenty minutes length.*
3. *Should be a five-star vehicle.*
   Original cast desired:
(a) Sam Buddwing	*Jack Lemmon*
(b) 50-yr-old woman	*Shirley Booth or Joan Blondell*
(c) Girl #1	*Natalie Wood*
(d) Girl #2	*Shirley MacLaine*
(e) Girl #3	*Geraldine Page*
4. *Must start in New York City in late April or early May due to story time and locale.*

For whatever reason, Jack Lemmon did not make the film and once again Jim, as second choice, got the lead. In this instance, however, it didn't matter because Jim was producing, not M-G-M.

The final budget for the picture was $2,829,049. The picture had a shooting schedule of forty-four days, with fourteen days on location in New York, twenty-fix in the studio, and four days in Los Angeles area locations.

In New York the company had all kinds of union problems. Although production had begun earlier, actual principal shooting did not begin until March 27—a Saturday. Problems began two days later while the company was shooting scenes in the subway station at Columbus Circle. An argument arose between the head grip and a worker over the manner in which a camera dolly was to be brought down the steps. Howard Horton, the location manager, called in a union representative from Local 52 in New York in hopes of settling the argument quickly and getting the production back on schedule. New York union officials resented "these Hollywood people coming in here and telling us how to do our jobs." What followed appeared to be an East Coast–West

Coast feud, and relations between the production company and the New York crews collapsed. Workers were unavailable when needed. Often search teams had to canvass the local bars to shoot a scene because the union men would take off without telling anybody where they were going. The low point occurred one day when the company was shooting scenes inside St. Malachy's Church. A man, claiming to represent the local union, came into the church reeking of alcohol, yelling and cursing and interrupting production. In a letter to the union written after he returned to Hollywood, Horton stated that the man conducted himself in "a loud and boisterous manner; the language was blasphemous and maledictory." E. C. de Lavigne, representing the producers, followed up Horton's letter, to which he attached statements about the conduct of union members of the New York local from Delbert Mann, James Garner, and Erich Von Stroheim, Jr. There were additional statements from other members of the company. The final paragraph of de Lavigne's letter summed up the aftermath of their horrendous experiences while shooting in New York:

> *Finally, may I say to you that the people selected to go with this company to New York were selected with infinite care because, if for no other reason, New York has never been too easy a place in which to work. Delbert Mann, himself, is a quiet sensible gentleman, easy to talk to, and the idol of our crews here because of his knowledgeability of the craft and his complete lack of any affectation or pompousness. He also was a resident of New York City for many, many years, and has always been very proud of it. James Garner, I can assure you, is one of the easiest gentlemen in the world to get along with, completely devoid of temperament or the usual af-*

*fectations that one associates with stars of his magni-
tude. The First Assistant Director, Erich Von Stroheim,
has handled some of our most difficult assignments in
the past and has always been a model of discretion and
known for his ability to handle men considerately and
intelligently. Parenthetically, may I add that he was
punched, and hard, by one of the Local 52 electricians,
in the stomach. He had the good presence of mind not to
retaliate, as he knew what a riot would have ensued.
The other people who went with the troupe to New York
were of equal caliber.*

Ray Klune, vice-president of M-G-M, further advised the
New York local that "unless Local 52 changes its attitude
with respect to our New York locations, we are going to do
everything within our power to avoid New York whenever it
is possible, and I would dare say that other companies may
feel the same way about it."

In spite of these problems the picture did get finished. The
stars and their salaries were:

James Garner	*$300,000 for 8⅗ weeks*
Katharine Ross	*$12,000 for 6⅖ weeks*
Suzanne Pleshette	*$60,000 for 1 week*
Jean Simmons	*$60,000 for 2⅕ weeks*
Angela Lansbury	*$10,000 for ⅗ of a week.*

Jim had the advantage of ownership and percentages.

The route taken by *Mr. Buddwing* to the screen was
lengthy. Principal shooting was completed in April. Four
sneak previews ensued: at Arlington Theater in Santa Barbara, July 23, 1965; M-G-M (Culver City), August 2, 1965;
Village Theater in Westwood, August 6, 1965; and Encino

Theater in Encino, August 20, 1965. Still, the picture was not released until October 11, 1966. This picture had to be good. With a string of pictures about to be released, Jim couldn't afford too many bad reviews. So the film was cut and edited and honed to perfection. But in the eyes of the critics, it didn't work.

The story was disjointed, no doubt as a result of the filming problems in New York. Jim played a character who wakes up on a park bench with no memory and only a telephone number on a scrap of paper in his pocket. He dials the wrong number, and the story goes on from there. In the end, of course, he remembers who he is and rushes to a local hospital to be with his wife, who has attempted suicide because of his rejection. In his review for the *New York Times* A. H. Weiler said, "A viewer even without benefit of Freud or a medical degree is bound to question the story's basic assumptions." As for Jim's portrayal, he added, "It is decent to divulge that our harried Buddwing, as played by James Garner, is a composer, but, unfortunately, his All American, genteel exterior completely hides his sincere, often energetic, efforts to portray a man driven to distraction by an all too-trying past." Only the audiences seemed to care—and that is a compliment to James Garner's drawing power at the box office.

The Art of Love, shot on location in Paris, starred Garner as a writer whose roommate (Dick Van Dyke) is a starving and unsuccessful artist. To bring him fame and, more importantly, fortune, Garner concocts a scheme to save his friend from the clutches of a wealthy woman he really doesn't want to marry. Garner's plan is to fake a suicide while he, as the go-between, would collect a fortune from sales of the "dead artist's" soon-to-be-famous works. Van Dyke double-crosses his friend and plants evidence to indicate that the "suicide" was actually murder and that Garner is the culprit. Van Dyke comes forward before Garner reaches the guillotine to which he was condemned and all ends well. The problem with the picture was that it had all been done too many times before. One critic assessed it as Universal's "still grinding them out from the same old mold." The picture was co-produced by Garner's Cherokee Productions with Ross Hunter, known for his lavish productions. There were many evidences of the Hunter touch throughout the picture. Eugene Archer of the *New York Times* described it thus: "It has the traditional dressy Ross Hunter production, with jewels by Cartier, photography by Russell Metty, actors by M.C.A., and backdrop courtesy of de Gaulle." Co-stars Ethel Merman (portraying a Parisian madam), Elke Sommer, and Angie Dickinson were very little help in salvaging this assembly-line formula effort. Carl Reiner's screenplay came in for some barbs as well. Truthfully, it was not a James Garner picture. Although he played a con artist, the role did not offer the typical Garner mischief and simply did not come off well. But as Jim has said many times, "One or two bad pictures will not ruin a career while one television series can."

A *Man Could Get Killed* received even more caustic reviews. Jim, as the victim of mistaken identity, is pursued by international spies who believe that he is a James Bond type out to get them. They are determined to get him first. It was a romp of a film but poorly constructed, and even a supporting cast that included Melina Mercouri, Sandra Dee, and Tony Franciosa didn't help. It was beginning to appear to some people, fans as well as movie makers, that Jim was out to "get the money and run" without considering whether he was making a good or even entertaining picture. Critics tore the picture apart. The *New York Times*, not known for flowery film reviews, nevertheless seemed to go out of its way to excoriate this one. Eliot Fremont-Smith's review began: "One of those tense little films Hollywood dubs romantic comedy, which are neither affecting nor funny, and some-times—as at this time—not even coherent. . . . Its message is 'A Moviegoer Can Get Taken.'" He concluded his critique several venomous paragraphs later by suggesting, "When Jack Valenti, the former White House aide, was appointed president of the Motion Picture Association of America, he allowed that he had never seen a bad movie come out of Hollywood. Now is his chance to begin his education."

With several films having been poorly received, even by audiences, Jim needed a morale booster, not a stinging comment involving his family life and his ability to handle being a father while spending so much time on location making motion pictures. Yet at that time Sheilah Graham chose to criticize Jim for a comment he had made explaining why he had taken his youngest daughter out of a progressive school in California and enrolled her in what he described as "a more conservative school in Massachusetts." He had added that, "She learned folk dancing and poetry and now I'm going to see that she gets an education." Graham fired back, "I know the name of the school in California and the fault, dear parents, sometimes lies not with the school but with the pupil. This particular school has sent pupils to some of the best colleges in America."

Despite Jim's disdain for fan magazines, often with much justification, one such publication, *Screen Album*, actually went to his defense when several columnists once again began questioning the Garners' marriage. Said *Screen Album*, "It makes exciting reading. It isn't true."

Jim continued to discount rumors that he and Lois were having marital problems and that they might even have a trial separation. "Look," he said, "I need Lois and I need the children." He added, "And I think they need me." For Jim that was almost an entire interview on his family life and as much as any one was likely to get on the subject.

Before embarking on his next picture, Garner took a couple of weeks off for a visit to Norman, Oklahoma, where he grew up. Almost a reprise of his 1958 homecoming following the initial success of "Maverick," his stopover in Norman while en route to Hollywood after twelve weeks in Europe was a welcome respite from so-so films and bad reviews. It was a chance to relax with relatives and old friends. He felt so good he even permitted an interview in the living room of his brother Charles's home, where he stayed during his Norman visit.

He fudged a little, or perhaps his memory was poor, when he told the interviewer that it was his first interview in eight years. Actually, the interview was beginning to sound a bit familiar. The glamour of movie making, he explained, "has been so built up that no one ever believes that an actor works hard," explaining that he often spent eleven hours on the set and was away from home most of the time when not actually filming because of promotions and business. Little wonder that rumors about a marital rift were abounding.

Jim took his opportunity to give one more reason why he wouldn't give fan magazine interviews. Some seven or eight years earlier, a movie magazine had written a story about him entitled, "Poor Jimmy, Poor Baby, Your Mommy Is Dead." He said the magazine purported to have quoted his father extensively. "My father," he declared, "wasn't even interviewed. He told me he wasn't."

Once again he took the opportunity to attack the medium that had made him a star. "I'm tired of television. 'Maverick' reruns are haunting me. I think I might do a once-a-year spot on some show—maybe a Bob Hope special. Otherwise I

don't want to do television." He commented that as an occupation the entertainment business was transitory. "I have
my own production company now and I'm on the board of
directors of the Silverlake National Bank. I'm almost in the
real estate business." He shrugged. "You know an actor has
to diversify. He's only as good as his last picture."

He discussed working on *The Children's Hour*. "It was a
depressing movie. Doing a film like that day after day can get
you down. It was the first time I had to cry in a movie and
that was difficult for me. I had to learn to do that. It is all
part of the craft of acting. You have to build up the mood in
order to cry. At least I did."

William Wyler, he revealed, was a hard taskmaster. "He
would comment on your performance but would't tell you
the reason for the commentary. He caught me totally by surprise one day by saying I had had a very good day." Garner
said he stayed awake all night trying to figure out "what I had
done really well" since the same scene had to be redone the
following day for closeups.

He confessed that not all his leading ladies were up to his
expectations. "There are only three that I would never work
with again, but I'm not going to tell you who they are. You'll
just have to figure that out yourself." He assured the press
that Audrey Hepburn wasn't one of them. Nor was Julie Andrews. "Julie," he declared, "is one of the sweetest, most
down-to-earth co-stars I've ever known. Audrey Hepburn is
wonderful, although she seems more up on a pedestal."
Other co-stars such as Doris Day, Shirley MacLaine, and
Lee Remick were not mentioned.

"I don't understand fans," he admitted. "Having never
been a fan myself, I have difficulty understanding their thinking." He avoided them, he said, by walking right by them.

"They don't believe it is me at first and by the time they realize who it was, I am gone."

Jim enjoyed a quiet family dinner while in Norman at his brother's house, with no more than twenty or so family members and close friends at the table with him. The following night, he said, he would be back in Hollywood having dinner with his wife and two daughters. "I look forward to that. I've been away for quite a while. It's always good to come home," he said, quite seriously.

XV

As far back as Garner could remember he had maintained a passion for fast automobiles. Ray Brown, a classmate at Hollywood High, was a hot rodder, and the two of them could be found from time to time drag racing out on the dry lakes of the high desert north of Los Angeles. From the moment he could afford one, Jim owned a sports car, and he has continued to own and race them throughout the years. But it was not until he made the motion picture *Grand Prix* that he was able to live out his racing dreams.

He was neither the first nor the most avid fan of racing in Hollywood. Metro-Goldwyn-Mayer had its share of actors crazy about cars or motorcycles: Clark Gable, Keenan Wynn, Douglas Fairbanks, Jr. There were also Jim's contemporaries, like Paul Newman and the daredevil Steve McQueen. Experts in racing seemed to agree that James Garner had the makings of a professional driver who could not only have made a living at racing but might conceivably have become one of racing's celebrities. The same has been said of him about golf. He must certainly have had a burning desire to be an actor. Though he has often said that he would rather play golf or race than act, James Garner, I believe, has always been starstruck and thoroughly enjoys the adulation he claims to want to evade.

Jim had wanted to do a racing film for quite some time, but the right picture had not come along. Furthermore, such a picture would require an enormous amount of preparation. Jim would never star in that kind of film without being thoroughly prepared. Too many bad pictures had been made in which racing and race cars were thrown in for excitement with no regard for technical accuracy. *Grand Prix* was the dream film for James Garner. He was the first of four male stars to be signed for the picture. Filming was scheduled to begin on May 19, 1966, at Monte Carlo, but for months prior to that, Jim was out on the circuits both in the United States and Europe adding to his already enormous reservoir of information and knowledge about auto racing.

Actually, the day after he signed to make the picture, he drove over the Riverside 500 Speedway in Riverside, California, fifty-five miles east of Los Angeles, where part of the picture would be shot. Cameras were being tested at the big track prior to taking the company to Europe, where most of the actual racing scenes were shot.

"The guys asked me if I'd like to hop in a car and take a ride. I had never been in a flat-out race car before, so I was real pleased. I was in a GT–40 with a camera mounted on it, and Frank Monise set up Formula Junior and Phil Hill was in a seven-liter Cobra. What we were supposed to do was have the Cobra follow the Formula Junior until we turned into the back straight-away and then he'd pass. Everybody took off like a bat out of hell. I got into the car with Phil and first off I told him. 'I know you're the world's champion. I know your whole background. The minute you put on your helmet and goggles and start the car, I'm truly impressed. You don't have to impress me any more than that.'

"He wasn't trying to impress me. Who the hell was I to impress, but I thought that's what he was trying to do. Believe me, I was impressed. Driving in a car with a guy like Phil Hill is an experience you don't easily forget."

Hill and Garner had to catch up with the Formula Junior, which had a head start on them. Hill took the car around the turns and onto the straight-aways until just before turn 6, where he caught up with the front car. Garner was so excited about actually being in the same car with Phil Hill that he completely forgot that he had no windscreen on his side of the car. (The Cobra's construction and design was for the benefit of one rider—the driver.)

Jim remembers it well. "It was a one-seater sort of situation, and the passenger has nothing to hold on to. I was diligently looking for something to hang on to but to no avail, of course. When we pulled in behind the other car I was already getting a face and mouth full of sand and dust, plus all the wind generated by their being in front of us. Then we passed them on a straight-away, and I'm saying to myself, 'Sure Jim, you're going to do this?' Of course I thought I was out of my cotton-pickin' mind and probably was, you know."

Only a week or ten days earlier, he had crashed his Ferrari in Palm Springs while attending and participating in a golf tournament. "Well," he grins, "I didn't actually *crash* it. Some dude was coming right at me. I was only doing about thirty-five miles an hour and I honestly tried to get out of his way, but he just totally wiped me out. A meter reader for the gas company was cutting across the lanes and I couldn't believe it but he was coming right at me. But he just kept crossing lanes and caught me broadside. I managed to barely get off the road about the same time he hit me."

By some miracle, Garner walked away from the demolished Ferrari without a scratch. He discussed the incident with Bob Bonderant, a Ferrari driver who later opened his own racing school. "I want to thank you for the safety features in your car. If that had happened with any other car I'd probably not be here telling you about it." The fellow laughed and lowered his voice. "Don't tell anybody, but we don't build automobiles. We build tanks!"

At the time Bonderant was driving Formula I cars and also working on *Grand Prix,* as were quite a number of professional car drivers. Jim drove right along with them at Willow Springs, north of Los Angeles, for about a month in preparation for the picture. "I went from the GT–350 to Formula III and then to what is now called a Formula A car. It had a huge five-liter engine in it and a tubular chassis; I think it was a Brabham. It was a squirrely thing. I spun out and bent a couple of things, but I didn't tell anybody about it. Why embarrass myself? I'm certain Bonderant was thinking I was an actor who drives a sports car who just wiped out his Ferrari and thinks he is hot stuff. He was probably saying to himself, 'I got a hot pilot that I'm going to have to teach how to drive a race car.' I'm dead certain he wasn't looking forward to his task. Of course, after my initial ride with Phil, I was sure I'd never be able to go that fast."

Jim had driven Cobras, but as an amateur, not as a professional race car driver. But he was an avid student. He wanted to know more about race cars. He'd been fascinated with racing all his life, and these cars were a far cry from the old '32 Dodge he drove in drag races when at Hollywood High School. They were among the best cars the racing world had to offer.

Jim was totally honest with his teacher, admitting that he knew how to drive a car but was totally ignorant about these big racing cars. His teacher was impressed with him. He had expected an egotistical movie star to come barging in, throwing his weight around. Instead, he found a professional from another field eager to increase his knowledge of racing to perfect his own craft. Teacher and student got along beautifully.

While making *Grand Prix* Jim spent five months in Europe on all the major racing circuits in Formula cars. He came to know the courses as well as the drivers who made their living racing on them. The production company spent five weeks in Monte Carlo working on sections of the course there, bit by bit. "We would take maybe three or four blocks at a time and spend the whole day on just that one small bit of course until we knew every crack and sprout of grass that popped through it. I got to where I knew every bump in the road, every speck of tar. I hadn't planned to get into racing the way I eventually did, but that experience converted me. I enjoyed it so much I simply could not stay out of cars for a long time after that. Hell, I was thirty-eight years old, a time when most drivers are looking toward something else. I had no business becoming involved with racing, but like Paul Newman, I just couldn't resist the challenge. It was fun."

His first time at Willow Springs also contributed much to his enjoyment of racing. "There was the first time I ever went around the turns doing it the way I wanted to. At turn four I looked to the next run and by the time I was at turn seven I was really into it, turning the revs that I wanted to turn at each corner, putting it on the line that I wanted to and coming out properly. When I finally did it as I wanted to, I came over the hump at seven where you get a little bit airborne. Going down that long straight-away I went 'Yaahooooo' just because I did it my way. The way I wanted to do it. That I had learned enough to do that. It was a great feeling."

For filming *Grand Prix* in Europe, Jim's car was equipped with butane tanks to create flames and smoke bombs to create the illusion that the flames were out of control. Either the butane tanks themselves were to be ignited, or their jet stream of gas, by an electrical switch. The idea was to simulate a fire, but what happened was the real thing.

The scene was created and engineered by Carey Loftin,

one of the great stuntmen working on the picture. According to Jim it was originally intended to split the shot and have Loftin do the stunt work and Jim cross the finish line in the closeup. "We decided that I was a good enough driver to bring it off and besides, I wanted to do it." He grins and continues. "Lloyds of London would probably have had a heart attack if they had known about it, and the only way they would know was if we had an accident, which we almost did."

Jim, then, did the scene, crossing the finish line at well over a hundred miles per hour. With the smoke bomb and the two butane tanks in place, smoke and flames were being emitted from the back of the car. As the car slowed down after finishing the race, Jim turned off the ignition key and braked into a skid. With one hand he attempted to hold the car steady toward the camera so that when it came to a stop he would be caught in a closeup. The moviegoer would then have no doubt that Jim himself had driven the car and not just slipped in for a closeup on a quick cut from the action. It was a noble idea, but risky.

The car had been rigged so that Jim would have an opportunity to cut off the butane tanks as he came to a stop to prevent a blowup. "I reached down," he said afterward, "and cut the left butane tank. I knew I had only four or five seconds for the remaining butane fuel to run through the tube before it cut off completely." With time running out as the car slid to a stop, he managed to reach down and cut off the second tank and also the electrical switch. "I was just jumping out of the car when everything blew up at one time. All the butane in the tubes came through at the same time and I was enveloped in one hell of a ball of flame. The fire must have shot up fifteen feet without warning."

Jim came out of the car headfirst in flames, and the special effects men, standing by in case of just such an emergency, sprayed him with a battery of fire extinguishers. The fire in the car stopped as suddenly as it had erupted since it had been caused by the last spurt of butane. The tanks inside had already been cut off by Garner. It was all over. Garner took off his helmet, and a wide grin crossed his face. His director heaved a sigh of relief.

Jim was impressed with the end result. "Oh, I thought the business involving the cars was very authentic and probably the first time a theater audience had ever seen anything quite like that. It was unique, although I don't think the story and performances compared with the actual racing. I'm not going to put down *Grand Prix* because so far as racing is concerned, it was the best movie ever made."

Grand Prix, a Joel Productions–JFP Productions–Chero-kee Productions and M-G-M release, was directed by another veteran of the movie wars, John Frankenheimer, from a screenplay by Robert Alan Aurthur. The cast, in addition to Jim, included Eva Marie Saint, Yves Montand, Toshiro Mifune, Brian Bedford, Jessica Walter, Antonio Sabato, and Claude Dauphin plus many other foreign actors, lending an international flavor to the picture. For authenticity, many well-known international race drivers had major roles in the film. These included Phil and Graham Hill, Bob Bondurant, Dan Gurney, and Bruce McLaren.

For a change, the *New York Times* film critics, as well as other critics around the country, agreed with Jim's assessment of his picture. One of them, Bosley Crowther, said the film "is a smashing and thundering compilation of racing footage shot superbly at the scenes of the big meets around the circuit, jazzed up with some great photographic trickery." He hardly commented on Jim's *personal* performance, but his overall assessment that the film effectively communicated the excitement of the Grand Prix Races was enough to pack the theaters. It was a great lift for Jim, who had truly put more into this picture to make it authentic than he had at any other time in his acting career. In this picture the director really had to rely on his star more than star on director; it is impossible to yell "cut" when a pack of race cars are speeding down the track at over a hundred miles per hour. This was a major accomplishment for Jim, and he seemed ready to face the world afterward.

Despite protestations that he was finished with Westerns, Jim climbed back into the saddle as both star and co-producer of his next picture, *Duel at Diablo*, made from the book *Apache Rising*. The project had several different names before reaching the screen. The original owners of the film rights were Stuart W. Cramer and Michel Grilikhes (husband of film star Laraine Day). The first-draft screenplay, written by Marvin H. Albert, was rewritten with Grilikhes as collaborator. (Grilikhes was a polished screenwriter, Albert was not.) The entire package was sold for $75,000 to Nelson–Engel Productions, a joint venture by Brien Productions, Inc., and Rainbow Productions, Inc., which became co-producers with James Garner's Cherokee Productions.

The picture was shot on location in Utah. One day Jim had been shooting a scene inside a building decorated to resembly a sheriff's office. He emerged into the bright sun, eyes squinting, ready to talk to a newspaperman, Dick Kleiner from the now-defunct *Hollywood Citizen-News*.

"Everybody wonders why I don't do Westerns," he began. "Truth is, I've been looking for a good Western for a long time. This is a good one and when it came along I decided it was time." He praised the director, Ralph Nelson, as "one of the best in the business." The picture boasted an all-star cast: Garner, Sidney Poitier, Bibi Andersson, Dennis Weaver, and John Hoyt. Nelson and Poitier had worked together before in the award-winning *Lilies of the Field*. Nelson also directed the television trendsetter "Requiem for a Heavyweight."

Jim was in a good mood, and when he is in a good mood, he talks, even to the press. "You know," he said, sipping a can of diet soda, "I hate locations, but you really can't shoot a Western in Los Angeles, now can you?"

He had developed a new philosophy about making motion pictures. He was looking ahead—beyond acting. "I'll let you in on something," he said. "Eventually I want to produce. That's where the money is. Producers can buy and sell actors." He had never forgotten Jack L. Warner and the way he treated his contract players.

The picture's story line wasn't new. It had been done hundreds of times in the history of Hollywood Westerns: The cavalry is ambushed by Indians and bloody battles take place until the rescue a few reels later. There was one big difference, however. This picture had James Garner, and Garner in the saddle was pure gold at the box office. But the film received critical acclaim, too. Even Jim's old nemesis, the *New York Times*, graced him with a good review, written by Robert Alden: "Garner, a man of experience at the Western trade, is a plainsman whose blood is red and who bleeds when he is beaten, who suffers agonies when his Indian wife is killed, whose tiredness with the pointless struggle is evident in every line of his weather-beaten face." He concluded the review by announcing that it was not for the fainthearted. "Much of it is raw and ugly, yet it is a film that will grip you, a film that will have a shattering effect by the time you go back out into the street."

Jim couldn't remember how long it had been since a critic in New York had treated him kindly. Whether or not he would admit it, he really did need a good review. If he truly meant it when he said that he wanted to get out of acting and only produce, then he would have to establish a good track record. Though he declared that what critics had to say didn't bother him, he knew that being bankable depended on critical as well as audience approval.

Back home in Hollywood, Jim settled down with his family before taking off to another location. As if to atone for past behavior, several fan magazines began an almost concentrated effort to assure readers that the Garners' marriage was happy. There were quotes, said to be from Lois Garner, in which she admitted that there were times when she was a "golf widow" but that she didn't mind because Jim was such a golf buff and she wanted him to be happy. She was also quoted as giving this advice to wives of other celebrities. "My advice to any wife who shares this situation with me is don't complain when your husband plays golf, or goes bowling or fishing. It's better than having him hang around a bar with some blonde. Just thank your lucky stars that he's a sportsman—not a playboy!" It is doubtful that Lois Garner even thought those words, much less said them.

Lois wasn't the only one quoted. Doris Day's comments were included. "Jim," she said, "is a wholesome, clean-living, good man. He loves his family, enjoys his work, plays golf, and has more fun than anyone I know."

Even Jack Kelly's past comments were included. It was such an obvious ploy that it might have embarrassed Jim. He was confident that stars no longer needed fan magazines—if they ever did—and he wasn't soliciting any compliments from them. He would have been just as happy if they never mentioned his name.

With *Duel at Diablo* both a critical and a personal success for Jim, he plunged right into a second Western. *Tombstone*, whose name was later changed to *Hour of the Gun*, was the last of his three-picture deal with Mirisch Corporation–United Artists. It was also the second film he would make for director John Sturges. He felt a particular loyalty to Mirisch because it had been the first company to hire him after his legal problems at Warner Brothers, which made possible the rest of his career. Jim's loyalty is renowned. His salary on *Hour of the Gun* was by his own definition "not much," but he had made the commitment some time back and would keep it. "I don't go back on friends," he declared.

Jim also felt like talking about *Grand Prix* at that time. "You know it was an all-location picture and we shot 600,000 feet of 70mm film in six countries. I don't know how many pictures have that kind of content. We covered five actual racing events plus one that was staged. That was quite an accomplishment and I'm proud of it." He also revealed that while they were shooting in Belgium a representative of Lloyds of London caught him doing his own stunts and canceled his insurance coverage for the duration of the picture. "My business manager's efforts kept my personal coverage from being canceled also."

He declared that when he completed his next picture he would be making all of his future films in Hollywood. "I'm tired of traveling," he said. "That's it! When this next location is finished I'll have been away for seventeen or eighteen of the past twenty-four months and I'm tired of being away from my home and family."

He revealed that his company, Cherokee Productions, was already into other ventures besides motion pictures. They had produced a record and two television pilots, which, he said, "I'm sorry to say, have not as yet been sold, but we have many good projects ahead for this company which will keep me in Hollywood."

Hour of the Gun, shot on location in Mexico, began principal photography the first week in November. Sturges's job was made all the easier by his having worked previously with Jim and others in the film. Mexico, he says, "was not a bad place at all to make a picture if you're doing a Western because the Mexicans are all terrific riders and they've got their own horses. That eliminated the need to bring down a lot of riders and horses, which can become an expensive proposition. So that saves money. Also, the hotels are okay to stay in. So, for that particular kind of picture Mexico is a pleasure and while we were there the weather was good."

Of Jim he says, "He's amiable and a hard-working fellow. There isn't any effort he wouldn't put out to get something done, but he doesn't like to get pushed around. He's a guy that's a little pugnacious. He's part Cherokee, you know, and when he has a few drinks he tries to take the country back." Jim would probably to be the first to agree with that statement. It's one of the reasons he hasn't drunk very much in quite a few years. It not only helps keep his temper in check but also helps prevent a recurrence of the ulcer that once caused him constant pain.

If he had any difficulty during this period, it was that another fan magazine was attacking his marriage once again. Under a story banner that asked the question, "Is $ucce$$ Ruining Jim Garner's Marriage?" the publication rehashed the old rumor that his long stays away from home were destroying his marriage. Every disparaging remark about Jim and Lois that had been made over the years was resuscitated and the story itself resembled a patchwork quilt of bits and pieces of gossip from the Garners' married life.

The story closed, however, with a supposedly direct quote from Jim in which he restated his desire to protect his family from public scrutiny. "I will never let anyone or anything hurt my wife, my marriage, or my children. . . . I was a nobody for twenty-seven years. I once sat in the corner of a bus station and hung my head. I was a healthy man and I didn't have a dime. I had no roots and no one outside my father and brothers cared a damn about me. . . . Today I have what I want and I'm going to keep it."

Hour of the Gun wasn't released for almost a year. Its story line, which concerned Wyatt Earp and Doc Holliday, was one Sturges knew well. He had directed the now-classic Burt Lancaster–Kirk Douglas film *Gunfight at the O.K. Corral*, based on the same true story. *Hour of the Gun* dealt with the aftermath of the gunfight. The picture opened with credits over the gunfight and went on to the courtroom where the Earps' murder trial took place. Jason Robards, Jr., played Doc Holliday to James Garner's Wyatt Earp. It was sensitive casting that brought together actors with contrasting yet complementary styles. The film ends with a "revenge gunfight" wherein Earp kills his archenemy Ike Clanton, played admirably by Robert Ryan. The picture introduced a young actor named Jon Voight,who has gone on to considerable renown.

The picture received excellent reviews, as did most of the cast and director. Yet this was not one of Jim's better efforts. He played the role of Wyatt Earp stiffly and seemed to be out of his element. Perhaps he was nervous and uncertain because he was so far out of character. The jovial, humorous performance that Jim usually offered was missing. He was not believable as a vengeful Wyatt Earp out to right what he believed to be a wrong. Jason Robards was so good as Doc Holliday that he overshadowed the less dramatic Garner. Even Jon Voight in the minor role of Curly Bill Brocious was more successful and was singled out for praise by the critics. The picture did very well at the box office, which seems to have been the Garner formula for success.

Jim could at least take some consolation in being named first in a list of the ten best-dressed men of the year by the Custom Tailors Guild of America. With the money he was amassing by "working cheaper," he could well afford to dress well.

On February 10, 1968, he completed *How Sweet It Is*, a co-production by Cherokee Productions and National General Productions that was distributed by National General

Pictures. Jim was back on more comfortable ground. He and co-star Debbie Reynolds made the most of a hilarious script that cast them as husband and wife. The picture was replete with all the madcap miscues that characterize a Garner comedy, and there can be little doubt that he played well against the vibrant and energetic Debbie Reynolds. Garry Marshall both authored the screenplay, which was adroitly brought to the screen under the aegis of Jerry Paris, and produced it with Jerry Belson. All these gentlemen would go on to distinguished careers in television. The cast, too, read like a cross-section of Hollywood's future television personalities: Paul Lynde, Elena Verdugo, Penny Marshall, and, way down the list, Erin Moran.

Almost true to his word not to leave Hollywood to make pictures, Jim had to spend a few days filming in Acapulco, which served as the French Riviera. Otherwise the picture was shot in Los Angeles. The reviews were good and the picture fared well. Jim was playing Jim Garner, a character he does better than any other.

No sooner was his last scene shot than Jim was busy putting together an automobile racing package. So anxious was he to get the Corvette team on the track that he invested in the deal what was described as "a hefty amount" of his own money. He went first class with proven pro drivers like Ed Leslie, David Jordan, Scooter Patrick, Dick Guldstrand, and Herb Kaplan and had plans to enter the Sebring races, Daytona, and French Le Mans in the coming season.

James Garner rarely criticizes another actor in public. Thus, his doing so when the Academy Award nominations were announced in February was news indeed. With the Hollywood community leaning heavily toward Warren Beatty, Faye Dunaway, and *Bonnie and Clyde* for the top awards, Jim voiced his objections loud and clear. "Everybody knows," he said, "that it's Keystone Cops with some music, but my argument against the picture is that it is amoral." He roared, "They're making heroes out of criminals. Look at it. They've made Bonnie and Clyde, and the John Dillingers and Pretty Boy Floyds into some kind of heroes. They were not heroes. They were public enemies. They were space-fillers in the papers when the news was dull. When people seeing that picture watch them get killed on the screen and say, 'Oh, that's too bad,' something's gone wrong."

He didn't let up. "It's not a true story of our time," he argued. "They were not just hippies or protesters. They were outlaws, bank robbers, and killers, and that's different." He seemed to have forgotten that Hollywood more often than not glorified legendary criminals. He had only to consider how many late-nineteenth- and early-twentieth-century Western gunslingers were glorified on the screen and given sympathetic love interests. Belle Starr and Billy the Kid come immediately to mind.

"I'm saying exactly what I feel," he responded when some-one commented that he was "coming on pretty strong." Beatty, he continued, "is disliked in this town and as bad as he is disliked the tendency is for people to slap him on the back and say, 'Well, he went out and did it,' and give him a lot of credit."

"I don't think Warren really cares," he added, "but if you want to know the reason for his unpopularity, I think it is his attitude. Besides, I don't think awards are very important and I don't see any reason to give them. I've been there. I was nominated a couple of times for Emmys. I went to one cere-mony but I didn't bother the second time. I don't say they were rigged, but they sure were loaded." He was asked to explain what he meant by "loaded." "What I mean is, every-body voted for his own program or for his company's pro-gram." He concluded, "I don't know how many people told me that Elizabeth Taylor got the *Butterfield 8* award not for the picture, but for pneumonia. And that Julie Andrews didn't get it for *Mary Poppins* but because she didn't get the leading part in *My Fair Lady*."

Jim made himself unpopular in much of Hollywood not only for attacking Warren Beatty but for suggesting that the Academy Awards were in some manner, legally or otherwise, rigged. He had critics of his own, some of whom were commenting in private that Garner was jealous of Beatty's success in quality pictures. It is true that Warren Beatty did not make many pictures, but those he did make were quality productions while Jim was becoming more known for quantity. There seemed never to be any pause, nor does there now, for taking stock of what he was doing and what his pictures were saying about him. For instance, within a month of completing *How Sweet It Is*, he plunged into another picture, giving some credence to the opinion, held by an increasing number, that he was in the business for the money and not for artistic excellence. The issue, though debatable, never quite reached an open forum. There was also a part of the film community who considered Jim something of a rowdy whose answer to every disagreement was his fists. They didn't want to take him on at that level. Very few of his antagonists would have cared to meet him with bare knuckles—and he knew it.

XVI

The Pink Jungle was one of the most forgettable films in Jim's career. He co-starred with a little-known actress named Eva Renzi, playing a fashion photographer on a location layout with a high-fashion model in Africa. Repeating the theme of so many of his films, Jim, initially a bystander, becomes involved in intrigue, diamond smuggling, and a minor revolution. The Garner sense of humor did little to save him from a bad plot with bad writing. Delbert Mann, who directed the debacle, should have taken one glance at the script and known better. He was fresh from directing the classic *Cool Hand Luke*, which starred Paul Newman in what is generally considered his greatest role.

Only George Kennedy, whom Mann had directed in *Cool Hand Luke*, came in for any praise from the critics. Veteran critic Vincent Canby said, "Movies that aren't much good have a way of looking uninhabited, which is several degrees worse than just being empty." That was the better part of the review. To Garner he gave this caustic one-liner: "Garner is a tall, incredibly coy actor whose way of emphasizing a comic line is to arch an eyebrow." Kennedy, who had won an Oscar earlier in the year as best supporting actor for his performance in *Cool Hand Luke*, was given credit for "the only real vitality" in the film.

Steve McQueen's cult film, *Bullitt*, opened to raves the following day. The chase in *Bullitt* was the chase after which all future chases would be patterned. Garner, McQueen's good buddy, was promulgating no such patterns.

Jim's humor simply wasn't working with the rebel-rousing, antiestablishment, thrill-seeking young moviegoers of the mid-sixties. He had his values and was determined to hold onto them regardless of fashion, though previously he had opted for "going where the action is," moving from films to television and then back to films when he decided "that's where the good writing is today."

His criticism of the Academy Award nominations added to the feeling that Jim had somehow lost touch with the times. Reviewers and movie makers alike were asking the same question: How many times had *he* been nominated for an Academy Award? It would take more than a so-so film to redeem him in the eyes of the artistic elite of Hollywood.

Jim wasn't all that worried about his adversaries or about those who thought he was less than a Barrymore. He was making over a million dollars a year and had begun a long-term investment program that included banks, land, and oil. The oil investment would prove to be unsound. He suffered considerable losses when Saxon Oil fell on hard times.

He was enthusiastic about the American International Racing Company, which he had founded. It was sponsoring entries in all the major auto races around the world. This he was doing for love, not money. "Hell," he shrugged, "if I won top money in every race we entered I wouldn't come close to breaking even." He even considered entering some of the races himself, so he went back to racing school to brush up on the expertise he gained while preparing for and filming *Grand Prix*.

Racing became a cause for Garner. "I want to upgrade the sport," he declared. "After football, it is the largest spectator sport in the world. It needs to be brought to the public's attention, and I can do that because I have the public's attention."

Many people were aware of racing, but it was a sport whose appeal seemed regional; most people who knew a lot about racing lived in parts of the country where race tracks existed: Sebring, Daytona Beach, Riverside. The Southwest and Southeast were the big racing centers in the United States. "They easily draw 85,000 in Riverside," Jim explained. "Even a small town of five thousand like Rockingham, North Carolina, can draw 50,000 for a race on Sunday afternoon."

Jim had other thoughts on the new venture. A chemical company was going to sponsor his racing setup. "We're almost signed. It'll be good for me and my image, but it will also be very good publicity for them—even if we don't win." He was anxious to return to his "nonactor" image. He was like a politician who runs for national office on the premise that he is "not a politician" but just an average citizen who wants to get into the thick of things and clean up the mess.

Jim had already raced two of his cars at Sebring and Daytona in the spring. Scooter Patrick, one of his drivers, led the pack at Sebring, setting track records for the ten- and twenty-lap distances. He might have gone on to set national records if a flat tire hadn't taken him out of the race.

His plans for the Le Mans classic in France during the summer included entering two new English-made Lolas that he had just purchased. He complained about the money it cost him for such an expensive sport. "Eighteen thousand dollars. That's what it cost me just for the chassis of the Lolas plus five grand for the engine."

With four expert drivers he hoped to have an impact on racing world. "It takes six mechanics and several others to complete the team. That's costing me $75,000, so you can see why it would be nice to get some sponsorship." He admitted that he recently slipped behind the wheel of one of his cars at Riverside and "let it all out," but added, "It wasn't any more fun than being a kid and challenging somebody at a stop sign to race them for their pink slip." Some of the slips were for speeding, not ownership. Jim seemed to enjoy recalling numerous incidents of derring-do over the years.

He didn't mention the South American locations for his last picture. But he was willing to discuss his recent efforts in Westerns. Yes, he was aware that *Hour of the Gun* had bombed at the box office. He admitted that there was a new generation of moviegoers out there. He added that there had been changes in the way movies were made. "It used to be," he detailed, "a director would shoot a master shot, then a two shot, over-the-shoulder shot and finally the closeups. No more. The camera has to move around and so do the actors."

A prominent theatrical writer and Hollywood analyst described Jim as ". . . a kind of three-way contradiction. On television—and in the kind of second-rate movie he seems to inevitably inhabit—he comes on very mild. . . . But he's more of a follower than a leader, full of easy charm, . . . and a little dilapidated." She declared that every wife knows a man like Jim—her husband. He is grumpy, she states, but "not evil or uncooperative or mean"; since married women know the type, "they sure don't have to go to the movies to find it." She did, however, admit that Jim was a star.

Jim speaks frankly, when he finally sits down to be interviewed by someone who has been thoroughly checked out by his public relations people. He let Carolyn See know what was on his mind during an interview for *TV Guide*.

"I am more diversified now than I used to be," he said. "The banking business bored me but I have other things going. I've got some ranch acreage up in northern California.

One of these days I'd like to subdivide it and put in tract houses."

Jim had also quietly purchased race horses. His hobbies were expensive, but he was a man who had worked awfully hard to have the things he wanted since his earliest days at the old country store and mail drop where he spent part of his childhood.

He doesn't like to talk about his movies—particularly the ones he considers less than good. But in a roundabout way, Carolyn See was able to get some response from him, albeit limited. "I don't like *A Man Could Get Killed* and I don't like *The Art of Love*, and I don't like to talk about them. I didn't like them when I made them. I don't like hearing about 'Maverick' all of the time. I haven't done a 'Maverick' in ten years and still people come up and talk about it." Both *A Man Could Get Killed* and *The Art of Love* were already running on television, which didn't surprise or please Garner. "There's nothing worse than seeing a bad movie unless it is watching yourself on television in a bad movie. I try not to watch any of my pictures on television."

In 1968 he didn't like the idea of movies coming to television, declaring that the reason so many films that had been recently made were being shown on the tube was because they were such failures at the box office and the studios had to cover some of their losses. Jim himself was guilty of doing exactly that, for some of the movies being viewed in living rooms about the country were produced by his own company.

Still, he was willing to go all out in his condemnation of bringing movies to the small screen, declaring that to do so was a disservice to each medium. "I don't think movies even belong on television. How's that for an opinion? The studios sell maybe thirty of them in a package and maybe two or three are really any good and God only knows where the actors are that appeared in them." When a studio is losing money on a picture and tries to dump it to recoup its losses, it will get rid of the film any way it can. "They'd sell them to nudie houses if they'd buy them," he said.

Television, he declared, was ruining motion pictures. He was unhappy that people no longer dressed up to go out to see a good movie anymore. "They wait until it comes to television," he said, pointing out that such habits contributed to the loss of money on good films shown in movie houses. "What people don't realize," he went on, "is that only the worst movies get shown because the really good movies are held back for four or five years," being rerun in the movie houses before finally being released to television.

Continuing his interview with Ms. See, Jim declared that Portugal and Italy, countries he had spent considerable time in on location, were not his favorite places. "It was hell," he growled.

Jim had just completed *Support Your Local Sheriff* and was quite excited about its chances of doing well. It was a Cherokee production, and the company was backing the film with its own money. *Support Your Local Sheriff*, another Western, cast Garner as a sheriff reluctantly recruited to settle unlawful and disorderly conduct on the part of the local citizenry after the mayor's daughter (played hilariously by Joan Hackett) discovers gold in an open grave at the town's cemetery. The film was a Western cops and robbers, and Jim, with his obvious lack of enthusiasm for doing personal harm, was at his humorous best. The film was funny. James Garner was funny. Joan Hackett was funny. The film was aided by established character actors who gave it some substance: Walter Brennan, Harry Morgan, Jack Elam, and Bruce Dern, who today is a major star in his own right. The film was directed by Burt Kennedy, who has praised James Garner as "one of the finest actors I ever directed. He is also one of the finest men I have ever known and working with him was a pleasure."

Support Your Local Sheriff, like so many movies, had a different working title from the one with which it was released. Originally, it was simply called *The Sheriff*. The picture was budgeted at $1.6 million plus the cost, if any, for a female star in excess of $100,000. Salaries were held pretty much in line on this Cherokee production. Kennedy was guaranteed twenty weeks for $100,000. Bill Bowers, who wrote the screenplay, was paid $100,000 for his rights to the screenplay and an additional $35,000 as "an individual producer" on the picture, plus 10 percent of any net profits. If there should be a sequel (which there was), then he was to be paid an additional $50,000, and if he wrote the sequel screenplay, Cherokee Productions had the right of first negotiation for his refusal. Later, there was some heated debate about the second picture, which brought Jim's agent and later executive producer, Meta Rosenberg, into prominence because of her negotiating ability. Meta Rosenberg, who was becoming increasingly important to Jim's business, would later be executive producer of his successful television series "The Rockford Files."

Before *Support Your Local Sheriff* was even off the ground there were problems. Paramount Pictures obtained a copy of the screenplay and immediately fired off a letter to United Artists, the distributors of the film, declaring that the opening scenes of the picture in which the female lead finds gold in the open grave were "not only similar to but closely paralleled the opening scenes of the musical film *Paint Your Wagon*," a Paramount picture, "in characters, situations, plot development, and details. Any use of these similar scenes will be detrimental to the rights which we own and to our proposed motion picture play and will constitute an infringement of our rights."

United Artists, surprised and somewhat rattled by the Paramount missive, quickly shot off a message of their own to James Garner and his Cherokee Productions, claiming that in view of the accusation by Paramount, "United Artists Corporation reserves all of its right and remedies against Cherokee under the financing and distribution agreements or otherwise in connection with this alleged infringement."

Jim turned the matter over to his attorney, Martin Gang, who notified Paramount that in his opinion there was no infringement, that the questioned passages of the script were contained in a previous work, "Recollections of the California Mines," and that the production would continue. He then sent Jim a reassuring memo that apparently settled the question of infringement: "I find absolutely nothing in the script of *Support Your Local Sheriff* which has any real relationship, or unreal for that matter, to the play *Paint Your Wagon.*" Production continued without difficulty, and although there was some correspondence between Gang's office and Paramount, it diminished in intensity after each exchange.

Reviews were mixed. The *New York Times*'s Vincent Canby declared, "Its comic images are unimaginative, sometimes as blunt as a human torch." However, he felt it was "unoffensive" and "very television-oriented" due to the number of television personalities among the cast.

Variety gave it a better review, which reached a much more limited audience than the *New York Times* review since *Variety* is aimed at the entertainment community, not the general film audience. The trade paper found it "a funny, but adult, Western that comes close to annihilating every cliché of this usually serious genre. James Garner and Joan Hackett head an excellent cast. Should make it big." The critic expressed surprise, however, that the film had been given a "G" rating by the MPAA because "much of the dialog is on the adult level, and two or three remarks even beyond that." Jim, they said, was "delightful," and Joan Hackett was deemed "excellent." Another critic declared that the film, "with its exceptional cast and script . . . remains one of the best films from director Burt Kennedy."

In his next film, Jim played Philip Marlowe, a character created by mystery novelist Raymond Chandler. Other actors had played this character, a private eye: Robert Montgomery in the unique *Lady in the Lake*, which had Marlowe lurking behind the camera for effect; Humphrey Bogart in *The Big Sleep*, a film that sizzled because of the scenes between Bogie and his co-star, Lauren Bacall; and Dick Powell in another classic, *Murder My Sweet*.

The film was shot in Los Angeles over a two-month period, so Jim was able to go home at night to his family. The nearest he came to "going on location" for the picture was to a penthouse in Santa Monica and a local office of the California Department of Motor Vehicles. Jim's good friend Paul Bogart directed the picture on a $2,642,959 budget.

Garner wanted Raquel Welch for the female lead but she didn't like the part and turned it down. Several other women turned down the role, mostly because of prior commitments. Gayle Hunnicutt was by no means the first choice to play Jim's leading lady. Jim received good support from a strong cast that included Rita Moreno and Carroll O'Connor. He seemed always to have the very best talent available when he made a film, both on the screen and behind the camera, but there always seemed to be something missing from his pictures—something that would make them truly great pictures.

Critics were hard on *Marlowe*. One review, which reflected a consensus among reviewers, said, ". . . Philip Marlowe is in need of better handling than either producers

Gabriel Katzka and Sidney Beckerman, scripter Stirling Silliphant, or James Garner in title role, have provided, if he is to survive as a screen hero. . . . Garner walks through the picture mostly with knotted brow."

Roger Greenspun of the *New York Times* pointed his sharpest barb at the star of the film. "Except for Garner," he wrote, "the cast is excellent and appropriate." The *New York Times*'s entire staff of film critics had at one time or another criticized Jim as a somewhat inept, "walk-through-the-scene" actor who would always be mediocre on the big screen.

Whether or not he liked it, or would admit it, Jim's greatest moments had been in television, not motion pictures, and what he needed to do was evident: Pay more attention to the quality and selection of his films or go back to television, where nobody seemed to care as long as the show came in on time and under budget.

With Jim so busy grinding out one picture after another, his partners were holding down the business activities of American International Racing, of which he was the director. John Crean, president; Don Rabbitt, vice-president; and Wilson Springer, director of public relations, were running the business. Still, the organization almost halted operations for a short time when Jim was unavailable due to pressing film commitments.

He took AIR, as the organization came to be known, seriously. John Crean and his wife Donna had raced as a team the previous year during the inaugural run of the Mexican 1000 race, which ran from Tijuana to La Paz at the tip of Baja. It was a tough, grueling course and Donna was the only female entrant who finished the race. Crean, like Garner, had his own empire to run in southern California, where he headed up an expansive mobile home business. Racing was a fun thing for him just as it was for Garner.

Business pressures had forced Crean to withdraw from

competition at the last minute as a driver in the Stardust 7–11 off-road race the previous summer. Ed Pearlman, president of NORRA, asked Crean to leave the buggy he was going to drive in the race and find another driver. Pearlman thought that perhaps he could lure Garner into replacing Crean.

"I had no thoughts of driving in that race," Jim declares, "but when Ed called and said I could drive John's car, I shucked whatever I was doing and got hold of Scooter Patrick to go along with me as co-driver." As it turned out, the desire to be at the race proved more important than Crean's pressing business affairs, and he deserted work and flew to Las Vegas to be a part of Jim's pit crew.

Jim's interest in racing went far beyond just hopping behind the steering wheel and tearing up the track. He was concerned about the inner workings of auto racing. "There is a lot of money invested in auto racing, but too often a good share of the money doesn't stay there, or it isn't poured back to take care of much needed improvements." He wanted to change that and believed that he could do so by setting an example. He and AIR had employed the best people available. "They are professionals and are compensated as professionals. We consider the fact that they should be paid not only for the work they do but for the invaluable experience they bring to our organization."

AIR had outside help now. Goodyear Tire and Rubber Company, one of the biggest car accessory companies in the world, had been brought in as a sponsor. The Goodyear people recognized the value of having Jim's name associated with them. Not only was he making a big splash in racing but he was a television and movie star with an instantly recognized name beyond racing circles. It was a good relationship between AIR and Goodyear, and both were profiting from it.

At this time Jim also accepted an invitation to become a

member of the board of the Oklahoma Medical Foundation. Given all his aches and pains over the years, he was instantly the subject of numerous medical jokes. He didn't mind because it only increased his personal publicity.

With Jim spending more time on the golf course and in racing cars, he was making fewer films. Between 1970 and 1974, only six Garner films were released—quite a contrast to the three or four Garner pictures released per year in the early sixties. Moving into the seventies had caused Jim to stop and assess where he was and what had happened in his life during the turbulent sixties, a decade in which he had seemed out of step with the times. He was still making pictures that reflected the mores of the forties and fifties.

In the back of his mind, Jim began reconsidering doing television. He had vowed never to do another television series, but he was certainly not setting the world on fire with a deluge of mediocre movies. The idea continued to germinate as he prepared to do his next film, in which he played a heavy. It was another Western with another European location. The film, *A Man Called Sledge*, was a Dino De Laurentiis production directed by actor-director Vic Morrow. Most of the filming took place in a small village called Polopos forty miles from Almería, Spain. Although Almería was a popular American film makers' locale, most of the villagers had never traveled very far from home and knew little or nothing of film making.

Jim wrote to a friend in Hollywood, reporting what he was seeing and how it impressed him. "It is amazing," he wrote. "These people didn't even know there had been a Spanish Civil War, and they didn't even know about World War II until several years after it was over." He was taken by the simple life-style they enjoyed, their uncomplicated lives, and their religious commitment. "I admire them," he said, "because of their self-dependency." Hard-working farmers, they grew most of the food they consumed on small plots of land.

In one scene, a reenactment of the portrayal of the death of Christ, known locally as "Penitente," was required. Jim was to be involved in a shootout during a crucial part of the pageant. "These people are very religious and brought a rare truth to the scene. They were amazed when the guns started to go off. Being unsophisticated, it was difficult for them to separate from fiction and understand that what we were doing was make-believe. It was that very puzzlement, however, that made the scene the most realistic in the film and one of the most realistic I've ever seen."

The villagers were able to make more money during a few weeks' shooting than they might make in a year.

"During the time we were in the village," he said, "we were all affected by these simple people. Who can say who has the better life? They were generous to all of us. They offered us food and water and a simple, natural hospitality without strings. Their life is hard but they have none of the taxes, tensions, or temptations that are part of our daily lives. Who can say who has the better deal?" Jim's observations may have reflected the frenetic pace of his own life, which brought him money and material goods but not enough peace and serenity of mind. He saw something in this poor village that did not exist in Hollywood.

A Man Called Sledge was described as having "violent action. A Western programmer starring James Garner as a downbeat, bad man pulling an impossible gold heist."

Playing the bad guy was not exactly typical of Jim, but apparently he was trying anything that came along to get back on the right track and make films that suited his personality and did better at the box office. It was his first film in some time in which Cherokee was not a co-producer. It was released by Columbia Pictures.

Once again, the cast was excellent. He was supported by Dennis Weaver, Claude Akins, John Marley, and his old friend Wade Preston—another line-up of television stars. The violent story, out of character for the cast, earned the film an "R" rating. "Garner and his cronies," wrote one reviewer in *Variety*, "are really bad guys, who kill merely for gold, without any sort of moral or romantic justification. . . . Garner and his number-two man, Weaver, give flat, underplayed performances of cold, cynical hard-drinking men. . . . It does not really create dramatically engaging or sympathetic characters."

Roger Greenspun of the *New York Times* said, "A Man Called Sledge is a bit better than most Italian Westerns and quite a bit better than many recent American Westerns—and that is still not good enough to satisfy the demands of its type."

Jim had always shied away from playing killers on the screen. It was a radical departure from what has become known as "the Garner wit," and shocked fans more than it entertained them.

Pictures seemed to be a means for Jim to make money to finance his avocation, racing. He was a familiar and popular face at all the off-road races, the Mint 400 on a Nevada alkali flat, for instance, or the tormenting Baja Peninsular run—a thousand miles of sheer torture. A man with bad knees and a bad back, he appeared to be putting both to the ultimate test of endurance. No football game or movie stunt that Jim ever participated in jolted him the way the pock-marked trails through Mexico did.

The Mint 400 Del Webb Desert Rally is a demanding race. It is a grueling two-day, eight-lap battle over a rugged, fifty-mile course, the worst possible desert terrain. There are no roads, few trails, hills to surmount, rocks, and sagebrush borne by the wind, which blows often and fierce. Only 12 of the 294 competing vehicles finished this particular race, which included jeeps, dune buggies, and modified passenger cars. Veteran drivers say it is America's toughest endurance race for man and machine—and James Garner loved it.

Jack Scagnetti, a writer and veteran Hollywood watcher, was attending the Mint 400 run and paid particular attention to Jim while there. He wondered why a film star who possessed fame and fortune would risk his life and career in such a serious and competitive sport. Lois Garner, who had come along with her husband and daughter Gigi, spoke with Scagnetti about her husband's interest in racing. "He takes racing quite seriously," she said. "Not just as a driver, but the sport overall. He's interested in what goes on behind the scenes as well. This has become a big thing in his life and it fills the gap left from not playing golf anymore." Golf, she said, had become a dull sport for her husband.

At the Mint 400 in 1970, driving a prototype fiberglass sedan—a souped-up 442 Olds V8 that bumped and bounced at breakneck speed across the desert floor—he was fully aware that a yellow jeep was right on his tail and he didn't like it. Better to let the guy by and and make a move to pass him later. He eased up on the gas and motioned the other driver to pass. It wasn't to be that easy. The yellow jeep careened past Jim on the right and smacked broadside into his blue and white racer. It was hard to tell what was going on until the dust settled.

When it did, it revealed Jim crumpled like a sack of potatoes behind the wheel of his crushed and motionless vehicle. Clutching his shoulder in agonizing pain, he leaned his head against the steering wheel and cursed. This was no stunt or publicity gimmick.

On the day of Jim's accident, Lois seemed unperturbed as

she lounged, seemingly totally out of place, in the pit area waiting for Jim to finally cross the finish line. "I don't worry about his racing. He's doing what he enjoys doing." Jim, she pointed out, "is basically a cautious man by nature. He won't try anything just to get hurt. He has to be confident that he will do it well. I don't think he would take chances on anything he couldn't handle. So what's to worry about?"

If anything, Lois Garner was more concerned about their daughter Gigi's interest in racing. "She's crazy about coming out like this with Jim and watching him race. I'm sure she'd hop right in with him. She's far more impressed with his racing than his film career."

Jim's tenacity held that day. It was first reported back to the pit area that he was down with his car and had possibly sustained serious injuries. Ten minutes later, however, a report came in from the next checkpoint that he had stopped for some water and parts and would continue on to the finish line. He did just that, and mechanics and spectators crowded around him when he pulled into his pit. Emerging from the banged-up vehicle, Jim grinned to show that he was okay. His face was caked with dust turned to mud by sweat and redried. He shook his head and said, "It's like riding under the surf out there. Just unbelievable."

He explained what had happened. "I was moving along watching the water gauge, which looked like it was about to jump right out of the dash, when some joker in a yellow jeep blasted me. I had waved him past on the left, but he decided to hit me on the right just as I moved over to let him by. Why he went to the right, I don't know. But I would sure like to have some words in private with him."

Jim asked fellow driver Drino Miller who owned a red Corvair. "He wouldn't let me by him for nothing. I was behind him for thirty miles and he just poked along at twenty-five miles an hour but wouldn't let me pass. Going slow like that didn't help the heating problem."

Drino admitted that "they shouldn't let those Sunday drivers in a race like this." Garner nodded his agreement.

It was decided that if the overheating problem could be taken care of, he would be able to go on with the race. "I think if we could get two more laps in today we'll be okay," he said.

One of the first in the pit to greet him was his young daughter Gigi, who was waiting for him with a cold soft drink. "Are you okay, daddy?" she asked.

"I'm just fine, sweetheart," he said with a loving smile. Jim moved as if to embrace his wife. Observing his mud-caked face she laughed, "Don't kiss me."

"It's only good ol' clean desert dirt, honey," he said.

Lois and her daughter returned to the hotel after learning that Garner was going to give it another try if they could clear up the overheating problem. The sun was blisteringly hot, and she'd been waiting around for three hours in the open desert air.

Later, after his car had withdrawn from the race because of the inability to solve the overheating problem, Jim relaxed and talked. He looked like a completely different man once he'd showered and freshened up—hardly the daredevil who would take on the heat and dust of the desert just "for the hell of it."

He modified Lois's earlier statement. "It isn't that golf is dull," he explained. "I still enjoy playing golf, except that I find the twisting and the way you have to hit a golf ball affects my back. I've got two ruptured discs in my lower back. I'd go out and play golf when I'd have a couple of months off between a picture, and within the first week I'd just ruin my back. So there would go my vacation. I just kind of laid off of it and found something else that I can really sink my teeth into—racing."

He particularly liked off-road racing. "I feel that we're onto something new and that's always a challenge. I just turned down a Formula Ford ride in Talladega, Florida. I would like to have gone but not on that basis. It's a professional ride. It takes time to prepare for something like that and I don't have the time right now. I have to be competitive or else I don't like to race."

It had been eight months, he said, since he'd last raced in a Formula car and he would have to "get that feeling" before taking to the track in a Formula race. He was proud, he added, that both he and Steve McQueen had organizations of their own formed for the advancement of racing. "I think," he beamed, "that we have stimulated automobile racing all around the world. Also off-road areas, too. It's a good thing to be a part of."

A week earlier, while practicing with his new Olds racing car, Jim had rolled his car at ninety miles an hour. What had happened, he was asked. Did it bother him?

"Not really. I came down off a little ridge and hit a flat spot where the road is very hard. Also it is strewn with pebbles and stuff like that, which have the same effect as going over marbles. The engine in my Olds was powerful and I just stepped on it too much. My right front wheel caught in some very soft sand. I tried to power out, but that didn't work. The car's rear end caught up and I couldn't correct it because of all the soft sand, which I was catching more and more. Then I got the left front wheel caught in the soft stuff and popped the bead on the tire. There was nothing I could do so I just decided to hell with it and let it spin in. I shouldn't have flipped. But when I started to spin in the rear wheels caught in the sand and popped a bead on another tire. That was it. Bang! Bang! Bang! I rolled over three times.

"I tore hell out of the muscles in my shoulder but that was from the shoulder harness digging in." He laughs. "I guess three is my number. That was not the first time I've flipped three times in a car. I was in Utah once with a girl driving and we went end over end twice and sideways once. Walked away from that one, too."

Jim figured that from the time he started to roll until after the third roll he never touched the ground. Regarding the Olds roll a mechanic said to him, "Don't the horizon look funny going around like that?"

Jim in true fashion, responded, "How the hell would I know? I had my eyes closed!"

Jim's cars are the safest in the country. He practices safety above all else. "I have a lot of people who I'm responsible for and I take that responsibility seriously," he explained. "So I have to protect myself for their sake. Hell, I've got a NASCAR roll cage in that thing. There's just no way that car can be made any safer. I have one of the very few off-road race cars that have NASCAR fuel tanks as precaution against fire. I'm no dummy when I climb into a car. I always wear a helmet, shoulder harness, and fire protective suit. I've been thinking of including full fire protection, including face protector."

As an independent producer without obligation to any film studio, he boasted that no one could tell him he couldn't race cars. He admitted, however, that those involved with his pictures discouraged him from racing when he had acting chores to complete. He got around insurance problems by driving at rallies only. "I'm not really driving professionally," he said. "Now if I'd taken them up on the offer to drive in the Formula Ford, I might have run into some insurance problems."

Garner admits he hates to lose, but during the Mexican 1000 he gave up winning to help somebody else. "We always try to help others if it isn't going to interfere with our cars. We helped the SAAB team by welding both their cars together. They went on to finish first and third. We were second. I don't mind that. On the other hand, we would have won easily." For his efforts, the SAAB people took a shot at him in their later advertising. "I don't go for that sort of thing," Jim said, a frown flitting across his face momentarily. "But the next time a SAAB comes to us for help they might just as well bypass us." Jim wasn't concerned about himself but went to the ready defense of others who were belittled in ads later run by SAAB. For instance, one read, "Alas, the poor Maverick took forty-eight hours." That incensed Garner. "What kind of statement is that? What about the couple of hundred guys that didn't get to finish? At least the Maverick finished. By God, that's something. They might have been a couple of guys out for the first time and someone like SAAB who has been doing this sort of thing for years attacks them. I don't like that kind of stuff and it sure as hell ain't fair play."

Of Garner, they jibed, "With James Garner driving an Oldsmobile Cutlass, how's it possible SAAB won in Baja?" Jim responded quickly, "They brought their great Swedish rally driver, Eric Carlson, out of retirement for the race and we beat him and his car—he was the guy who came in third. Hell, our car had two blocks of practice time. I gave it the try, brought it in, and said 'Bleed the brakes. We got no brakes. Paint it and let's hit the road to Mexico.'"

James Garner is not a man to be crosseed. Stick to the facts and he will be gracious, but deviate from them with the intention of hurting someone and you might as well walk into a nest of hornets on a hot August day. He doesn't care if you're one of the largest corporations in the world. That's one of the reasons he is respected by so many—and feared by some.

Jim had come a long way from those lessons at Riverside

and his first real competition in the Stardust 7-11 desert race in 1968. He considers that one of the toughest races he ever ran. "Scooter Patrick was my co-driver and neither of us had ever driven an off-road car. That buggy had only one testing before that."

Jim arrived on the scene a few days early to check out the terrain and was immediately awed. "That buggy we're driving," he said, "is too heavy and it's not prepared properly." He was right. They had completed 135 of the 700 miles when the car fell apart, the engine falling out and the distributor falling off. "Good little buggy," he admitted, "but much too heavy for that kind of stuff. It was overloaded with luxuries and not enough necessities. We needed more stability. But we learned from that. I was never discouraged. You're going to make mistakes. I've made them, but profited from them. I try not to make the same one twice. You have to keep in mind that you're not wheeling around the corner in your Cadillac. If you have a crack-up under those conditions, you could be badly hurt. The reason I've done so well is that I am always careful. If you ever watched 'Maverick' you know that I don't cotton to unnecessary danger."

Jim had plunged into producing and directing *Support Your Local Gunfighter*, something of a sequel to *Support Your Local Sheriff*. This was a co-production with his old pal Burt Kennedy. Jim would star while Kennedy would co-produce and direct. The screenplay was from an original unpublished story called "Latigo," written by James Edward Grant. The project passed from the Grant heirs to Garner by way of Brigade Productions, a company connected with United Artists. The budget was not to exceed $1.172 million. Jim deferred $250,000 of his salary, taking only $75,000 up front. Profits were to be divided 35 percent to Garner, 25 percent to Kennedy, and 40 percent to United Artists, the releasing company. Jim's contract was later amended, bringing his up-front money to $100,000, with $225,000 deferred.

Some old acting friends of Garner's shared the spotlight in this picture: Suzanne Pleshette, Jack Elam, Joan Blondell, Marie Windsor, Henry Jones, John Dehner, and Chuck Connors—again, a line-up of television stars with the exception of Joan Blondell. Was he edging closer to television again? Perhaps, but he was still not letting on.

The *New York Times* didn't give the picture a rave, nor did it tear the film to pieces, as with other Garner films. *Variety* saw it as a welcome relief to a "G-starved family audience." The film journal observed that "James Garner again stars in the light comedy groove he does so well with . . . a company of comedy-perfected supporting players."

Coupling pleasure with work, Jim completed a film about racing called *The Racing Scene*, which he hoped would be compared with *Endless Summer*, which presented an unusual insight into surfing and was critically acclaimed.

LEFT: James Garner and Katharine Ross in the 1966 movie *Mister Buddwing*, which later aired on "The CBS Friday Night Movie." *CBS-TV.*
RIGHT: James Garner seeks comfort from Angela Lansbury in this scene from *Mister Buddwing*. *Doug McClelland Collection*

Melina Mercouri and James Garner on the run in A *Man Could Get Killed* (1966). *Kenneth Norris Collection*

James Garner and Bibi Andersson in *Duel at Diablo* (1966). *Doug McClelland Collection*

A mustachioed James Garner takes aim in *Hour of the Gun* (1967). *Larry Edmunds*

Garner's daughter Gigi greets him after he finishes the grueling Stardust 7–11 off-road race in Las Vegas in 1968. He drove a high-powered modified Oldsmobile. *Jack Scagnetti*

LEFT: George Kennedy restrains James Garner in *The Pink Jungle* (1968). *Kenneth Norris Collection*

RIGHT: James Garner and Sharon Farrell have a serious moment in the Raymond Chandler detective thriller *Marlowe* (1968). *Larry Edmunds*

Garner and Debbie Reynolds find a lifeboat a good place to share a nightcap in *How Sweet It Is* (1968). *Kenneth Norris Collection*

Garner hits one down the fairway in a celebrity fund-raising event for the Latin American community in Montebello, California, in 1972. *Jack Scagnetti*

James Garner and Joan Hackett in *Support Your Local Sheriff* (1968). *Doug McClelland Collection*

Garner and *Health* co-star Lauren
Bacall backstage at a Willie Nelson
concert during a break in filming on
location in Florida. *Tampa Times*

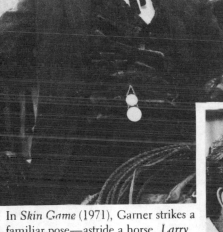

In *Skin Game* (1971), Garner strikes a
familiar pose—astride a horse. *Larry
Edmunds*

Garner discusses a problem with Rita
Moreno during one of her frequent
guest appearances on "The Rockford
Files." *Larry Edmunds*

James Garner, Julie Andrews, and Robert Preston in the Blake Edwards film, *Victor/Victoria* (1982). *Larry Edmunds*

James Garner and Julie Andrews in *Victor/Victoria*. *Larry Edmunds*

James Garner, Joan Hackett, Bobby Fite (left), and Blake Tannery starred in *The Long Summer of George Adams*, which premiered on NBC in 1982. Garner played an Oklahoma railroad man whose job is threatened by plans to replace steam engines with diesels. *NBC Photo*

James Garner receives comfort and assurance from C. Thomas Howell in the film *Tank* (1984). *Larry Edmunds*

Garner makes a rare appearance at one of Hollywood's splashy awards shows. *Dick Biegert*

Tom Selleck credits his recurrent appearances on "The Rockford Files" with being the launching pad for his phenomenal success as the star of "Magnum, P.I." *Dick Biegert*

James Garner as Navy Commander Norman Grant in James Michener's *Space*, a 13-hour, 5-part mini-series. *Stone-Hallinan Assoc.*

XVII

James Garner had been out of television for over ten years. During that time he had made nearly two dozen motion pictures and had raised a family. He was no longer a Hollywood tyro—if, in fact, he ever had been. Warner Brothers Studios, where he had begun and had achieved fame in "Maverick," were no longer owned by the famous brothers. Jack L. Warner had long since abandoned movie making. Gerald Leider, now president of Warner Brothers Television, had no quarrel with James Garner and welcomed the cooperation of new production companies.

In early August 1970 a joint statement was issued by Gerald Leider and Meta Rosenberg, now executive producer of Jim's Cherokee Productions, Inc.: Cherokee had signed for a joint venture with Warner Brothers that would involve Jim not only as a producer but as an actor. One part of this venture would be a network series to premiere on NBC in the fall of 1971. Cherokee would produce the series in association with Warner Brothers Television at the Burbank Studios, where "Maverick" had been filmed. Beyond the network showings, Warner Brothers would maintain worldwide distribution of the series.

Jim and Warner Brothers also agreed jointly to develop and

co-produce other projects for television, exclusively for the NBC Network, for future seasons. The contract also called for Jim to star in several films in the coming years, with specific details to be announced in the months ahead. It all sounded more like a wedding announcement than a business contract. Jim assured everyone that it was "good to be going back home."

He wasted no time getting back into the saddle. His first film placed him in a "Maverick"-like situation. James Garner was back at his old stance as a con man, but he was operating in the pre–Civil War era. Lou Gossett played Jim's sidekick in *Skin Game*, the film's premise being that he was sold from town to town as a slave and then escaped 'to rejoin Jim for the next con job in a different location. Susan Clark played the perfect female accomplice. It was vintage Garner without the nuances or sharp detail of a Roy Huggins. Still, the film moved well under the direction of Paul Bogart, who was familiar with Jim and his humor. Every joke and con trick displayed to perfection Jim's ability to be humorous without force. The critics had mixed emotions about the picture, but the reviews generally praised Jim. *Variety* commented that ". . . that character blend of likable rascality, or near-rascality, remains his [Garner's] most effective screen image. Many another film player never finds the right pitch. Herein, Garner is at his best in years." They lauded Lou Gossett's performance in a role that calls on him to "shift rapidly from the characteristics of a northern-born free man to those of a Dixie lackey." Jim *had* come home—and to good notices.

The cast was completed by Ed Asner as a slave trader, Andrew Duggan as a cold-hearted villain, Brenda Sykes as Gossett's girlfriend, and Henry Jones as a slave buyer attending an auction interrupted by John Brown (played by Royal

Dano) and his raiders. Talia Shire's husband, David, provided the musical score, which also received plaudits.

It was interesting to read reviews of Ed Asner's performance as a black-hearted slave trader while at the same time he was being declared "the comedy find of the year," in his role as Lou Grant on "The Mary Tyler Moore Show." Playing a slave was not a new adventure for Lou Gossett, who had recently been cast as a freed slave in the television series "The Young Rebels." These two supporting actors could have been stars of their own films. Again, James Garner had firmly and decisively surrounded himself with star-quality talent. Even though Meta Rosenberg was executive producer of the picture, it was Garner who made every important decision. In the future Meta would be Jim's front woman in other areas.

The *New York Times* wasn't impressed with the talent Jim had amassed to cash in on his "Maverick" image. In his review Roger Greenspun complained "It isn't a very consistent movie, and its comedy misses much more often than it hits. . . . Sometimes it is pretty funny." Garner and Gossett, he wrote, ". . . are equals, buddies, who enjoy a kind of personal freedom that it is difficult to credit given the times, and given the country." Garner, he said, was "appealing at first and finally tiresome." However, others totally disagreed.

When he left Warner Brothers Jim said that he would never work at the studio again. At the time he was asked if he would ever do another television series. He sharply responded, "Are you kidding?" Kidding or not, he was returning to the same studio and to another television series. This time, however, he was on the lot as a tenant, not as a studio property. And other things had changed. "Too many are gone from every studio," he said as if in some sort of mourning for the past. "I'm sorry about that. The commissary at one time was filled with the people that make a studio live—actors, directors, technicians. There are so few here now that they don't even open up the whole area. Part of the commissary is closed off. It is a shame to see this happen."

After all the years he had been in Hollywood, his reputation as a nice guy was intact. But he still fought tenaciously for his rights if he felt the studio or network was infringing on them. "The only thing I've allowed them to do to me is keep me out of racing cars. That's in my contract. I'm getting too old to race," he laughed. "Besides, there's no demand for a guy whose knees are so busted up he has a hard time bending them."

However, Jim demanded of his writers that there be no messages or causes espoused in the TV series. "I am against actors publicly making speeches and that sort of thing. It is wrong for stars to get involved in all that stuff." Stars, he contended, projected two images. The first was the personality projected on the screen, whether it be movies or television. The other was the real person. "Most of the roles we play are designed to make us look good. Roles that flatter us beyond who we really are. Therefore, when [a star] gets up on his celebrity soapbox and starts mouthing off about whatever cause he happens to be hysterical about at the time, he's throwing an unduly strong and clean image behind it. Since he is Mister Right in front of the cameras, all too often people believe he is equally right when he puts his mouth and name to a cause. That's wrong. You can't judge a star or other type celebrity by what you see when they're performing, and how does the average guy on the corner know when the actor is acting and when he is being himself?"

Jim's new series was called "Nichols." It was a well-researched series that boasted excellent writers, good or at least competent directors, and James Garner. Jim the producer-star was less reclusive regarding the press. To run his own show he needed media coverage, and he cooperated with media writers to his own benefit. "Nichols" was conceived by Frank Pierson, a writer-director who came to the series with excellent writing credits that included *Cat Ballou*, *Cool Hand Luke*, and *The Anderson Tapes*. As producer of the show for Garner, he wrote the first script and directed the first episode on location near Lancaster, California.

Acting as Jim's agent, Meta Rosenberg sold the series to NBC. In other words, she sold Jim Garner to NBC for a series. That sale was based on James Garner the con artist and pseudocowboy. Jim turned to Pierson to tailor a series to his particular type of humor.

"Two things made it attractive," said Pierson. "The movie business was so totally shot that I knew directors, and good ones, who were going two and three years between pictures. Creative people must work to justify their existence."

"Nichols" was a period piece, taking place in the Southwest just prior to World War I "The times were right," Pierson said. "It was the American dream in full bloom." Henry Ford was boggling the American imagination. Progress was everywhere. People were energetic and optimistic, and were beginning to resist Victorian morality. The saga of cowboys and Indians was fading. Pierson's Nichols was a career cavalryman accustomed to the relaxed life-style of a peacetime army that did nothing more exciting than exercising horses while pursuing the legendary and elusive Pancho Villa. "Nichols knows it is all over," Pierson stated, "the first time he sees a water-cooled machine gun mounted on a flatcar. It is the end of the romanticism of the cavalry soldier. Innocence has been replaced by machine and Nichols decides it is time to be mustered out of the army into civilian life."

Returning to his home in Nichols, Arizona—founded by his grandfather—Nichols is coerced into becoming the county's sheriff. It seemed custom-made for the star of "Maverick." As in his previous series, most critics felt that James Garner as "Nichols" was simply playing James Garner. While Brett Maverick was described as "a gun-fearing card-sharp and agitator who could squirm out of anything—to laughs," in "Nichols" he was profiled as "another kind of freewheeling slicker, operating in the fading West just before World War I. Conning and strewing confusion, a blend of W. C. Fields and the Earp brothers—managing to stay alive."

A crony at the time elaborated. "Jim," he said, "is like that in person. He's cagey. He's always dissembling." He related an instance in which Jim was playing against Sam Snead in "Celebrity Golf." Snead seemed unbeatable, having knocked over amateur golfers like Andy Williams, Dean Martin, and Donald O'Connor. The friend recalled, "Jim showed up with a bad back, bad swing, and hopeless chances. It was a deceiving look. Snead had to eagle a hole and sink a forty-foot putt—and that was just to tie Garner, who defeated him. Jim is slick." Slick, incidentally, is his long-time nickname.

Pierson said, "Jim Garner is like Wally Berry in his prime." Known as a roguish, the-hell-with-it sort when he isn't in front of the cameras, he plays such characters disarmingly when he is. In one segment of "Nichols,"—and remember, he is the sheriff—he swindles a saloon owner out of his bar, money, and bed while at the same times he owes the fellow $400. On another occasion he plotted to sell cracked church bells to the gullible citizenry. No other actor could carry off such unorthodox—and illegal—activities on screen and get away with it. Bigger than life on the screen, he is still Peck's bad boy and loved for being who he is.

Roy Huggins says such descriptions of Jim are inflated. "Jim personally wouldn't cheat anyone," he says. "But he is slippery as an eel with a mind like a steel trap. He never forgets anything. Many people think he is beady-eyed. He isn't. He squints at you and those eyes, like beady little dots, penetrate deeply. Don't whisper around him. He has ears like satellite saucers. They pick up conversations out of the air."

Just prior to the advent of "Nichols," Jim had made three humorous Westerns in which he played a cowardly drifter of lethargic bent who always seemed to be the cause of somebody else's grief. By wile and guile he survived victorious. "Nichols" was considered a frontier detective show, which gave Jim great latitude in his portrayal—perhaps too much. As the production chief he could overrule others who saw flaws in the show and in his performances from time to time.

The cast was a good one. Neva Patterson played Ma Ketchum, a tough frontier lady and matriarch of the town she had inherited from the last departing Nichols. Stuart Margolin, a close friend of Jim who later gained fame as Angel in "The Rockford Files," portrayed Mitch Ketchum, Nichols's slovenly deputy. Mitch got the job through Ma Ketchum, who used blackmail and coercion to force Nichols to become sheriff in the first place. Margot Kidder was cast as the whiskey-voiced but beautiful barmaid that is always found on this type of show.

There was only one problem with "Nichols." The public ignored it. Several episodes into the season, the show's name was changed from "Nichols" to "James Garner as Nichols." It was hoped that Jim's name would carry the show, but it did not. By November, a little more than two months into the season, the show was in trouble. It was on opposite the ABC series "Longstreet," which starred James Franciscus as a blind insurance investigator. "Longstreet" was a respectable sixteenth in the Nielsen Ratings, while "Nichols" was a dismal thirty-seventh. In what many considered a senseless panic, the network quickly began shifting programs around, hoping to improve the standings. Four shows were immediately placed in new and in some cases far more competitive time slots. They were "Ironside," "Nichols," "Funny Side," and "Sarge."

Jim was livid. He was given the rawest deal of all by having his infant series shifted from Thursdays at 9:00 to Tuesdays at 9:30. If "Longstreet," a mediocre show which died about the same time as "Nichols," was considered heavy competition for Jim's show, then moving to Tuesday was a disaster. The show would now be facing ABC's "Movie of the Week" and "Marcus Welby, M.D."—two of the most popular shows of the time. Additionally, he had to compete with William Conrad's increasingly popular "Cannon" on the CBS Network. It appeared that the network was attempting to sabotage "Nichols" or else had written it off and was placing it where it wouldn't hurt anybody.

The lead-ins on the new night were dreary, with little chance of survival: "Sarge" (fifty-third in the ratings) and "Funny Side" (which sustained a not-so-funny sixty-eighth position out of a possible seventy-three). Jim was in some good company. Shirley MacLaine's show was rated seventy-third at the bottom of the heap.

The postmortems were coming in months before the series was given an execution date. The network contended that the lead character spent too much time involved in get-rich-quick schemes, which negated the "Garner image." Some efforts were made to change the direction of the show, but they were insufficient. Nichols was finally killed off in a barroom brawl in December. After New Year's he was brought back as his own twin brother, Jim Nichols, who was the antithesis of Nichols: capable, brave, heroic, and definitely not a con artist.

The show was canceled by NBC early in 1972 and went into limbo after the August 1, 1972, episode. In trouble with ratings from the very beginning, it was unceremoniously dumped by NBC, leaving an embittered James Garner. Many of his contemporaries believe his bitterness was justified. The network executives were not compassionate. Garner, they said, knew the rules of the game. For every success in television there are dozens of shows that don't make it. Better luck next time.

Jim vented his frustration soon and often. "The show," he argued, "was five or ten years ahead of its time. The sponsor and the network both did things that were a sheer cinch to deep-six the show before it ever appeared on television." Jim had gone to Detroit to show his sponsor, the Chevrolet Division of General Motors, the pilot for the series. "What surprised me more than anything else was that they were expecting 'Maverick.' As a matter of fact—and I don't know where they got the idea unless it was from the network—they *thought* they were getting another 'Maverick'—maybe a clone, I don't know. But they were way off base. They never gave the show a chance. In my opinion it was at an intellectual level beyond their comprehension—way over their heads.

"They thought it was a bad show without even looking at it and they were wrong. The initial ratings weren't bad. We were getting ratings in the mid-thirties, comparable to other successful shows then on the air. When the network juggled us around we lost our audience. People didn't know where to look for us and when." Jim believes that "Nichols" was the best television series he ever appeared in.

Roy Huggins has other views. "I laugh when I hear or read

the various dissertations on why 'Nichols' failed. I'll tell you why it didn't work. It was one of the worst shows ever made. It made hits out of shows that it was opposite. 'Longstreet' was a big hit as long as its opposition was 'Nichols.' As soon as 'Nichols' was moved to another time slot, replaced by a better show, that series with Jim Franciscus as the blind detective failed and it was canceled.

"Jim Garner stopped at that point of his life. He became obsessed with 'Nichols.' He also became obsessed with me. He felt that people were saying, 'Ha. Jim Garner comes back into television without Roy Huggins and fails—again.' 'Maverick' failed after I left. Now he comes back, alone, with 'Nichols' and it fails spectacularly. Garner began to give interviews about how 'Nichols' was one of the best shows ever made—ahead of its time and all that. Better than 'Maverick,' he said. Then he began to make personal cracks about me. He was searching for something or somebody to blame. His film career, artistically, has been disastrous."

As to NBC's supposed indifference, Roy disagrees. "NBC did everything they possibly could for the show. Gave it new time slots, for example—and Garner will tell you that's what caused it to fail. Not true. The network didn't intend for the show to go down the chute. No network does that. It was simply something that wouldn't work no matter where they tried it. It was a terrible show. Good shows don't fail—especially when you leave them on for a whole year. 'M*A*S*H' is a classic example of that. It was a good show that didn't catch on the first year but showed some promise so the network carried it. 'Nichols' had nothing to show for the future. NBC was not at fault. More and more Jim's obsession with his own failure began to include me."

Many people disliked Meta Rosenberg, some with good cause, but she was loyal to Jim. She knew him well, having

been his agent long before helping him form Cherokee Pro
ductions. Originally a literary agent and one of the first
female executive directors of a production company, she understood Hollywood; she knew how to be tough and how to
handle the "hatchet jobs" that a star must have done from
time to time.

Meta was a woman in what was predominantly a man's
world and smart enough to know how tough she had to be to
survive. She was younger than most of the men with whom
she had to compete. "I'm sure some people were shocked
that I would be picked over other male candidates, but Jim
was looking for what he thought would be the best for his
company," Meta says. "He looked for the right person and
wasn't worried about gender. He's different from most of the
people one deals with in this business."

Meta often intervened for Jim, whose temper, in those
days especially, went off like a Roman candle on the Fourth
of July when something nettled him. His fists did the talking
and often Meta had to do the explaining. Meta did what she
could to prevent such outbreaks, and over the years Jim began to see the merit in letting her handle the tough situations
while he stayed behind the scenes. At the time, Jim said,
"Meta helps me sleep at night. She does my worrying for me.
When a guy gets up at five-thirty every morning he needs at
least seven hours' sleep—at least I do."

During the "Nichols" era Jim was reported to have separated from Lois for several months, leaving the family home
in Brentwood and taking up residence on the Warner Brothers lot in his dressing room. Neither Jim nor his wife would
discuss their marital situation.

It may have given Jim some peace of mind that his film
They Only Kill Their Masters, which he had made earlier in
the year, was released in November following the final epi-

sode of 'Nichols.' This picture boasted cameo appearances by June Allyson, Peter Lawford, Ann Rutherford, Edmond O'Brien, Arthur O'Connell, and Tom Ewell. The main cast, led by Jim as the local chief of police, included Katharine Ross (her return to pictures after a lengthy absence), Hal Holbrook, Harry Guardino, and Christopher Connelly. Jim turned in the kind of performance that audiences have come to expect. He made it all look so easy that one had a tendency to forget that he was acting.

During his battles with Warner Brothers, Jim had developed an ulcer, a recurrence of which almost hospitalized him when he was having difficulties with "Nichols." "I knew there was something wrong," he said. "Ever since that ulcer popped up the first time I get this aching feeling in my gut when things begin to get screwed up." Disgusted with his most recent encounter with the networks, Jim returned to making pictures again but did not, as he had after "Maverick" rule out television in the future. "Who knows," he said, "what's in the future? I said I wouldn't race cars anymore, but that doesn't mean I won't. It 'suggests' that I won't." He winked when he said it.

Despite the canceled television series, Jim was receiving considerable publicity. When "Nichols" premiered, his personal star was installed in the Hollywood Walk of Fame directly in front of the renowned Chinese Theater, and *Skin Game* was having a world premiere as Warner Brothers' fifteen-hundredth picture. Most people cannot remember "Nichols" or what it was about, but folks don't forget James Garner. He has always been thought of warmly by fans. The star still shines brightly.

In an article published in *Entertainment Weekly* while "Nichols" was still running, Jim declared that motion pictures were permissive and he wanted no part of it. "I don't think that's my kind of thing. I think that TV is more creative at the moment than motion pictures, so at this stage I felt working within the framework of television was more rewarding than making motion pictures where *everything* goes." Such was his explanation for returning to the medium he had so soundly denounced a dozen years earlier.

"Permissive films," he declared, "are a fad, and they'll pass. In the forties there were the John Wayne war pictures. Then came a stretch of meller-dramas and a stretch of comedies like the Doris Day things of the fifties. It goes back and forth." He felt that movie makers would have to return to good stories that would provide solid motion picture entertainment.

In an effort to make "Nichols" more popular with audiences, Jim gave more interviews and talked more about his private life than he ever had before. Whether by design or just because he felt like talking, he discussed his relationship with Lois with several writers. He appeared to be a happily married man.

"Paul Newman said it," he declared, "but I said it first. My wife and I have a good marriage because we have nothing in common."

His marriage had a solid foundation, he said, because "my wife permits me to do what I want to do. She never nags or makes scenes." He admitted that she did not share his avid interest in sports, especially auto racing, "but she occasionally accompanies me." Later he said she'd only been to races in which he participated a couple of times. She much preferred him to be sitting on the bench with the jocks at a football game than jarring his system by racing over terrain not fit for man or beast.

He quickly agreed that his household revolved almost exclusively around him. "I like it that way, and apparently my family does, too."

"I don't impose my will on others," he explained, "but by the same token, I don't take kindly to someone trying to impose his or her will on me. I think that's why—or at least one of the reasons why—Lois and I get along so well. She doesn't impose her will on me, plus she has respect for me. And that's mutual. That's what makes a marriage nice."

He revealed that he spent much more time with the girls than with their mother. "I'm king at home and why not, with a houseful of women competing for my attention. Lois and the girls see plenty of each other so it is natural for them to each want my attention when I'm there. I try not to get involved in the arguments they have between them. Mother—daughter competition for the man's attention is normal. I know how to handle that.

"Every individual has needs and in a marriage you try to fulfill the needs of your partner," he says. "I need freedom. My wife understands and gives me that freedom. A lot of women would be complaining if her husband didn't spend more time catering to her needs. I know my wife's needs and I think if she wasn't satisfied I'd hear about it—and I haven't."

Going on in greater detail than he had before, he said that Lois "needs the freedom to run her house the way she wants to and it's a job she enjoys. She also enjoys her social life with her girl friends. She's very close to ladies like Suzanne Pleshette and Hank Fonda's wife, Shirlee, so it's not like she's been deserted when I go on location. She has a full life, just as I do, and we both enjoy it that way."

Worrying about his kids becoming involved with drugs was something he very definitely did not do. "What's the use?" he asked. "If you give a child a basic sense of values, by the example you set before her, then you've done the best you could as a parent. If they know they're loved that's a big plus. If they don't turn out okay, then there's nothing you can do to change it until they decide to make the changes themselves."

His elder daughter, Kim, had tried pot but found it not to be the high it was purported to be. "She put it down," he said. "No big deal. I never had any doubt about that. I suspect most kids *try* it, but not that many make it a life-style. My wife has been very involved in drug-abuse programs and she knows what goes on. She's seen the really bad situations and worries about them as if they were her own kids. That's a caring lady."

XVIII

In an effort to promote "Nichols" in hopes of an unlikely second season, Jim and his publicity people permitted the press to literally line up at his door. NBC public relations types were on hand at Warner Brothers to guide the interviews, cautioning the somewhat jaded feature writers not to ask routine questions whose answers could be found in any one of a dozen or so Garner biographies that had been prepared for every picture he had ever made, plus the new one that had been prepared for "Nichols." Still, the same questions did get asked, the most common one being, "How does it feel to be returning to television?" Undoubtedly Jim felt revulsion after hearing the question asked a hundred times.

An issue that came up constantly was salary. Jim's "Nichols" salary was estimated to be as low as $40,000 and as high as $100,000 an episode. He argued that people were confusing his salary with the show's weekly budget.

Although there was already talk by mid-season that "Nichols" probably wouldn't make it, even though the early ratings were good for a new show, Jim wasn't too concerned. "If NBC drops me," he said, "I'll be heading to Mexico and the next Baja 1000. I can't race right now because the network won't let me—that was my only concession to this series. So if they drop me, I'll be free to race again."

Reconsidering his life, Jim offered some slight variations of previous accounts: "My formal education stopped at the ninth grade, and I finished high school in the army. When I was sixteen I joined the Merchant Marine, then I was in the National Guard, and a few years later I had the distinction of being Oklahoma's first draftee for the Korean War. In the guard, I tore a cartilege in my leg and I reinjured it in Korea. It still acts up, so I just had an operation on my knee. I also have three disintegrating discs in my back, so I can't play golf anymore."

Jim likes to leave an interviewer with something to ponder—usually a philosophic one-liner. This time was no exception. "You know," he said once, "I don't think there is such a thing as a TV *star*. . . . I think a star is Clark Gable."

Meta Rosenberg often became the person to be interviewed, not Jim. Other times she warmed up the interviewer and tried to shield Jim from questions that did not deal with "Nichols," his television series being the reason for the interview in the first place. Some found Meta's position offensive and brash.' *New York Times* writer Paul Gardner went through Meta's warm-up for his interview with Jim hoping that they would be able to get down to the nitty-gritty of who James Garner really was. It didn't work. Meta told him, "Garner is a real professional, he doesn't goof off, he's generous. I know this is boring and I may sound like Pollyanna, but *goddamn*, he's a pleasure to be around."

Gardner wrote, "Garner is . . . a relaxed, humorous, self-deprecating actor who certainly does not need Meta's hosannas . . . but I could not very well say, 'Aw, knock it off, Meta.'" Somewhat like a good press agent, Meta declared that Jim's favorite film was *The Americanization of Emily* (which everybody already knew) and that judging from the preview in Topanga, where she had heard the applause of a thousand people, Jim's last picture was a success and his popularity with moviegoers assured. Meta explained that "Nichols" came about because the network had offered Jim a lot of money to return to television "in any series he chose. I assigned three writers to come up with something. One prepared a detective series; another created a lawyer show; and Frank Pierson was the winner with the pre–World War I Western. That's the way it happened." That discounts earlier statements supposedly made by Jim that Pierson was "chosen" to come up with a show. The media often slant a story if it makes for better reading.

Once he knew the show was not going to make it, Jim attacked the ratings system. "It is nothing new for me, not believing in ratings," he stated. "I didn't believe them when they showed me on top of the heap with 'Maverick.' That hasn't changed. It is an antiquated system and everybody knows it, the networks as much as anybody. Still we are forced to live by them. Here you have grown men—businessmen—acting on something they don't even believe in. Interesting, isn't it?"

Jim wasn't the only star who was failing on the small screen. His situation was, however, unique in that he had been a giant star on television before abandoning it for films—films that for the most part sank into the sunset. That he understood. What he couldn't seem to fathom was what many critics saw immediately, although he himself had declared that there were no television stars because television actors were in your living room every week. In truth, there was a glut of Garner both in the living room and the movie houses. His "Maverick" series was playing in syndication around the world, theaters were saturated with his films, and some of his films were competing with "Maverick" for television space. Under the circumstances, had it been the greatest series in years, "Nichols" would still have had a tough time. Jim's personal ratings were spread over too wide an area to be representative. At some point there may have been more people watching Jim in their homes than any other star, but Neilson calculates its ratings differently.

He resented the way Neilson obtained its ratings. "Don't tell me that 1,200 sets around the country, placed in locations nobody knows about, can possibly reflect the taste of 200 million viewers." The only reason there were outside ratings in the first place, he stated, was because "the networks don't trust their own judgment."

Jim had his own ideas about ratings. He wouldn't toss them out but would use a different means to obtain them. "I would throw the current ones out. I was involved with a research and development company that has the right idea, and it works. You'd have to have airplanes, a scanner, and a computer. It would cost more, but to keep a good show on the air in preference to a bad one makes it worthwhile. What you have to do is fly over the area being tested. The scanner will give an accurate account of what's on each set because each channel gives off a different beep."

Almost simultaneously with NBC's decision not to renew "Nichols," Garner and Steve McQueen filed separate lawsuits in California Superior Court against Image Films for the use of their names in a picture entitled *Mexican 1,000.* Both claimed an invasion of privacy and requested that segments of the race wherein they appeared be immediately deleted from the low-budget film. Garner claimed that his reputation would be damaged by release of the picture, which concerned road racing in Mexico.

Cancellation of "Nichols" gave him the opportunity to do exactly what he said he would, and he promptly signed up for the Baja 500, racing out of Ensenada. Once more he said he could "do what I want. Nobody owns any part of me."

The Baja 500 was becoming a happening rather than a race. More than three hundred people entered the contest, driving motorcycles, cars, trucks, and dune buggies. Jim and his co-driver, Slick Gardner, were sponsored by Andersson's Split Pea Soup. Jim took his frustrations with network television and threw them into one hell of a road race. It was the one way he could be violent without hurting anybody other than himself. By the end of the run he could simply relax with a cold soft drink and forget Hollywood—which he did.

The failure of "Nichols" caused Jim to slow down and alter his schedule. He cut back to about one film a year and seemed to spend more time on business and with his family. A man in his forties, he *had* to curtail some of his athletic activities. He rarely played golf, he was watching football from the sidelines, and though he could still shove the stuntman aside and say "let me do it," he knew that if he continued tackling the increasingly rough off-road races he might suffer some genuinely serious injuries or worse.

But he continued to test his luck. While filming *They Only Kill Their Masters*, in which he played a small-town police chief investigating a murder, he insisted on doing his own driving in a scene that involved cracking up a police car. He found nothing wrong with taking risks that might handicap him, depriving his family of a healthy, functioning father and husband. A teen-aged mentality appeared to be operating in Jim's middle-aged body.

"I enjoy finding out what a car's limits are, what my own limits are, and running with that." Stating that he wished that he had gotten into auto racing at an earlier age, he said

"I'm getting a little too old now. Forty-four. I only get to run an average of two races a year because of picture commitments, and it is difficult to stay in shape in between."

They Only Kill Their Masters was not a Cherokee Production. Metro-Goldwyn-Mayer produced and distributed the picture. James Goldstone directed with a budget of $1.551 million. It had a short schedule of forty-four days with location scenes shot at St. Andrews by the Sea in New Brunswick. Kim Novak was anxious to play the lead, which eventually went to Katharine Ross. Ann Rutherford came out of retirement for her first film role in twenty-two years to play the wife of a policeman for the studio she had called home throughout her acting career. It was quite a homecoming.

Why did Jim choose to make a film that Cherokee Productions did not produce? Was his production company failing him? A well-made film based on a good story and screenplay that employs good actors working to capacity is what a producer-director wants. *They Only Kill Their Masters* more than met these criteria. Both audiences and critics lauded it.

In the film, a divorcée is found dead, believed to have been killed by her pet Doberman until the police chief unravels the mystery, discovering her murderer. The deliberately low-key film was in the best tradition of Hollywood murder mysteries. "Garner," reported *Variety*, ". . . again projects well his serio-comic dramatic abilities, now enhanced further by good, strong facial lines (not lines of age, but of definition)." Further, the paper found the film to be a relief from "the uptight, frenzied crime melodramas of recent years."

The *New York Times*'s Howard Thompson penned what even Jim would have to call a "rave review." "This," Thompson contended, "is the most original and likable whodunit I have seen in years. . . . Front and center is

Garner in his most becoming performance, low-pedaling that blandness with just enough amusing bite." As to the rest of the cast, he found that "they're all good."

Yet James Goldstone, the director, was not happy. Shortly after the picture's completion he wrote a bitter letter to Daniel Melnick, vice-president in charge of production at MGM, recalling that he had asked to be relieved as director at the beginning of the film since he and the studio, particularly Melnick, had disagreed on how the picture should be handled. But the critics thought Goldstone had done a superb job. Thompson gave him high marks, declaring, "The tone, text, and mystery have been set up and sustained with exquisite sensibility by Lane Slate's script and James Goldstone's direction."

In December 1972 Garner decided to take off a few months from work. A writers' strike in Hollywood created a slow-down in production, and he could rest easy with the success of *They Only Kill Their Masters*. At this time he treated his brother Jack and daughter Gigi to a vacation with the folks back home in Oklahoma, once again staying with his brother Charles rather than at a hotel. He has never liked hotel living nor felt truly comfortable when staying in one. He likes homey situations and home cooking.

In Oklahoma he began to play golf "once in a while," and "tried some tennis. My knees bother me too much for tennis. That's a fast-action game." Looking tanned and healthy, he seemed to have mellowed some since his last visit to Norman. He was like a transplanted southerner whose accent is lost until he meets another southerner or returns to the South for a visit.

He had little inclination to discuss "Nichols." "We were doing what I consider to be good work. It was their loss," referring to the NBC Network. "There were some good things that came out of the series." It was a brief comment on a personal work. As a matter of courtesy or brotherly pride, he played up his brother Jack's film career, ticking off the television shows he had appeared in. "We used him in 'Nichols,'" Jim said, "and he's done other shows that I wasn't involved in, like 'Mannix,' 'The FBI,' 'Lancer,' and 'The Doris Day Show'—and that doesn't count the movies."

Jim was cautious about making any long-term commitments during the next year or so. Producer Alan Landsberg signed him to host and narrate a ninety-minute racing spectacular for ABC-TV. It was something different for the athletic Garner, but his geniality and easy way of talking with people would be an asset when he interviewed the racers (most of whom he knew personally), mechanics, wives, and numerous others who are involved in assuring that races come off.

He made two pictures in succession for Walt Disney Studios, which were nice, folksy, "G"-rated films that the whole family could view. *One Little Indian* was a Western comedy-drama, ideally suited to Jim's style. He played the part of a U.S. cavalry corporal who is unjustly arrested for disobeying orders but escapes on a camel borrowed from Uncle Sam's Camel Corps and is involved in a number of comedic escapades throughout the film. The second picture, *The Castaway Cowboy*, cast him as Lincoln Costain, a shanghaied Texan who ends up becoming Hawaii's first cattle rancher. The film was in the same genre as "Maverick" and other humorous Westerns he had done so many times before.

Both films were given excellent reviews and recommended for all audiences. *Variety* praised *Cowboy* as a "topnotch, lighthearted Disney entry for family trade particularly; excellent grosses foreseen." Howard Thompson also had high praise for the picture and singled out Jim for praise: "The film's rudder is James Garner, whose leathery, laconic expertise (minus the pat blandness) winningly sets the tone and flavor."

Jim seemed to be on a winning streak with the critics. The timing was excellent. He was planning to return to television, a move that would again bring him into the living rooms once a week. It would also pair him again with the man who had had more to do with his phenomenal success in "Maverick" than anyone else. That man was Roy Huggins, who tells an intriguing story of his reunion with Jim.

Roy's brother-in-law Luis Delgado had been, and still is, Jim's stand-in and close friend since the early days at Warner Brothers. Even though relations were somewhat chilly between Roy and Jim, it was inevitable that each would be reasonably aware of the other's activities. Not everything that happens in Hollywood makes the papers—even when the press knows about it—but to insiders there are no secrets.

Thus, Roy was aware of Jim's dissatisfaction with his recent films and was not surprised when his brother-in-law approached him about Jim's availability to do a television series again. It was a subtle effort at reconciliation. "I found it interesting," Roy recalls, "because it was about the same time 'Nichols' was canceled that he went back into his disastrous film career—and it was almost always just that. I've known him so long, so I feel I can be more objective about him than perhaps others can.

Luis Delgado told Roy, "Jim Garner would like to come back into television, Roy, and he wouldn't be averse, the way he put it, to doing it at Universal. He didn't say he wouldn't be averse to doing it with you, Roy. Just that he wouldn't be averse to coming back and doing it at Universal."

"I nodded," Roy said, "understanding there must be some difficulty on Jim's part to come to me directly. So I said,

'Fine.' That's the way it began and it went on from there. I was producing at Universal so it was easy for us to connect. I came up with the story for the pilot of 'The Rockford Files.' Don't believe anything you have heard about how it came about. It came from me. Actually, 'The Rockford Files' was simply 'Maverick' as a modern-day private eye. That's all. Played by the same character. He was a guy who didn't like to put himself in danger. Didn't like to work too hard. Had a wry sense of humor. Somewhat cowardly. Was not a superman or superhero. When he hit the villain with his fist he would wince and go 'Oww!,' which is what Maverick did.

"That's the way I came up with the character. Doing 'Maverick' in modern-day circumstances meant that I had to have a guy who is kind of an outsider, which is why I made him a former convict.

"As a prisoner, or ex-con as it was, he was an outsider because of his background, whereas Maverick had been an outsider by choice. In both he maintained a certain sense of humor. Garner humor—and that's the difference."

Roy proceeded to create the characters around Rockford. Joe Santos, for instance, his friend on the police force, was Roy's idea. "Having a friend with the police department is a bit of a cliché, as is the relationship, but it was needed in this case. All private eyes need the guy on the police force. They're still doing it. Mike Hammer has his friend in the department."

When Roy Huggins comes up with stories they are not brief sketches. He tapes full treatments and has them transcribed by a secretary. "My treatments are screenplays in treatment form. Then I turn them over to writers. That's how I work. I had been using a guy named Steve Cannell and I turned the story over to him. Steve invented the character of Angel, who was played admirably by Stuart Margolin. Angel was a funny, bizarre kind of character—typical Steve Cannell. Angel always got himself and Rockford in trouble."

Roy explained why the screen credits read "Created by Roy Huggins and Steven Cannell." "His creative credits come about because of a legal situation which says that whoever writes the script get credit for 'created by.' Steve deserved creative credit, however, because he did create the character of Angel. I was so impressed with his understanding of the characters, I made him the producer of the show."

In any event, there was now a script, which Roy sent to Jim. Jim immediately saw himself in the script. "I knew he'd go for it," Roy says, "because it worked for him before and there wasn't any reason it wouldn't work again. It still boils down to writing and writers preparing characters and scripts that fit the Garner personality and natural ability to be humorous in his own right.

"Jim had an agent, Meta Rosenberg, who had become his personal manager. When he and I met he told me right away, 'Roy, I want to do this, but I have a problem. I have promised Meta that if I go back into television she would be the executive producer.'"

Roy did not have a high opinion of Meta's work on "Nichols." "She hadn't helped much on 'Nichols,' but nevertheless she was there. I told Jim that was no problem as long as he understood one thing, and I made this extremely clear at the time. I didn't mind who had title credits but I wanted it understood that I would be the producer during the first year.

"'Jim,' I said, 'I have often produced shows without taking a credit. There was a very successful show called 'Kraft Suspense Theater' and I did it without credit because I chose to. So that's not a problem "

Explaining why he would allow someone else to have credit on the screen, he added, "I wanted to get some very good producers on there and to entice them to come in—like Robert Altman. I explained to Altman that I wouldn't be taking credit so that when it says 'Produced by Robert Altman' he would be belittled by a second credit that will say 'Executive Producer, Roy Huggins.' I'm not going to put my name on it at all.'

"Besides, everyone in the business knows who did what and who gets credit. You leave a certain imprint after a while."

So "The Rockford Files" was launched. "I think," recalls Roy, "there were something like twenty-four of them done. I wrote seventeen story treatments—absolute originals. The rest I found based on books and other material. I make this point to emphasize the need for James Garner to have the right kind of material to be successful at television—or movies."

Roy has always written the shows he produced in that manner—with nearly absolute control over story content—and his hits bear out the formula as a winning one: "Run for Your Life" and "The Virginian" are instances. Roy's modest side is reflected in his use of twelve different pseudonyms because he doesn't like to see his name on the screen two or three times for a show.

The Huggins–Garner team was off and running, and the series looked good immediately, ranging from twelfth to first out of eighty shows rated the first year. Jim was delighted.

Tanned and jovial but carrying ten pounds more than he found comfortable, Jim talked while having iced tea and what was called a "sunshine salad" at the Universal Studios commissary. His ulcer, he said, was acting up a bit also—an unpleasant reminder from the "Maverick" days. Speaking of "Maverick," he revealed a new and previously unpublicized aspect of his battle with Warners'. "I was offered a million dollars to continue the series, but no way." He allowed a twelve-year-old girl with an autograph book to interrupt his lunch. After signing his name he directed her to another table where Peter Falk, then starring in the extremely popular 'Colombo' series, was eating. "I'm sure Peter won't mind," he winked. After the youngster had moved away he said, "I only did that because she's twelve years old. I think she would have been terribly disappointed to find out he was here and she didn't get his autograph."

Jim has done the same thing to Paul Newman and Steve McQueen, both of whom were notorious for not liking to sign autographs. "If I signed one right in front of him, I don't see how Paul could refuse—now could he?" Probably not.

"The Rockford Files," with a contented James Garner at his best, debuted on NBC on September 13, 1974, and would run in prime time through July 25, 1980. It would have an abrupt and name-calling ending, with ups and downs along the way and more downs than ups after the first year, and was the show that finally made viewers forget Jim as Maverick. Now, practically a generation remembers "Rockford" more vividly than "Maverick." Jim had always contended that television has no stars, only personalities who are forgotten quickly.

XIX

While working on "The Rockford Files," Jim lived out of a trailer parked on a public beach in Santa Monica. But his home away from "Rockford" was something quite different. His Brentwood mansion is described as "a fortress with iron gates and entrance doors twenty feet high." The house took five years to build, mostly under the supervision of Lois while Jim was away on location. The builders, she said, were not easy to deal with, "but when Jim spoke, they jumped."

The Garners had earned their home. Both had worked long and hard to be able to have the space and seclusion they desired. The house wasn't even visible from the road, so that unlike so many Beverly Hills celebrities, when the Garners went out into the front yard, they did not find tour buses lined up along the street hoping to catch an idol in pajamas or hair curlers. Three stories high, the home has become a model of celebrity living, with decorator and home magazines vying for the right to photograph it. It was quite unlike the early days when their Belair home was snubbed by a home magazine.

The house has something for every member of the family, but the family lives mostly in the library, with its polished wood and fine, leather-upholstered furnishings. In an interview with Muriel Davidson that included Jim, his wife, and their younger daughter, Gigi, they revealed that it was Jim's ritual, when working in town, to call home before leaving work at night so that they could all eat together. It was the same consideration that he had shown his family when working on "Maverick" and as a vice-president of the Screen Actors Guild. Sometimes, Gigi said, "we have our dinner on TV trays and hold conversations," which might cover the day's news or a planned picnic—but never Jim's work.

The house boasts a living room that turns into a movie theater with an enormous screen. There is also a pool table where Jim and his friends spend some relaxing moments. With all its size and family warmth, the house has, as Davidson described it, "a curiously impersonal, transient quality about it."

The one room in the house that reflects Lois's true personality is the master bedroom, which is lined with photographs of family and friends—dozens of them. Included are the Henry Fondas, the Joel Greys, Steve McQueen, and parents and grandparents from both sides of the family. There is also an oil painting of Gigi at six.

Jim has a few men friends, but it is the women in his life who have most influenced him. He once said that pretty women scared him, but there has rarely been a time in his life not affected by women, beginning with his mother's long illness and death. His family life of course included Lois and the girls, and in many of his films his leading ladies were bigger stars than he was. In business he has depended on Juanita Bartlett, "my script genius," and of course Meta Rosenberg, who acted almost as an extension of him. The fact that she was sometimes unpopular with the men around him and yet survived them pleases him. He likes strong, self-confident women who do not need a man around twenty-four hours a day to assure them that everything is okay. Jim believes in women's liberation without fanfare. He gives them the room to be liberated, as long as they do the same for him.

"The Rockford Files" was a success. Meta Rosenberg was the executive producer and James Garner the star under the banner of "A Roy Huggins–Public Arts Production in association with Cherokee Productions, Universal Television, and NBC-TV." Roy Huggins is a "take-charge" producer. As producer, he is concerned with only two things. "Script and postproduction. A movie or television film is always written three times. First, in script form. It is written again by the director and his actors and then it is written a third time in postproduction when you edit the show and put in the music and sound effects. That is my business and that's why 'Maverick' and 'Rockford' were so successful in the beginning. I always knew how to present Garner in a story that was specifically designed for his personality and completely polished before it was released for screening."

Roy usually employed jazz great Pete Rugulo to do the music for his shows, but for "Rockford" Mike Post and Peter Carpenter did the music. As Roy recalls, "I did not want to interfere with those aspects of 'The Rockford Files.'" Later on, this was to become an issue.

Throughout the first year of filming "Rockford" Roy Huggins states that there was little or any direct contact between him and James Garner. "There was no use. He was doing his job and I was taking care of mine. The show was the important thing. And we were lucky to have a show. I had trouble selling 'Rockford' to NBC because of 'Nichols.' I had quite a lengthy meeting with the president and vice-president in charge of programming at NBC, during which I had to go through the whole story of 'Maverick' because they were not going to do 'Rockford.' Their position was that they had already lost a fortune. 'We've been burned by this man,' I was told."

Roy assured the network executives that he would not be leaving this show. "I'm going to do this show." He neglected to add that he planned to leave after the first year.

The show was taken to ASI, a preview house where audiences are brought in off the street to test new shows, commercials, or anything else with television potential. "We did the preview and the average over there is about sixty-four on up for an acceptable show. We scored in the eighties."

Even so, NBC felt they were taking a gamble, but the president of NBC agreed to give the show a try. "Roy," he said, "we're probably out of our minds, but we're going to buy 'Rockford.' Remember that the experts had advised Henry Kaiser not to buy "Maverick," but he did and made history with it.

The show ended the first year with a solid twelfth position in the ratings. Roy Huggins felt that the series was in good condition and that he could go on to other things without jeopardizing it.

Frank Price, who happens to be Roy Huggins's son-in-law, was head of production at Universal at the time. One day at the end of the first year, Roy was in Frank's office and Frank asked, "Jesus, what's eating Garner? He came up here in some kind of a huff and said you didn't keep your promise."

Surprised, Roy asked what he was talking about. "He said you promised him that Meta Rosenberg would be executive producer and you didn't keep your promise and you're off the show. He won't have you on the show anymore."

Shaking his head in disbelief, Roy laughed. "Frank, I told Jim I was only going to do the show for one year. I have no idea what he's raving about. I don't intend to do the show anymore. They've got a guy named Steve Cannell who is very talented, and they don't have to worry about it. Steve can produce and Meta can do her little thing. She can sit in the casting section and she can direct a few of them. I don't think it's going to be devastating."

Roy has had second thoughts about that. "It was devastating," he says, regretfully. "Check out the ratings after I left." During the show's first year, two private eye shows finished in the top twenty: "The Rockford Files" and Mike Connors's "Mannix." The private eye series was losing popularity; there would not be another private eye show in the top twenty in prime television until the eighties. When "Maverick" was made, Westerns were at their peak and quickly diminished thereafter. The private eye show had already begun to decline and would never be as strong as it had once been. Crime dramas on television began focusing on the police department, perhaps reflecting the growing conservativism of the United States. While private eyes had been shown skirting the law in many instances, the new genre was strictly law and order in its approach: "Starsky and Hutch," "Baretta," "Kojak," "S.W.A.T.," and "The Rookies," and on into the eighties with award-winning shows like "Hill Street Blues" and "T. J. Hooker." Consequently, when considering Roy's assessment, there is always the public's mood, ever fickle and fluctuating, to consider.

Roy ticks off ratings like a computer. His accuracy on dozens of shows and where they were at any given time over the years is uncanny, and he was right on target with "Rockford."

"In the second year the show dropped out of the top twenty. All right. It was about thirty-five. By the end of the third year it was down in the forties and faced possible cancellation. I asked questions. Why did NBC continue to pick up 'The Rockford Files' when the ratings were so low? I wasn't complaining. I was happy because they were still paying me my full fee. My contract assured that I would get my production fee whether I was on the show or not. I was the creator, so I was delighted to have it picked up, but what I couldn't understand, as a pragmatic film maker, was why a network would carry the show when it was getting close to fiftieth in the ratings and perhaps no more than a twenty-four share of the audience—a very low share for a prime-time series."

A television executive from another network explained to Roy what was happening. "Can't you see?" he asked. "It isn't just 'Rockford.' NBC hasn't got any shows in the top twenty anymore." NBC had begun its slide into third place in the battle of the networks. CBS and ABC had moved ahead of the giant RCA network.

Steven Cannell assumed the over-all production duties following Roy's exit from the show, and over the several years there was a galaxy of directors, including Meta Rosenberg and even Jim Garner himself. The show boasted dozens of guest stars, some with recurring roles. Robert Donley, who portrayed Rockford's father in the ninety-minute pilot, which aired in March 1974, was seen in only that episode. He was replaced in the role on the series by Noah Beery, Jr., as an easygoing, folksy, retired trucker, always around to pick up the loose ends when Rockford returned from his wild chases and narrow escapes. Gretchen Corbett, also a regular, was Rockford's girl friend. She happened to be a practicing attorney and was always available to bail him out of jail when he stepped on the toes of the police. Detective Dennis Becker, played by Joe Santos, maintained an uneasy relationship with Rockford; it was often his toes that the private eye trampled.

Recurring roles included Pat Finley as Becker's wife, Kathryn Harrold as Jim Rockford's blind friend, James Luisi as a lieutenant in the Los Angeles Police Department, and Dennis Dugan as a novice detective. Garner's old buddy Stuart Margolin enjoyed the plum role of Rockford's slightly crazy

friend who was always in some kind of trouble, usually drag-
ging Rockford along with him. His was a memorable, somewhat bumbling character. Tom Selleck, a rival detective who
sometimes gets on Rockford's nerves, credits his appearances
in "Rockford" with catapulting him to the stardom he now
enjoys as Magnum P.I. and as a film actor. Rita Moreno as
Rita Capkovic, a heart-of-gold prostitute who periodically
comes to Rockford with problems working prostitutes never
hear of, gave the show a warmth and compassion from time
to time that was appealing to viewers. As always, Jim was
surrounded by the best that money could buy in terms of cast
and crew.

Audiences who followed the show regularly knew that Jim
Rockford lived at the Paradise Cove Trailer Colony at 29
Palm Road in Malibu and that his telephone number was a
nonexistent 555-2368. They identified with Rockford's humorous, often bungling efforts at solving crime, which resembled the efforts of an armchair detective who couldn't
figure out whether his kid was on pot or merely going
through a phase.

As Rockford, Jim was nominated for an Emmy five times
in the category of "Best Actor in a Dramatic Series." In
1975–1976 Peter Falk won for "Colombo." In 1977–1978
Ed Asner won for "Lou Grant." Trailing him in number of
votes were James Broderick ("Family"), Peter Falk, Garner,
Jack Klugman ("Quincy, M.E."), and a new entry, Ralph
Waite ("The Waltons"). In 1978–1979 Ron Liebman took
the award for "Kaz," followed by Ed Asner, Garner, and
Klugman. Garner's last nomination came for the 1979–1980
season. Ed Asner won again that year. Nominees that year
included Klugman and Larry Hagman for the "nasty guy"
role in "Dallas," a newcomer.

In 1976–1977 Jim won for the first and only time, beating
out tough competition such as Robert Blake in "Baretta," Pe-

ter Falk, Jack Klugman, and Karl Malden in the popular police drama, "The Streets of San Francisco." They were tough
opponents, all popular, but Jim finally received the award
that he so justly deserved for his many years in television as a
star.

For the 1977–78 season the show won Emmys for several
people behind the cameras: Meta Rosenberg (executive producer), Stephen J. Cannell (supervising producer), and David
Chase and Charles Floyd Johnson (producers). In 1975 the
"Rockford Files" theme was nominated for a Grammy Award
and was even on the hit parade. That music would later play
an important part in a confrontation between James Garner
and another producer that ended in violence.

Regardless of NBC's status in the network ratings or its reasons for keeping "Rockford" on the air (it was considered by
most critics to be one of NBC's best entries in prime time),
James Garner's popularity with the general public was never
at a higher point. He belonged to that select group of public
figures whose names and faces were instantly recognizable.

Even though he is partial to independent women, Jim
Garner can be protective at times. Meta Rosenberg tells of an
instance that occurred on the set of "Rockford." It was a
cold, damp California night. A nighttime scene was being
shot on the beach. "The special effects men were setting up a
tricky shot involving kerosene doused over a car with a wiring
device to blow it up at the proper time. Jim was worried that I
was going to catch a cold because it was so chilly. I assured
him I was all right, but he kept insisting that the scene could
be dangerous and I could go on home if I wanted to. I didn't
want to. I wanted to watch the explosion."

Just as the blast went off, Garner jumped in front of Meta,
shielding her from the fireworks. Meta, infuriated, yelled at
him, "Why did you do that? You wouldn't do that to a man!"

Jim firmly answered, "Yes I would!" He walked away until Meta, fuming, had a chance to cool off.

During the second year of "Rockford" Garner returned to golf. In April, as tournament chairman of the first California Celebrity Golf Invitational, he proved he could still swing a club by winning his own event with a 5 over par 76. Fellow actor Richard Long took low net with 67.

Jim appeared more relaxed than he had in years. Talk of family strife had all but disappeared from the gossip columns. Lois was deeply involved in community causes, Kim was now out of college and working in preschool education, while Gigi, fresh out of high school, was looking forward to college. The pressure of bringing up teen-aged daughters behind them, Jim and Lois could now have some time for the two of them, probably for the first time in their marriage.

As Jim had planned, Cherokee Productions was producing films in which he did not star. He was not even listed in the credits of some of them. For instance, in the fall of 1976 a Cherokee movie of the week was aired on NBC that might have been left over from the "Maverick" scriptbook. *Scott Free*, an adventure drama pilot, involved a gambler who wins some acreage in a poker game. Meta Rosenberg and Stephen Cannell were joint executive producers. Mike Post and Peter Carpenter, who had successfully written the "Rockford" theme, provided the music. Michael Brandon and Susan Saint James (a particularly successful television actress) just couldn't bring it off to the satisfaction of network bosses, so it never became a series and can now be seen as a syndicated rerun.

Occasionally he guest-starred on NBC as part of the contract he had with them. There was "Superstunt," described as a "documentary–informational special," which brought stars together to show off what they could do. Most were weekend jocks, but not all. Lee Marvin hosted the show. Jim shared the limelight with a variety of stars from Jane Fonda and Angie Dickinson to Robert Conrad, Lee Majors, and Burt Reynolds. It was more social gathering than documentary and showed that Jim was becoming a bit less reclusive. A few years earlier he would not have bothered with such a program.

For the fall season of "Rockford," Garner purchased a $12,000 GMC Siesta Classic pickup to use as his vehicle on the show; $7,000 went for the truck, with $5,000 for accessories such as a $2,000 paint job, special tires, wheels, bumpers, mud guards, roll bars, and off-the-road lights. It helped to strengthen further his image on the show as a renegade of sorts but really just a "good ol' boy" at heart. Contrary to what anybody may think, James Garner is one of the shrewdest actors in the business when it comes to getting publicity that *he wants*. Jim Mahoney and Jerry Pam, who have handled publicity for him over the years, are not amateurs and they don't come cheap. Jim has spent huge sums exploiting, as well as protecting, the image he has created for himself. He has failed in this regard only when he lets his temper get the better of him. Even fights with studios can have a backlash. It is one thing to be the underdog, another to keep beating a dead horse. There are times in Jim's life that he has done the latter. His incessant criticism of Jack L. Warner and his big studio, which gave Jim an opportunity to show what he could do, is perhaps one of them.

When Jim, annoyed by the tour buses that seemed to slow up along the tour when they reached his dressing room, suggested that part of the money earned by the tours of the Universal lot be diverted to an actors' welfare fund, the operators thought he was crazy. "All I wanted to do was have them compensate the actors, who were appearing for the tourists for free." He was quite serious. So serious, in fact, that he sent a letter to Universal's front office declaring that the next time he became the focus of a passing tour bus when he stepped out of his trailer, he was going to bill them for five grand. "That's what I get for personal appearances," he declared through his attorney. It is doubtful he ever sent such a bill. The letter was written off as an instance of his dry kind of humor.

At forty-eight he was still attesting to his insecurity in the business he had been working at for over twenty years. "I don't feel one bit more secure now than I did twenty-three years ago, and that's a fact. I always think my last job was just that—my last." Racing was no longer a high-priority item. The tragic race track death of his close friend Peter Revson gave him one of the great jolts of his life. If it could happen to a younger man, then it could more likely happen to him. That did not prevent him, nevertheless, from continuing to do his own stunt work on "Rockford." The wild auto chases on his series, he said, "give the show action without violence. I don't fight so much in this series. All those fist fights were beating the hell out of me. You can only fake so much, you know." During the first fifty shows he allowed only a couple of characters to be killed off. "My motto is jail 'em, not kill 'em." "Rockford" often began with a murder victim the audience never saw.

He hadn't given up on movies. "If I find something I like, I'll appear in pictures that can be made during the hiatus of my series. It's done all of the time, so why not?"

Jim has a habit of getting along fabulously with studios for which he is making motion pictures and running into all kinds of trouble on television. He has fought with his bosses on every television series he has starred in, and has criticized the networks as well. In fact, his assessment of network vice-presidents in charge of production is as scathing as his commentary on fan magazines.

It is not surprising, therefore, that in the third year of "Rockford," long after Roy Huggins's departure from the show, Jim was finding fault with Universal Studios. He claimed that his quarrel with the studio was not his first one. "During '74 and '75 I had trouble with them, trying to establish the Jim Rockford character as an easygoing guy and the show as a sort of semispoof. I can tell you this, I've had more trouble with Universal than I ever did with NBC. I had terrible problems with them the first year and a half—the attitude of the scripts, the content of the scripts. They don't have much of a sense of humor out there." He said he had told the studio to take care of its business and he'd take care of "Rockford." "I've been making pictures for twenty years, so I told them to get the hell off my back."

Roy Huggins believes that Jim has the story all wrong. "Garner didn't have trouble with Universal—at least not at that time. His problem was between James Garner and Roy Huggins. He was still embittered, as he is today, about the failure of 'Nichols.' He can't face the fact that he had one television series on his own and it was a great big nothing—right down the toilet—and had two years of success in "Maverick" and one year on "Rockford," and it was Roy Huggins behind the scenes running things in both cases. There was nothing wrong with the scripts that first year. If there had been the ratings would have reflected it."

If not philosophical about his employers, Jim was jovially so about his work on the series. "I am able to do some of the things I never would do otherwise. Everybody knows I'm not the most outstanding actor in the world, but I think I do pretty well for a boy from Oklahoma who did a lot of kicking around before he settled down to what he wanted to do for a living. I enjoy the work. Nobody tortures me. I have this thing that says you either want to work or you don't. I like work and I like going out to the studio in the morning. You might say it is a form of relaxation."

Arthur Hiller noticed Jim's enjoyment of his "Rockford" work as well: "I bumped into him at Universal Studios one day when he was working on the "Rockford" series. The sheer joy and ecstasy I saw in his face. He had just finished his first day of directing and he was in heaven. He was in love with the whole thing and I could feel from him that he really had done a good day's work. He was just shining—so thrilled."

Jim's spats with Universal did not keep him from enjoying himself. As far as he was concerned his show was doing fabulously. He liked to say that he didn't really need to see the reviews, good or bad. He didn't believe that a weekly review told the story of "Rockford" or any other show. He was a better judge of the series. "You have to watch it week after week. You have to get to know the people in it." There were some people, he declared, who watched it every single week and noticed if a single digit in Jim Rockford's phone number was given incorrectly.

He was nearing his fiftieth birthday and admitted that there were a few gray hairs here and there. "I pluck them out because they draw attention," he revealed in a rare moment of public vanity, "but I damned well don't dye it. The color is my own." His youthfulness, he said, came from keeping fit and healthy. "Fonda has always had that secret, although he's had several operations that would inhibit a man of his age who wasn't in great shape. My God, the man just returned from fourteen weeks on the road in a play. I wouldn't attempt that. Look at Bob Hope. They have terrific energy because they've kept fit and continue to."

Jim worried about losing his hair but figured his hairline had probably receded as much as it was going to. His only real physical problem was the recurring pain from injuries he sustained while playing football, in Korea, and in automobile accidents. He told one writer from a national magazine, "Sometimes I'm taped and bandaged up when I do a scene the same way I was when I played football. My pain is real."

Jim has claimed that he has done everything he could to minimize discussion of his injuries. "That's why I have publicity people. I mean I employ them to keep publicity away from me. I've managed to do pretty well over the years without it."

He discussed his attitude toward the numerous movie scripts he was given. "I'm not soliciting movie scripts. Not that I wouldn't like to do a good movie, I would. But I read dozens of scripts—or I have—and it is all the same old thing. Sex and violence and that's not what I'm about." He didn't understand, he said, why producers continued to deluge him with scripts he wouldn't do. "They all know what I'm looking for, but I don't see it. My series has nothing to do with making movies. When somebody presents me with a story that is what I do—I'm not going to compromise my integrity as an actor to do pictures I wouldn't want to see or ask anyone else to see."

Those who knew Jim were concerned. Whenever he spoke publicly of being relaxed, it usually meant that a storm was about to break. It was just a matter of time, they agreed, but when it would break only James Garner could say. The only hint was his complaint about Universal's lack of understanding and compassion.

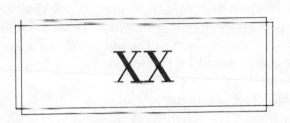

XX

Jimmy Lydon, who had a recurring role in "Rockford," has made some valuable observations about Jim and the inner workings of his series. Regarding rumors that Jim hates certain people in the industry he says, "I don't think Jim Garner hates anyone. He dislikes certain people professionally because of how they operate, which is not Jim's way of operating.

"Remember that Jim has owned his own company for years. Even there he does things that I can appreciate, because I've been a producer and a director and a writer for many years. Jim is all of those things, too, but he doesn't say he is. He purports to be an actor and an actor only, but he's not. Jim is a consummate producer, he's a doggone good director, and he's a pretty good rewrite fellow."

Meta Rosenberg's directorial efforts were not all her own, Lydon declares. "Even there Jim really directed them. She sat in the chair and as soon as the assistant would call 'action' and they'd shoot the scene, she'd say 'cut' and look at Jim. If Jim nodded, she's print it. If he didn't, they'd do another take. That's the way it was. He was always in control."

To Lydon, Jim was and is a very decent man who does not like to be the heavy in situations. He left that to Meta. "Meta Rosenberg," he explains, "was the hatchet in Cherokee Productions. I mean that in the sense that if anyone had to go, anyone had to be fired, anyone had to be chastised for having done something wrong or costing the company unnecessary money, Jim remained in the background and Meta took care of the nasty business, which is correct. He had the image of the star. He was the hero of the series and his image to the viewing public would be in joepardy had he been out front officially running his own company."

Unofficially Jim did run the company, like a controlling silent partner. "He was behind the scenes in everything," Lydon recalls, "and he is very wise regarding production. He knows both sides of the camera equally well and I'm sure other actors would agree with me that Jim Garner is one of the two or three finest and nicest men or women to work for or with in this industry."

Meta Rosenberg talks often of Jim's generosity and his caring about "his people." There are dozens of examples; the following is merely one.

A long sequence was being shot for "Rockford," and it was about five o'clock on the last day of shooting. The crew went into overtime and were scheduled to stop at seven. The actors were also into overtime and went into penalty time shortly thereafter. Jim returned to his dressing room while the scene was being set up and the actors were rehearsing. He didn't like to bother anybody on the set while these things were being done. About 6:45 Jim came on the set.

The assistant director was screaming and yelling at everybody. "Let's get this done. Come on now. Let's get that done." It was nerve-racking for everybody. Jim stood around for a while and listened to the assistant's tirade. Meanwhile Larry Doheny, a kind and gentle director, was going about his business getting the scene rehearsed.

After Jim had heard enough, he very quietly called the assistant aside and said, "Listen! Don't you ever rush a man when he's trying to do his job for the good of this show. I know we're going into another overtime and I know it is going to be expensive, but the show is more important than that. From now on, you let him alone. I don't care if it goes until ten o'clock tonight. You let him alone and when he's ready, then you call action, but don't you rush anybody from here on."

The completely subdued assistant said, "I'm sorry, Jim."

Doheny finished at about 9:30. It probably cost another $7,000 or $8,000 to shoot the scene, but the care and attention Jim showed was enormously important to everyone involved. And he had done it very quietly, without disturbing the set.

Lydon worked on that show and saw the entire affair. "Certain producers," he said, "will scream and yell at you and get the thing finished on time and on schedule because that's really all that is important on television—realistically. There is no way you can hide going over schedule or over budget on a television show. On features you have some leeway, but not in television. You get the same amount of money for that one hour show as you do for all the other twenty-three that year. So a producer has to budget accordingly. There are no excuses for going over. But Jim Garner is very wise and gentle. He does not officially wield his power. He does it very gently and quietly in the background so as to not throw his weight around or offend anyone."

According to numerous people who have worked with him, the only thing that irritates Jim is professional dishonesty for whatever reason. All of Hollywood heard about one of those times when Jim decided he had sufficient reason to be irritated.

Meta Rosenberg received a telephone call from Jim one night after she'd gone to bed. "Meta," he said, "I think I'm going to jail."

Meta woke up fast. "What happened?" she asked. "What did you do?"

"I just beat up Glen Larson."

Glen Larson was and remains a very prominent producer. He had created the popular "Smith and Jones" series for ABC and also created "B.J. and the Bear" and "Battleship Galactica." Garner and Larson didn't care much for each other, and Jim avoided him whenever possible. The fight had started on the set of "Rockford" and ended at the Universal commissary, or on the set of "Rockford" or, elsewhere—depending on whose story one chooses to believe.

Jim has spoken about the incident from time to time but never so explicitly as he did on a cable television talk show in the fall of 1983. Larson, he said, had been stealing scripts from him. "He stole twelve scripts from 'Rockford,'" Jim told CNN's Sandi Freeman, "and put them into another series. Before we caught him he already had one on the air. I found out about it when one of the actors, a girl, came to me." The actress had just finished working on a Larson series. "Jim, we just did a 'Rockford,'" she said.

"What do you mean?" he asked.

"I know the dialogue. I played the same part on 'Rockford.'"

"And she had," Jim said. "They hadn't changed anything but the names. Evidently the producer had been told by the other studio to get more like 'Rockford,' and the best way to do that was go take our scripts and rewrite them. I didn't do anything about that. I let the producers handle it, and Larson was censured by the Guild and had to change the name for the writing and all, because he had put his name on the writing and was collecting money for having written those scripts. I think he only got one or two of them done before we caught him.

"Later, he did a pilot for a television series with the 'Rockford' music in it. He used to be a musician, and of course, now he'd written a song and he put it on there and again somebody told me about it. I obtained a copy of it, played it, and then called him and told him to take the damn thing out of there because it was an absolute out-and-out steal. He knew it. I knew it. I said, 'I'm not going to listen to any excuses anymore. Just take it out.'"

Larson came on the "Rockford" set one night, which further incensed Garner. "I really shouldn't go into all of this, but anyway I asked him to leave. I didn't want to talk about it. I just wanted him to take it out. But he stayed there and stayed there and stayed there and I asked him about eight or nine times to leave. Finally I got so hot I slapped him and he wouldn't do anything about it. So yeah—I punched him!"

Admitting that he does have a quick temper, Jim added, "It builds up and up and up to a point where there're no holds barred. I will cut off my nose to spite my face. I'll do things with no regard whatsoever for the consequences."

Jimmy Lydon heard that the incident happened in the Universal Commissary, which was the story that went around. In Hollywood location isn't always what's important. What matters is the *incident*. Lydon, like others, had an opinion. "I doubt there is any way Jim can actually prove what occurred at that time, yet I think all of us who are conversant with both sides of the camera know exactly what happened. It was not unique. It has happened many, many times. What script is brand new? Everything is a steal on everything else. Jim was angry—sure—but he knew it occurred often. It had occurred in a partnership he was involved in.

"So he was already angry. The second thing that angered him was that it was so blatant. One can change a situation, can change a member of the cast, and can change things around so that it looks to all intents and purposes that it is a brand new theme—different. This one was almost the same, apparently, line for line, word for word, and since Jim had no other recourse I guess he went to the commissary that day still steaming and happened to run into Glen Larson, had some words with him, and Jim decked him. It was one of the few times in his life he lost his temper and belted someone. I might add, Jim is quite formidable. He's a big man. He's very strong. Very athletic. Plays a great game of golf."

Lydon believes that Jim is one of a small group of television stars who successfully crossed the line and became major film actors. "Certainly," he said, "the only one of any content, besides Jim, would be Steve McQueen. McQueen, in a sense, was a little bit like Jim. McQueen was one of the nicest human beings in the world off the sound stage. On a set he was an absolute monster because he controlled everything he did, even to the lining up of the shots or rewriting the script right on the sound stage. So, like Jimmy Garner, he was a very nice man personally and like Jimmy Garner he had that one extra thing that none of the rest of us knows anything about. I've been almost fifty years in the business at this time and I don't understand it. It's just that there is something that an actress or actor has that comes across as warmth and appeal to all ages and sexes. Jimmy Garner and Steve McQueen appeal to little children, to grandmothers and grandfathers, and to everything in between and it is not a learnable part of acting. It is just some innate something that comes across on the screen. We don't understand it."

Jim is indeed that particular breed of actor with whom people so immediately identify that he can start a new television series tomorrow and the next day go out and make a big motion picture and the public will accept him in both. Most stars (not including the journeyman actor) have difficulty maintaining their status in even one medium, much less two.

When Lydon was appearing on "Rockford," he was anxious to direct an episode. Lydon had been raised by a director and had spent his whole life wanting to be one. When he got his director's card he was working on "Rockford." For months he pestered Jim to let him direct a show. One of Lydon's friends had directed several, and Lydon wanted the opportunity. When he appeared on "Rockford" he spent hours observing the director.

"Jim never turned me down directly," Lydon says. "Not one time. He would say, 'Jimmy, talk to Meta about it. Meta makes the decisions.' Jim could have told Meta, 'Jim Lydon is going to direct a "Rockford."' But Meta was the executive director and she had the dirty job.

"Now some people would say that I have a right to be mad at Jim Garner—and some people would have been. But I wasn't. My feelings weren't hurt at all because he was so professional. He kept our personal relationship out of the business. That was Meta's job, and I appreciated the way he handled it. Jim was that way with everybody. He always sought out the proper way and nice way to do it. I've never found him to be anything but a wonderful, very likable, solid professional."

Probably the most loved member of Jim's personal entourage was Luis Delgado. Delgado had been with him longer than anyone else. A classic example of the way Jim shows his affection for others involved Delgado. Delgado was working with Steve McQueen on location in Texas, where Sam Peckinpah was filming *The Getaway*, which starred McQueen and Ali MacGraw. Mrs. Delgado planned to surprise her husband upon his return to Los Angeles with a new van—something she knew he wanted. Jim thought that was a nice idea and asked if he could go along with her to pick it out.

As they looked around Jim began to get excited. He was

like a kid out Christmas shopping. Finally, he decided that it was just too nice a gift to delay receipt and asked if it would be all right for him to deliver it himself.

"All the way to Texas?" Mrs. Delgado asked.

"Sure," Garner beamed. "Why not?" Why not, indeed. When driving Jim Garner was a man out of his cage. The trip would give him a chance to get out on the road, as he did in the old days, without being bothered by studios, scripts, or the necessities of Hollywood, and so he took off.

Delgado was absolutely flabbergasted but overjoyed to see his friend.

Jim told Peckinpah, "Well, since I'm down here and you know how I like to work, why don't you let me do something in the picture?"

You'll never see Jim if you watch the reruns, but he was there—doing something his insurance company would have viewed with displeasure. He was driving a stunt car. After it was all finished and he'd had a lot of fun and a good visit with his buddy McQueen, he went to Peckinpah and said, "I'd like to be paid."

Peckinpah looked at him, scratched his jaw, and asked, "How much do you want?"

"How much you think I'm worth?" Jim replied.

Peckinpah pulled some bills from his pocket, peeled off three, and handed them to Jim. Jim said he would have paid to have had so much fun. It had been a long, long time since he'd been so completely free of restrictions. He returned to Los Angeles in excellent spirits.

Jim remembered Jack Kelly, his brother on "Maverick," when he was producing his own show, "Rockford." "He had me on the series five or six times," Kelly says. "It was sort of reunion time but our relationship was contingent on his lead. I never tried to impose on him. You can't do that with Jim Garner."

Jack has appeared with Jim twice since, once when Jim made *The New Maverick*, a movie for ABC's "Sunday Night Movie," in 1978 and again when Jim fulfilled a commitment to NBC by reviving his old character and returned to television in a short-lived series, "Brett Maverick." Jack was happy to do the movie. "It sounded like fun. We were going to do it on location and I wasn't doing anything else."

The New Maverick was filmed near Tucson, Arizona. One day both men had the same day off from work. Jim rented a car and took Luis Delgado and Jack Kelly for a ride. "I had no idea where we were going or what he was up to. He just said 'Hop in,' and I did. This is the kind of rap that Garner and I have. We piled into the car and went out to that old airplane morgue they have down there—just the three of us—and spent the whole day together going through an airplane graveyard. Can you imagine that? And we had one helleva time looking at the artifactual materials in the museum; walking through all those piles and piles of old airplanes. Vintage aircraft—and vintage Garner."

By the end of the 1979–1980 season, Jim says, "I was worn out. My legs and back were a mess I went to Fred Silverman, the new head of NBC production, and asked him not to pick up the sixth-year option. You see, I had a contract with Universal for six years, but I wouldn't have had to do a sixth year if the series wasn't picked up because Universal's deal with the network was for five years—unless the network decided to go for the final year."

Silverman, Jim says, knew that he had a good show. NBC was having great difficulty trying to improve its ratings, and why get rid of a show that was one of the network's better ones? "He had a winner in 'Rockford.' I understood where he was coming from. I have never had bad feelings about Silverman. He was just doing his job. I probably would have done the same thing under similar circumstances."

The summer of 1979 was not a good one for Jim, though on the surface everything looked fine: a popular series renewed for the coming season, more work offers than he could possibly handle, and a wonderful family and home life. Beneath the surface, however, were numerous problems, soon to become apparent.

Jim signed to star in a Robert Altman film during the hiatus of "Rockford." *Health* was an outrageous spoof on nutrition faddists and health nuts in general. Jim knew all about Altman and admired him. *Health* would be a change of pace, a chance to do the kind of picture he had never done before, to get away from television, and, hopefully, to get out of the pressure cooker that had been his life for the past few years.

Altman's roots were in television rather than motion pictures. Few know that he directed a one-season series called "The Troubleshooters," which starred Keenan Wynn, in the late fifties. Jim knew. He felt comfortable working with Altman and with the cast that was assembled for *Health*: Carol Burnett, Glenda Jackson, Lauren Bacall, Dick Cavett, Paul Dooley, Donald Moffat, and Henry Gibson. Some were or would become good friends.

The film involves the election of a president of a huge trade organization called HEALTH (Happiness, Energy, and Longevity Through Health). Glenda Jackson described her character, a candidate for the presidency, as an idealistic woman dedicated to health and democracy. "She says all the right things, but their very truthfulness makes them negligible in the world in which she wishes to function." She's considered a loser. Jackson declares, "I think she's also a bit crazy." Jackson's rival for the office of president is portrayed by Lauren Bacall, "an eighty-three-year-old virgin who doesn't look her age because she's religiously hooked on health food and believes that sex is a killer." Jim Garner's role was that of a campaign manager–press agent for Lauren Bacall's character. The movie can be seen as a spoof on the 1952 presidential race between Eisenhower and Stevenson.

For Jim it was a romp. His aching back and joints soaked up the St. Petersburg, Florida, sunshine (in between the freakish February storms for which the area is famous). When not working he joined his friends just to lounge about and relax. Almost all of the film was shot in and around the Don CeSar Hotel, so Jim was able to do what he likes best—and play at the same time.

The film wasn't released for a year and as a result of less than mediocre reviews had a limited run. Even Altman's adversaries felt the critics had treated him badly. Lauren Bacall, a tough critic herself, didn't agree. "I can't wait to see this movie. It's a madhouse, my dear."

Charles Champlin, a tough critic who was nevertheless always fair to the creators, had great difficulty saying anything positive about the film. He said the picture had easily won the year's "Listerine Prize for lousy word of mouth." Further, he declared, "It would be hard for any film to live down to the negative rumbles about *Health,* but *Health* is pretty ill, and there's no other way to say it." His consensus: "It . . . conspicuously wastes the time and the talent of a large number of good people, Lauren Bacall, James Garner, and Glenda Jackson being key sufferers."

It was Jim's rule not to read reviews, and he ignored this one.

In June Jim announced that the next season would be the last of "Rockford." "It's a killer. You get tired of it." At a press conference at which the announcement was made, Jim was accompanied by the actress who co-starred in his Polaroid commercials, Mariette Hartley, giving rise to new rumors that the Garners were having problems. Hartley took to wearing a T-shirt that read: I AM NOT MRS. JAMES

GARNER. She declared that she wasn't anything else to Jim, either, except an actress and friend who worked with him in a series of commercials. The rumors flourished, however, when it was announced that Mariette Hartley would appear in a fall segment of "The Rockford Files."

Even before his work for Polaroid drew unwanted rumors Jim had always been wary about doing television commericals. His first was a Winston cigarette commercial in which he takes credit for making the grammatical error, "*like* a cigarette should," which led to a series of follow-ups with other actors repeating the catchy error.

Plain spoken, as usual, about his involvement in a project, Jim said, "I am cautious about the commercials to which I lend my name or talents. I've learned something about that over the years. Don't look for commercials that feature me selling extermination products or bathroom accessories. If I did a commercial for a medical product it would probably make people ill. I'd never be very convincing. I have to, if I'm going to do commercials, pick and choose the right ones that suit my ability to be honest." Jim simply cannot sell something he doesn't believe in. Mostly he sells himself. And that's what the public has been buying over the years, for he has remained popular though many of his films have been less than stupendous. Jim was the draw—not the vehicle.

He says that he is always being asked to endorse products but rejects most requests because he doesn't believe in the product, doesn't think he could do it justice, or simply doesn't want to get involved. When he agreed to do the Polaroid commercials, which have become some of the most popular commercials in the history of television, it was because of the company and its track record. "They had class," he states. "They didn't do anything cheap." He had been preceded as spokesperson for Polaroid by Perry Como, Candice Bergen, and Sir Laurence Olivier.

Garner's idea of how to do a commercial was innovative. It had nothing to do with the mechanics of the product. His idea was to show the audience the Polaroid camera, tell a joke, and leave the audience feeling good rather than trying to hit it with a hard sell. "I wouldn't buy something that was shoved down my throat, so why should I expect anybody else to?

In a sense, Jim became his own producer, director, and sales manager of the commercials he agreed to do for Polaroid. He wanted a lot of commercials shot so that the same commercial would not be repeated over and over and over again. He didn't want the audience to tire either of him or of the product he was pitching. He knew all about overexposure from his own career. "I don't want the audience to get sick of seeing me," he told the Polaroid ad people. Most importantly, he insisted that the commercials be light and frothy. Never has the Garner humor been put to better use than in the eight to ten dozen Polaroid commercials he has done since he first signed with the company to be its television salesman.

He hasn't always seen eye to eye with Polaroid's ad agency either, and he hasn't hesitated to tell the ad people what he thought about some of their schemes. His attitude was, "If I don't sell cameras—fire me."

Henry Fonda led the way for Jim's appearing in this type of commercial. Jim had been impressed with the manner in which Fonda had represented the GAF film company in television commercials and became incensed when Fonda's daughter, Jane, expressed embarrassment that her father had done the commercials. "Screw her!" he said. "That's snobbery." Jim had known the Fonda children since they were young and he could condemn Jane's statements without alienating the Fonda family. "God forbid," he said, "that Jane's career should go on its ass and she needed money to support her kids and the only way to get it was by doing a commercial. I'm sure she'd find a way to make commercials more palatable if her pocketbook was involved."

Since then, Jane Fonda has indeed found a justification for doing commercials. Her physical fitness studios and books, which have saturated the country, and her husband's political ambitions and the foundation she and he created have profited immensely from the success of her venture—and the hard-sell commercials that have helped create the success. Jim's thoughts on the subject were prophetic.

Jim had made several Polaroid commercials alone or with kids and animals before Mariette Hartley became involved. "I hate working with animals and kids," he declares, though criticizing himself for it, "and had just finished a commercial where I had *both* kids and dogs all over me. It was bullshit and I told them so."

Mariette Hartley had been making commercials and the occasional movie for twenty years. All the while her ambition was to be a full-fledged dramatic actress. Jim sensed her talent the first day they worked together. She was as relaxed as he and shared his sense of humor. They rehearsed the "one step," "two step" bit and the bit of nonsense that came out of it resulted in one of the hottest commercials on television.

Jim was first in line to praise Mariette and her ability as an actress. "There are few times in our business," he told an assemblage of press, "when actors are fortunate enough to come in contact with other actors or actresses with whom they have what's called chemistry."

The press conference was arranged by the Doyle Dane Bernbach Agency, the Madison Avenue company handling the Polaroid commercial account. Account executives Jack Dillon and Bob Gage were responsible for the content of the commercials, but both agreed that it was Hartley and Garner who made them work.

"Mariette and I understand each other," Jim said. "We like each other, we know how we play, and we both feel we're very, very fortunate to be able to have this contact. It's a rare thing in our business. We really enjoy it. We have a lot of fun."

The Hartley-Garner "marriage" was strictly an on-camera one. Jim had been married many years, and Mariette was married to Patrick Boyriven, a commercial director who was responsible for major accounts like Home Savings and Loan and Continental Airlines. The purpose of the press conference was in part to celebrate the completion of one year of Hartley-Garner commercials and to announce that Hartley would be appearing on a segment of "Rockford" in the coming season. Hartley said that the "Rockford" producers "would not have touched me before the commercials." It was as a direct result of appearing with Jim that she was cast as the female lead opposite Bill Bixby in the series "Goodnight Beantown."

It is generally believed that Jim's contract with Polaroid paid him $2 million, but he denies it, though he won't counter with a figure of his own. "I don't charge anywhere near what I could get," he said.

About a week to ten days after the press conference, the news broke that James and Lois Garner had separated. In a few days the details began to trickle out. Jim was reported to have moved out of the house and taken an apartment in the San Fernando Valley. The official release from Jim's company said he had taken the apartment to be closer to the studio due to the heavy workload he was carrying, which indeed he was.

Rumors of a relationship between Garner and Hartley immediately surfaced. No responsible person believed them. The one thing that James Garner was not doing was having an affair with Mariette Hartley, or any other woman for that matter. James Garner is a one-woman man.

Hank Grant, one of the most reliable and trusted newsmen covering the Hollywood beat and a columnist for the trade paper the *Hollywood Reporter*, was very positive and straightforward when telling the story of the Garner separation. In the first place, he stated, he didn't think it was permanent. "Regardless of how much breach there is, there has not been one breath of scandal involved in their marriage. There is no reason to believe that Garner has found another love."

He went on to say that Lois had never enjoyed the Hollywood party circuit while "Jim is the very outgoing, gregarious type." It was the first time anyone had ever put it that way. Most people had thought it was the other way around: that it was Jim who was the reclusive one, preferring home life to partying.

Lois referred all inquiries to her husband. Jim couldn't be located. He was on a trip to Europe with Bill Saxon and "nobody knows how to locate him." Jim's father said he didn't believe it and wouldn't bet any hard-earned money that the separation would last.

By the end of July, Marilyn Beck reported in the *Valley News* that "the James Garners are trying to work things out." She said that Jim had moved into the Sheraton Universal Hotel on the Universal Studios lot. This was apparently not the first time the Garners had separated, having been apart for three months a few years earlier.

There was never any formal separation agreement, and neither party filed for divorce. If anything was ever taboo with Jim, it was discussion of the problems that caused his separation from Lois. It turned out to be not such a short separation. When a *Playboy* interviewer asked Jim about it a year and a half later, in typical Garner fashion he answered honestly. "My marriage,'" he said, "is still not together. I'm not sure what I want to do with my career, I didn't want to talk about this . . . but the reason my wife and I are separated is that I was so physically and mentally exhausted from work that I said I had to take a sabbatical; I needed a hiatus. . . . And my wife understood that."

It was the most he had ever said to anyone publicly about his marital problems. Still, he and Lois continued to see each other regularly, having dinner together as if they were courting and talking on the telephone daily. Theirs was a strong marriage, built over twenty-three years, and it had too many good points to let it fall apart. So they did what most people don't: They worked at finding out what the problems were and correcting them. Very few marriages inside or out of Hollywood can survive an eighteen-month separation. The Garners' did because they love each other so much that neither could stand the thought of permanent separation.

But in the summer of 1979 it seemed like the end of the world to the both of them. It wasn't. Just the onset of more problems that had nothing to do with their relationship, although it was directly affected.

XXI

While Jim was preparing for the final fall season of "Rockford," Warner Brothers was dusting off the old "Maverick" scripts. The object was to bring back the series as "Young Maverick" with Charles Frank playing Ben Maverick, a cousin of Brett and Bart. But there is nothing like an original, which Warner Brothers soon found out. The series went nowhere.

Without James Garner there really wasn't a "Maverick," and without James Garner there wasn't a "Rockford Files." He held the show together, but what was being held together? It was a closely knit family of dedicated film makers: Stephen Cannell (Roy Huggins in the beginning), producer; Meta Rosenberg, executive producer; the writers; the cast regulars; special guest stars; and the crew.

Meta Rosenberg had begun as Jim Garner's agent twenty years earlier and had worked her way up to become one of the most important women in television—especially on "Rockford." She became Jim's official spokesperson on the series.

Like Luis Delgado, Roy Clark had been with the Garner company before there was a company. Garner's stunt coordinator and double, he had first met Jim at Warner Brothers during the "Maverick" years. Cherokee's chief electrician,

Gibby Germaine, had also met Jim then. While making the two pictures at Walt Disney Studios, Jim had become friendly with cinematographer Andrew Jackson and brought him to "Rockford." Makeup artists Dick Blair and film editor George Rohrs both were with "Rockford" throughout its entire run.

The official Garner family is completed by Juanita Bartlett. Hers is a remarkable story. Hollywood is known as a place where one comes up through the ranks. That myth was dispelled by Miss Bartlett when at Cherokee Productions. Juanita was the newest member of the team. She came into the production company as Meta Rosenberg's secretary. She has described herself, at the time, as "a writer with a drawerful of rejection slips."

Her career began with "Nichols." Frank Pierson, the producer, was always looking for new scripts and new ideas for the series. At one point he was leaving for location scouting in Arizona and didn't have time to read the script that the untried Bartlett handed him, so he crammed it into a briefcase with other "required reading." For all Bartlett knew that would be the end of her writing career. At least working secretaries are paid weekly. Hopeful writers sometimes don't eat regularly.

But Pierson did read the script at a lunch stop in the desert and it so excited him he called Juanita immediately. "I like your script," he told the astonished secretary, "and we'll use it." Jim declares that it was the best script they ever had on the series. Such was Bartlett's rapid rise from typing letters for her boss to writing scripts for her boss's boss. Juanita Bartlett went on to become a mainstay writer on "Rockford," establishing herself as a valuable asset to Jim and to the television industry. It sounds like an old Doris Day movie ending, but if she hadn't been good she'd still be typing letters for Meta— or someone else. As head of the company, Jim was the one who moved her up. He made the final decision on whose scripts were acceptable, and he believed this young woman had capability. It is little wonder that his "family" feels such loyalty for him—and almost adulation.

There has always been a dispute about who created "Rockford." Roy Huggins has said it was his creation—"Maverick" in a different setting. Steve Cannell says, "Roy and I plotted the character of Rockford in about six seconds. I had to write it in five days." He declares that he decided to break with the previous criteria for the television detective and go for broke. "My guy wants money, lives in a trailer, and doesn't have a pretty secretary but a truckdriver father who's embarrassed by what his son does."

Both Jim and Meta Rosenberg stand behind Cannell. Jim swears that Roy Huggins left the series after only a few episodes.

There were disagreements with the studio, the network, and Roy Huggins, but the set of "The Rockford Files" seemed a place of serenity and happiness for Jim. But that was about the only place he found any real peace and harmony. The physical and emotional demands being made on him were staggering, and he was working in constant pain, his ulcer problem having recurred. Consequently he found himself turning more and more to support from artificial means: drugs. He claims to have gotten them from the Universal first aid department. "They had me call up and find out how many pain pills and muscle relaxants they had over there to keep me on my feet. I was taking Percodan, codeine, Soma, Robaxin—whatever would keep me going until the show was done."

Jim was a physical mess, and everybody knew it. It was not Universal's problem. It wasn't NBC's problem. There were contracts to be honored, and those were the cold, hard facts of television production. The show is the thing and the actors are expected to comply. Lawyers will assure their compliance, or "reasonable compensation" if there is none.

Nobody can say exactly when Jim decided to quit the series. In October 1979, having taken everything possible to ease the pain he was feeling, Jim was trying to get through the week to complete the episode they were working on. Suddenly, without warning, he doubled over in pain and was taken to his dressing room, where a studio doctor was brought in to examine him. "The pain was awesome," he said. "I couldn't breathe because I was having trouble with my sinuses, and I was bleeding rectally. I wasn't an actor that day, I was a basket case."

The Universal doctor told Jim that his ulcer was back and that he needed further medical attention. After being given medication he returned to the set, where he completed shooting the show. Then he checked into The Scripps Institute Clinic at La Jolla, California, near San Diego, for a complete physical examination and treatment. He spent three days there just resting up and doing as the doctors told him. They told him if he did not take a couple of months off from work he faced continued illness—or worse. Jim got their point and did not return to complete shooting "The Rockford Files." The series was finished.

Jerry Pam and Meta Rosenberg became the outside world's only contact with James Garner. He talked to no one else. They said he had been very ill but would return to shoot the remaining "Rockford" shows—if the studio wanted him to. They did not. Right after Christmas NBC announced that Jim's series would be replaced in January 1980 by "SKAG," which would star Karl Malden. "Rockford" was ten shows shy of a complete season at the time, and the network wasn't willing to take any further risks with either Jim or his health.

Meta issued a statement on behalf of Jim in which she took an upbeat approach. "It's best to leave when we're still doing good shows," she told Howard Rosenberg of the *Los Angeles Times.*

While important decisions were being made about the show, Jim's health, and his future employment, another bombshell exploded. Through inadvertence or stupidity, somebody at Universal had sent Jim an accounting report after the new season had begun that indicted that "The Rockford Files" was $9.5 million in debt. It was the last civil communication between James Garner and Universal Studios.

Jim had been sitting and stewing. Once NBC announced cancellation of the show, he let his complaints about Universal Studios be known. "What they're trying to tell me," he fumed, "is that for almost six years my series has been a total financial flop and I'm telling them that's bullshit. I don't believe it."

It was the first accounting he'd seen since the end of the first year, when Roy Huggins left the show. He had assumed that everything was going well financially and that Cherokee Productions, which owned 38 percent of the show, was building up a multimillion-dollar investment for the future. "I don't think I was ever supposed to see those figures," he said, "and I can tell you something else. I'll bet the guy who passed the report on to me is digging ditches somewhere in Peru today." It was Jim's reasoning that Universal knew he had the report months before he became chronically ill and figured he would use that as an excuse not to work. He denies it. "I honestly intended to complete the show and then deal with the shortages. If they don't believe me, that's their problem, not mine. I think their attorneys know the truth."

Jim had rented the equipment used on *Rockford* himself to save costs. "I knew it would cost the studio a lot more than it would me. I know how to shop and save money. but it didn't do any good. All that economizing down the drain—and for what? I thought I'd work the series through to the end in spite of the pain and my deteriorating physical condition. I *thought* the series would make me financially independent."

He says that the same kind of bookkeeping has been going on in Hollywood for years and that studios should not be allowed to get away with it. "Look at what happened to Natalie Wood and Robert Wagner and their fifty percent ownership in 'Charlie's Angels.'" He said he made money on "Nichols" because he controlled everything about the series. "The only other people I know who have made money on a television series were Jack Webb and Raymond Burr." He gave an example of how costs were inflated to reflect a loss rather than a profit. "It's all on paper—in favor of the studio. Example: Say we buy something for the show that costs $100. By the time all the costs have been added, with each department tagging on a bit for 'their' profit, it continues to spiral until the final bookkeeping item shows $725 for the $100 item. They have something they call a 'generic account.' Nobody has any idea what the term means, and I don't think they do either. But it doesn't matter. They take one third of the inflated cost and add it on to the top of the figure and that's what's called their 'generic account' addition."

Jim wasn't the only one at Universal being manipulated. Frank Price was president of Universal Television when Fred Silverman became head of production at NBC. It is uncertain what happened, but Silverman suddenly became angry with Universal and began canceling all the NBC shows produced by the studio. The studio and the network had a deal at the time not unlike the one Warner Brothers had with ABC when "Maverick" was on the air.

Lew Wasserman, head of MCA (Universal's parent company), called Price into his office and put it to him directly. "Frank," he said, "we've got to bump you upstairs." Price didn't understand and asked Wasserman to explain. "You are now going to be in feature production. You'll have a title but you can't touch television."

Frank Price had a contract that ran for three or four more years and there was a lot of money involved, so he wasn't about to abandon Universal. It boiled down to whatever differences existed between Silverman and Price. "You won't be put out to pasture, Frank," Wasserman assured him. "But we have to appease the network by removing you from the television end so that we can sell Silverman some of our shows."

Price could have demanded that Universal abide by his contract, and Wasserman would have had to find a way to cancel it. That's the way the industry works: Mountains can be moved merely because they are in the way. Two weeks later, following the scandal at Columbia Pictures involving David Begelman's having forged Cliff Robertson's name to some checks, which he cashed and used for his own purposes, it was suddenly announced that Frank Price would be moving over to Columbia Studios. Price would be in charge of the studio's motion picture production.

According to an executive at Universal, "Frank began to look around for another job the day after his conversation with Wasserman." This same executive said that "when Frank Price left Universal, Mr. Wasserman had him sign a paper agreeing to never again be involved in television. Now that's illegal and everybody knows it, but Frank signed the paper and became president of the motion picture division at Columbia."

Another power struggle took place at Universal, resulting in the ouster of certain executives, and in no time at all Frank Price returned to Universal as president of Universal Pictures. He is a man much admired and respected and is considered to be a "nice guy" by those who have worked with him. But the inner workings of the industry affect everyone.

This is the kind of situation James Garner was facing when he decided to take on Universal and try to get back the money he felt he had been cheated out of.

The last episode of "The Rockford Files" was to be aired on January 10, 1980, although some of the episodes previously filmed were shown later in the year. But the only thing that concerned Jim were the legal battles that would be required to settle the financial dispute between Cherokee Productions and Universal Television.

In his column of January 4, 1980, Charles Parker, a columnist for the *Valley Times* (now the *Los Angeles Daily News*), asked the question, "Is Jim Garner sick or tired?" NBC, he said, suspected that Jim's mysterious ailment was greatly exaggerated.

NBC Entertainment president Mike Weinblatt issued a terse statement that read like an indictment of Garner. "The change has been made," he said, "because James Garner has not appeared for production of additional 'Rockford Files' episodes." It was cold and to the point and gave the distinct impression that Jim was the culprit.

After that, Jim didn't need the next highly publicized event in his life. It was about 6:30 or 7:00 in the evening on Wednesday, January 16, 1980. Jim was driving north on Coldwater Canyon Drive, going home to his apartment in the San Fernando Valley. He was still separated from his wife. Traffic was bumper to bumper, as it always is on weekdays at that hour, with tired, anxious commuters traveling single-file over the canyon road that uncoils through the Santa Monica Mountains between Beverly Hills and the mid–San Fernando Valley. Jim was aware that an El Camino was coming up behind him. "He was passing cars behind me. I saw that in my window mirror on the right hand side because that's where he was passing—on the right. Traffic was slow. Maybe six to eight miles an hour. Nobody was going anywhere very fast.

"Anyway, I saw this guy approaching me and I'm thinking, What the hell is this, anyway? I kind of pulled to the center of the road and sped up to let him get in behind me and the guy surprised me by attempting to pass just where the road narrowed down to one lane.

The El Camino smashed into Garner's 1979 vehicle at the right rear fender. The "vehicle" was described at the time in a police report as a "1979 Pontiac Firebird." Garner later said it was a TransAm.

It was nothing more than a fender bender. Garner pulled over anyway to check the damage and to exchange insurance information with the other driver. "He never had a chance," said police officer Steve Kegley from the West Los Angeles Police division. Jim was surprised that the guy behind him then tried to pass on the left. So instead of continuing to the right to park off the road, Jim pulled back into the center of the street to prevent the guy's getting away. For Jim Garner that was a big mistake.

He had set the brake, turned off the ignition, and started to open the door when he suddenly heard, "You motherfucker!" It was all he heard. The guy slammed his fist into Jim's face through the open window. The man hit Garner three times before Jim realized what was happening to him. According to the policeman's report, "The man jumped out of his car, walked over to Garner's automobile, reached in the window, used one hand to grab gold chains Garner wore around his neck, and used the other to pummel Garner about the head and face."

The officer further stated that after the chains broke and Jim was able to get out of the car to try to defend himself, he did so with "little luck." However, the two men struggled and wrestled across the roadway, where the driver of the El

Camino knocked Jim down and kicked him a number of times about the head, groin, and face. Officer Kegley said, "Mr. Garner's face was raw from the beating and he was extremely bitter because he did not have a chance to defend himself. He was a little stunned and surprised by the first blows and he did not get to get in any good punches."

According to Jim, a woman accompanying his assailant leaned in the passenger side of his car and grabbed the keys. She then said, "Come on, Aubrey. I've got the keys. Let's go." Jim continued, "I wasn't about to let go of that sucker. After he'd hit me about nine times I had pulled him up so close to the car that his face was on top of the roof. Then the chain broke." It was after that that Jim took a terrific beating from the man.

It was rush hour and traffic was heavy. Consequently a large crowd gathered, and even though Jim yelled for help, nobody volunteered. Nobody wanted to "get involved." Lew Wasserman's chauffeur, who happened to be in the long line of traffic, was finally able to come to Jim's aid along with another man, but by then the culprit had sped off into the evening.

Jim spent three days in the hospital, having sustained injuries over his entire body. He'd been kicked not only in the head but in the back and hard on the tail bone. He was totally out of commission. While he tried to forget the constant pain, the police were issuing all points bulletins for the man and woman in the El Camino.

Two days after the beating, the *Los Angeles Herald-Examiner* told the story under the headline, "Trials and Traumas of James Garner." As he lay in Cedars-Sinai accepting get well wishes and being entertained by visitors, he received another jolt. Universal Studios filed a $1.5 million dollar breach of contract suit against him, alleging that he had failed to complete eleven of the season's episodes for "The Rockford Files," which had caused NBC to cancel the series.

Jim must have groaned. His injuries included a fractured coccyx, a possible concussion and back injury, cuts, bruises, a gash in his scalp, and several loosened teeth. He still found time to inject humor into the situation. Speaking of his antagonist, he said, "I could tell he was getting tired. If he had kept it up for another five minutes, I'd have beaten the hell out of him." He also allowed that considering the beating he did take, "I'm in a lot better shape than I have any right to be."

Someone had the presence of mind to jot down the license number of the El Camino, and the police obtained "probable cause" warrants authorizing the arrest of Aubrey and Debbie Williams, a brother and sister, who were suspected of having beaten and robbed Garner. On January 22 the two suspects from Pasadena surrendered to police in the company of their attorney, who told the news media that his clients had taken independent lie detector tests that proved that James Garner had thrown the first punch. The attorney, Wesley Russell, said it was he who had delayed the surrender of his clients in order to arrange for polygrapher Theodore Ponticelli of Santa Ana, California, to conduct the polygraph tests "in an effort to prove their claims that they did not start the fight."

Los Angeles Police Detective Chuck Brown, the investigator assigned to the case, issued his own statement about lie detector tests. "It doesn't make any difference unless it is a police polygraph. You can buy a polygraph for $100 and get whatever results you want." Besides, he added, witnesses to the incident supported Jim's account "100 percent down the line."

The Williams couple told a different story. According to them Jim was driving about ten to fifteen miles per hour while they, returning from Beverly Hills, attempted to pass his car on the right. Jim was supposed to have looked at them and then swerved "so we couldn't pass."

Aubrey Williams said, "I went to his car and told him to get out of the road." He didn't know it was Garner and said "the man's size scared me. That's why I blocked the door." Jim, he said, told him, "You're in big goddamn trouble," further claiming that Jim had put his foot through the window and kicked Aubrey's head. Jim, by now recuperating at some undisclosed location in the desert, sent a message through his agent, Wally Beeme. "I guess it will all come out in court."

The Los Angeles County district attorney wasn't buying the couple's story and charged Williams with assault with a deadly weapon (his feet) with intent to do great bodily harm and grand theft—both of which were felonies—plus misdemeanor hit-and-run charges following a minor traffic accident. His sister was charged with felony grand theft involving two gold chains allegedly torn from Jim's neck during the incident.

The incident became a sort of "Rockford for real" situation, and the newspapers had a good time with it. Williams's attorney said that the prosecution was trying to turn a minor incident into a celebrated felony case simply because the victim is "James Garner, a star." He said, "I think maybe Jim Rockford doesn't know when he has a righteous script, one where he doesn't always win."

Before the month of January was over, Jim sued the brother and sister for $2 million dollars, charging assault. For a very private man he was getting a lot of the wrong kind of exposure in the media. A tabloid ran a feature story in which he was purported to have told them that his widely rumored romances with Lauren Bacall and Marcia Strassman was "pure bunk," that he frequently saw Lois, and that "she is still the main woman in my life."

His humor never left him. In June he appeared on a Barbara Walters special for ABC. When Barbara asked him, "How do you feel?" he let her know exactly how he felt.

"Right now I'm getting over a concussion and a few stitches in the head and I've got a ruptured vertebra—a disintegrating disc in the neck. I have three in the lower back. I have broken three, four ribs, most knuckles, both kneecaps. We were fighting the North Koreans and I was going south—I got shot in the rear end. And, of course, the knees—I have got six incisions in them. The feet? They're just hanging there. I'm constantly in pain. I have arthritis in my back and my knees and my hands. I had ulcers this year—once an ulcer patient, always an ulcer patient. I get depressed. Very."

Would he ever do a nude scene if the script called for it? "God, no. I don't do horror films. They couldn't stand the scars."

When Aubrey Williams, Jr., was brought to trial in August (all charges against his sister having been dropped), Jim took the witness stand to describe what had happened to him and there were snickers in the courtroom when he said, "I tried to act my way out of it by faking unconsciousness. I let out a moan, shuddered, and laid still, but he kicked me again." He later admitted it wasn't his best performance.

Judge Charles Woodmansee, hearing the case without a jury, listened to all the testimony and witnesses on both sides and ultimately found Williams guilty of beating up Garner. He sentenced the man to three years' probation, ordered him to spend one hundred days in the county jail, and fined him $500.

After the trial Garner told reporters, "I have no pleasure in the disruption of this man's life and I'm sure we both wish the whole thing hadn't happened."

A bitter Aubrey Williams was visibly upset by the verdict and sentence. "I was a captain in the service," he declared.

"I served my country; my record shows that I never committed a criminal act in my life. The judge reads all this, and says I still have to spend time in jail. This decision was made because it's political and because I'm black."

Later he softened his opinion. "I thought the verdict was unfair. But," he continued in a philosophical manner, "it could have been worse." He admitted that he had been a fan of Jim's and had watched him on TV. "I used to like him, but I won't watch him on TV anymore."

In October NBC-TV caught everyone by surprise by announcing that James Garner would return to NBC in the fall of 1981 in an updated "Maverick" series. What was surprising was that Westerns were being revived by the various networks with no success. But Meta Rosenberg disagreed totally with the "experts." "I think you should do what you're enthusiastic about and not worry about whether Westerns are in or out. I don't give a *shit* about the trend, and you can quote me on that."

The youthful Brandon Tartikoff, president of NBC Entertainment, defended the network's decision to revive the series that had been so popular twenty years earlier, stating that "Maverick" was not a Western in the usual sense "because it always maintained a contemporary attitude in its approach to comedy and drama. Besides," he added, "we're buying a known quantity—and Garner is the ultimate TV actor. We're not scared about Westerns. Western movies have done pretty well for us."

Tartikoff, the confident television executive, said, "We buy programs to fill time periods, and 'Maverick' is very compatible with what we're doing. It has a basically nonviolent theme and can be scheduled either early or late in the evening.

Jim's schedule during the fall was as hectic as ever. Early

in October he slipped into Nashville to record some country music for his old friend Waylon Jennings. "I never thought much about singing," he said, "until Waylon talked me into it." It was not a first for Jim. Real film buffs will recall that he sang a song on an Emmy Awards show many years ago, surprising everyone with his pleasant singing voice.

Stuart Margolin, his friend and co-star over the years, had written a script for a film he was planning to direct, and he asked Jim to star in it with Billy Dee Williams. Jim agreed. The film, *Pure Escape*, was being shot on location in Alberta, Canada, and Jim leaped at the opportunity to put Hollywood behind him for a while. But his plans backfired when the film, a couple of weeks short of completion, was shut down when the producers ran out of money.

"Nothing," he sighed, "seems to be right anymore."

Jim had managed to fit another movie into his bizarre schedule that year. The picture, in which he co-starred with his good friend Lauren Bacall, was called *The Fan*. He was passionately dissatisfied with it and expressed his displeasure loudly to anyone who would listen.

"I only did it," he declared, "to help Betty Bacall. Actually, I turned down the first three scripts they sent me. The ending was different from the one in the book and a lot of people think it was changed because of John Lennon's death. I disagree totally with that premise. I think they changed it before his death. They just thought it had a down ending and that it would be a total downer for people. That's my opinion, of course, and I'm entitled to it. But they didn't write a good ending to the film. I argued about it."

Jim finally approved a script and director. "After I was signed, they fired that director and rewrote the ending with a good deal more blood and gore—about everything they could get into it, and I told them no, I wouldn't do it."

The producer said, "Okay, Garner, we're going to shut the picture down and sue you for all the losses."

"I already had one lawsuit going with Universal and I didn't want another suit. As a matter of fact I had two lawsuits going at the time. I didn't think it would look good for me to have another one, so I agreed to do the picture, but I was never happy with the ending. They promised to rewrite it before I came to New York to do the filming, but they never did."

The producer refused to incorporate any of Jim's suggestions into the film. "I can't blame the director," Jim said, "and I shouldn't pick on him. He had never directed a film. He was a director of commercials. My feeling was that the picture needed a particular flare that could have been provided by the director they had fired. I think they ruined the film by not keeping the original director."

The film was produced by Robert Stigwood, a man of whom Jim was not fond. "He was kind of a little Hitler, I guess. The 'I'll do what I want' attitude and the hell with everybody else. He's the guy being sued by the Bee Gees for $137 million and I hope they nail his butt. It was a terribly fouled up production. I thought I could be helpful to Bacall by being in it with her."

When Jim reported for work on *Pure Escape* he received a call from Stigwood's office to come back to New York to re-shoot the ending. "I told him to go to hell," Jim said.

"I know next year has to be a better deal for me."

XXII

In 1981 at age fifty-two Jim was overweight, and his face reflected the pain he felt, both emotional and physical. He didn't smile as often as before; he was more inclined to snarl than to make humorous asides. His generally negative attitude resulted partly from career frustrations and partly from the failures in his private life, for which he was quick to shoulder all the blame. His first instinct, which dated back to his treatment by his stepmother Wilma, was to ask "What did I do wrong this time?"

He had been seeing an analyst for his deep depressions, more because he needed somebody to talk to than someone to help him. He had to solve his own problems. He knew that. He could solve them if there was just a break in the action—a breather. "I'm a stubborn son-of-a-bitch," he told a close associate. "I'm not the kind that cries. I fight back."

The studios had become intolerable to him. "The lawyers and computers are running the business now. Creative people no longer make the major decisions about creativity. That I resent. All they ever think of is the contract and the money—and how to steal it. Everything goes into a computer and if the machine says to star Shirley Temple and

Walter Brennan in a picture, that's what they do. Actors and writers and directors don't mean a thing to them anymore."

"Rockford," he said, was done "in spite of Universal. I hate liars and thieves, but I've had to work with them for six years. I did "Nichols" for only one year before it was canceled and made a profit—a series that was not considered high in the ratings by the people who judge such things. "Rockford" was highly rated for six years—it should have been making big profits and they tell me it is almost ten million dollars in debt. Bullshit!"

He figured that by the time the accountants and lawyers (including his own) went over all the books Universal would eventually owe him somewhere between $5 and $15 million. "They'll do like they always do, drag it out for years, but I have all the time in the world. I'll wait them out. Somewhere along the way they'll come to me and say, 'Hey, Jim, let's settle this thing without an argument. How about ten cents on the dollar?' I'll tell them to go to hell. The eventual profits will be so enormous that they can't hide them. They'll never buy me off for less than what I've got coming."

Jim was without a doubt an extremely wealthy man. All the movies that he had made that were either produced or co-produced by his own company were paying off, with handsome profit from foreign, television, and videocassette sales. He had other investments that brought in regular income monthly. Thus he could have decided never to act again—never to fight another Hollywood fight—without fear of poverty. But he would not give up that easily.

Roy Huggins reappeared in Jim's life at about this time— twice. The CBS Sunday-evening show "60 Minutes" got in touch with Jim to do a segment of the show. Mike Wallace would do the interview himself. Jim agreed. "That was the next step in my relationship with Jim Garner," Roy alleged. "He had been constantly libeling me in *TV Guide* and in interviews."

The public statements finally ended with the "60 Minutes" taping. "He still talks about 'Nichols,' but not Roy Huggins, and here's how that came about. Mike Wallace interviewed him first. Throughout the interview he complained about Universal Studios and Roy Huggins. Wallace asked him why Roy Huggins and he said, 'Well, Roy Huggins is collecting fifteen thousand dollars or whatever it is on every episode for doing nothing.'

"Wallace asked, 'Why would they pay him for doing nothing?'

"'I don't know why they did it,' he said. 'Some deal he's got with Universal. But he never did anything.'"

Wallace, sensing the kind of controversy that has made "60 Minutes" a Sunday-night institution, took his camera crew and motored over to Mandeville Canyon in the Santa Monica Mountains to Roy Huggins's house, where, once they were comfortably settled in his living room, Mike told Roy, "You know, Roy, Jim Garner said some very nasty things about you. He said he didn't know what you'd ever had to do with 'The Rockford Files.'"

Roy looked at him, thought a moment, and said, "Well, Jim Garner and I have a love-hate relationship. I love him. He hates me."

"And that was the end of that," Roy states. Jim, he added, "called me as soon as the show was on the air. He said, 'Hi Roy, how are you?'

"'Fine,' I said. He had created some superficial excuse to call me and he has been superficially friendly toward me from time to time, but only superficially. But he no longer

makes libelous remarks about me because of what I said on
'60 Minutes.'"

Roy believes that Jim hasn't changed. "There's something
eating him because of the failure of 'Nichols.' The failure of
that show is more important in Garner's life than the success
of 'Maverick,' the success of 'Rockford Files,' or any other
success he may have had. He is a natural-born sufferer and
he suffers deeply because he went on the air with a show and
it failed.

"Outside his obsessive preoccupation with his failure, I
think Jim lives a fairly happy life. We sit together at the Raiders' football games. Except that he's never in his seat. He's
down on the bench with the players. He's really a jock at
heart. I think he misses what might have been for him in
football—and he probably would have been quite successful
as a professional player if it hadn't been for the bad knees. He
hasn't done badly with golf and auto racing."

In February 1981 Jim made the papers again from the
ninth hole of the Fortieth Annual Bing Crosby Tournament
at Pebble Beach. A fight started between him and a spectator
from Laguna Beach during the final round of the tournament. According to accounts, the spectator was making comments from the sidelines while Jim finished off the last hole.
With his ball sunk, Jim took a punch at the heckler, and
sensible observers stepped in to prevent a brawl. Nobody suffered anything more than hurt egos, but because it involved
James Garner, who had a reputation for getting into fights, it
made the papers.

With a new series coming up and the old one behind him,
Garner talked more freely about his reasons for leaving
"Rockford," admitting for the first time that more than just
illness had made him quit. In an interview with Ann Salis-

bury for *Panorama*, he said, "When all those injuries finally caught up with me, that's when I quit 'Rockford.' I'd just had it as long as I could take it. I was going downhill, physically, extremely fast. . . . I was overworked."

He touched on his separation from Lois. "I haven't dated—as such. I have had dinner with other ladies and been out with other ladies, and whatever, but I haven't really dated. . . . My wife and I aren't mad at each other, but we're not living together. That's true." He revealed the previous separation, which had taken place ten years earlier. "Our separations have had to do with a lot of other things, not so much between us. The first time it was between us. We had to have some understandings, but we resolved that. I just need to have some time and space to get my head together. She's been wonderful about it."

He said that the past couple of years had been really hard on him. "I had a lot of problems businesswise and then I was ill and getting worse. It bothered me mentally. I was making bad decisions. . . . Things were coming into my mind that I know were not right. I was going to chuck everything. The business. The family. Everybody can go to hell. That kind of thing."

Asked if he thought of suicide, he said, "I wouldn't want to say that. But I guess you could. You could go deeper and deeper and it might end that way. . . . I was in a depression for a year and a half. . . . I have a history of depression. I saw a psychiatrist in Westwood." He said that he was on Elavil for a while and that he didn't want to keep taking that. Elavil is a mood elevator given by psychiatrists to patients suffering from deep depression. His psychiatrist, Jim said, had a great deal to do with his putting some distance between himself and his family. "I wasn't doing my wife or children or any of my friends or anybody else any good. Everything would have deteriorated and deteriorated until it was . . . ruined. . . . That's really my private life."

He confessed that in a sense he was his own worst enemy. "I don't know when to stop. When I make a commitment, it is to the end. They can put me in my grave and I'll still be trying to commit." He believes it has something to do with his roots—the part of the country where he comes from, where a man's word is his bond. "But I'm in a business where they don't understand that. They'd rather lie than tell the truth." That, he says, is why he has had so much trouble with studios and networks. "I don't think they know the truth anymore. They lie so much, they begin to believe it."

He subscribes to the theory that power corrupts. "Most people, when they get power, will abuse it." Eventually, he says, they will get careless and slip up. "Somebody with a little street sense will get to them eventually. Most of them are not that smart."

Jim has never gotten through a year without some kind of problem, emotional or physical, and 1981 was no exception. In August, while shooting a sequence of the new series, now called "Brett Maverick," Jim was injured again when he was thrown from a mechanical horse. He had cracked some ribs, and production shut down for three days while he recuperated. It was a bad way to start a series. He was working on the opening two-hour episode when the accident occurred.

Yet some good things had happened. Jim very quietly moved back into the family home and had reconciled with his wife and family. It was the best possible medicine he could have received. Jim Garner is and always has been a family man. The separation was handled in a far more dignified manner than most Hollywood separations in which press agents issue conflicting "trial separation" releases from both sides. The reconciliation was as dignified as the separation.

*   *   *

It was doubtful that "Maverick" could be revived twenty years later, but Jim said he had no choice but to try. "At my age," he said, "you don't get too many chances." It was a weak statement. He could do pretty much what he wanted to do, and he knew it as well as anybody.

Jim did his part to promote the new series, declaring that the new version was "better written, better plotted, but still funny." He issued a number of conflicting statements about the series. When he had the accident while filming the pilot he indicated he hadn't really wanted to come back in that show but was committed to NBC. But in November he told columnist Roderick Mann that doing the series again was his own idea. "I couldn't find anything I wanted to do more and I realized there were two generations who'd grown up never having seen me in the role, so I thought, why not? Let's do it."

That Jim had been in the business a long time was evidenced by his selecting his original stand-in's son to be his new stand-in. Luis Delgado had moved into an executive position with Cherokee, and his son Max became Jim's stand-in on "Brett Maverick." "We're all gettin' older," Jim grinned.

Westerns hadn't fared well on television for several seasons. "Father Murphy" and "Little House on the Prairie" were never considered Westerns in the true sense of the word but pioneer shows. So the consensus was that "Brett Maverick" would depend totally on James Garner's ability to draw an audience. Never before had his power to hold an audience been put to such a test.

He brought to the show his regulars: Luis Delgado, Roy Clark, Meta Rosenberg, and Stuart Margolin as a character named Philo who is supposed to be an Indian scout. Like many of Margolin's roles for Jim his was a dubious character. Margolin also directed the season opener. The regular cast was rounded out by Ed Bruce, playing an ex-sheriff with honest intentions who has recently been defeated in the town election. Maverick selects him to run a saloon he has won in a poker game. Darlene Carr plays the female interest—a newspaperwoman who like all of Maverick's friends involves him in her problems.

Jim had been busy that year, having made two television movies and one film for the big screen, all of which had not as yet been released. A false security was represented in the 23.2 Nielsen Rating the premiere segment of "Brett Maverick" received. The curiosity factor loomed large. Audiences wanted to compare the old "Maverick" with the new one. Also, new shows have a tendency to do well the first night. Year after year each network strives to get its new shows on the air first in order to capture the imagination of viewers. It rarely guarantees that the audience will stay with the show, but it does give the network, producer, and star of the show their evening in the limelight.

In the meantime Jim was making a TV movie. *Hangin' On* was a pet project of Jim. He'd had the script for ten years and always wanted to do it. When he had the chance, he took it. His new deal at Warner Brothers gave him the opportunity to do other things than "Brett Maverick." Interestingly, Jim had come full circle. He was at Warner Brothers making a "Maverick" series, and a Warner Brothers movie for NBC television. Only the network had changed in twenty years. And this time around it was not a disgruntled Garner who moved about among the crowd at Cushing, Texas, where he was on location shooting the NBC-TV "Movie of the Week."

His co-star was Joan Hackett, long a favorite of Jim since he had insisted that she appear with him in *Support Your*

Local Sheriff when he was the only one who wanted her for the part. He had rightly believed in her ability to be something more than a featured actress. She was a star, he had said, and deserved star roles. History proved him correct.

The story was set in Oklahoma in the fifties, when America was more serene. It was a time, Jim related, "when you could go anywhere you wanted to and not be afraid, and you didn't have to lock your doors at night." Being separated from Lois had changed his perspective on life. During their separation he had given a great deal of thought to values and priorities and had come to the conclusion that one shouldn't ever abandon the basic mores of American life: home, family, and peaceful co-existence with one's neighbors.

On location for *Hangin' On* (later retitled *The Long Summer of George Adams*), he ignored his fear of crowds and waded into them to sign autographs and make himself more available to the fans. He had always accommodated his fans, but he seemed now to take the extra step rather than to wait for them to come to him. For instance, while signing autographs before shooting a scene with Joan Hackett, he noticed a little old lady watching him from the crowd. He went to her, brought her over to the edge of the scene, and seated her in *his* chair. "You shouldn't have to stand up," he chided her gently, as a son might. "You deserve the best seat in the house, and this is it!"

There definitely was something different about Jim Garner. What had changed him? Age, maybe? More maturity? Appreciation, born of the loneliness he had endured while living away from home? One thing was certain. An already likable man was now even more likable.

The Long Summer of George Adams was aired on NBC's "Movie of the Week" on January 18, 1982. Jim, as a small-town railroad man facing mid-life crisis, gave one of the better performances of his career. In its review, the *Hollywood Reporter* said, "Stuart Margolin's direction elicits a deeper shade of vulnerability from Garner than evidenced in previous roles. It's not exactly angst, but Garner's Adams is definitely a man in transition with his identity on the line." The review continued, "The rush of resolution for Adams's summer of discontent is somewhat abrupt, but the denouement is at least symbolically rewarding."

Meta Rosenberg produced the TV movie, and Jim praised her abilities. "People like her," he said. "She is one of the most talented people I've ever met. She can look at a script and tell me in an instant if it's any good and whether it can be fixed and who can fix it."

Jim went directly from filming the *The Long Summer of George Adams* to London, where he co-starred in *Victor/Victoria* for Blake Edwards. His co-star was Julie Andrews, Blake's wife. Jim had made what many consider to be the best film of his career, *The Americanization of Emily*, with Julie Andrews. He enjoyed working with her.

Victor/Victoria is a farcical film. Julie Andrews plays an English singer without funds in Paris in 1934. She pretends to be a man so that she can secure work as a female impersonator. It was not the first time such a premise had been used on stage or screen. Four or five versions preceded it, the first being an English musical comedy made in 1935 called *First a Girl*.

Robert Preston, as an aging homosexual entertainer who teaches Andrews the intricate art of playing a female impersonator, carried the picture. Jim, in the role of a Chicago nightclub owner, believes he is in love with Julie but hides in her bathroom to assure himself that she really is a girl.

Julie and Jim are listed, respectively, as the stars of the film. But the supporting cast—Preston, Lesley Ann Warren,

and Alex Karras—stole the show. Critics were not unkind to
Jim, but they raved about Preston's performance. Julie Andrews received bad reviews. She was called "cold and emo-
tionless," and those were the kinder descriptions of her
performance. Still, the film—heavily laced with homosexual
innuendo and dialogue—captured moviegoers' fancy and
seems destined to become a gay cult film in the manner of
Some Like It Hot.

Similarly, not all the reviews of "Brett Maverick" were
raves. By February 1982 it was becoming apparent that the
series wouldn't work. Cecil Smith of the *Los Angeles Times*
summed up kindly what others were saying more ven-
omously. "'Brett Maverick' . . . seems like just a nice, easy
amusing show, something to kill an hour with if there's nothing better on—pleasant and forgettable. We thought the old
'Maverick' was hell on wheels. . . . Were we so naive?"

For what turned out to be the last episode of "Brett
Maverick," Jack Kelly was called on to appear as Bart
Maverick again. "I received a call from my agent," Kelly recalls, "asking me to do a segment with Jim. My first instinct
was to say, 'Sure. Fine.' I was thinking in terms of doing a
whole show like the one we had done over in Arizona. So I
told my agent, 'Okay. What's the deal? I'll have to arrange
my schedule, but that can be done.'

"'About thirteen or eighteen seconds at the end of the
show and they're paying $1,000.'"

"Fuck them!" Jack said. "Are you crazy? I'm a goddamn
mayor pro-tem. I'm a star down here! First of all, I've got to
do one day, which for me to travel from Huntington Beach
to Los Angeles is an hour plus. I don't want to do it."

"Think about it," the agent said. "It might reactivate your
career."

"Hey, baby," Jack said, "how many jobs do I pass up a

year? I get maybe forty-five calls to do work that would produce maybe eighty thousand dollars. I don't need one-liners for one day."

Jim made a personal call to Jack and explained why he was needed to do the show. "It is at the end of the show—actually the end of the series, I think. We've written ourselves into a tunnel and Brother Bart is the only way out. So come on, asshole, get up here and do the fucking thing. I've got to have you. There's no way to do it without you."

Jack said, "Oh, bullshit! Get off the phone. I'll be there."

"The only reason I did it," Jack explains, "is because Jim leaned on me.

"You look at the last frame of film and you'll see old ugly Kelly—Brother Bart—in there. There were only about three lines in the entire scene—it was mostly reaction. We looked at each other, recognized each other. I was in a carpetbagger's outfit and he was playing some kind of phony CPA on a swindle. I didn't like the play because it wasn't the essence of 'Maverick.' He was a fucking thief. He was providing scams to make a living out of scams. The real Maverick *never* did that!"

The last contact with Roy Huggins came when "Brett Maverick" was in trouble and starting to sink. Huggins refers to it as "the capper." Except for attending football games together, he says he never saw Jim. "I got a call one morning from my agent. Warner Brothers, he said, would like for me to take over producing 'Brett Maverick.' Now that didn't make any sense to me in light of all that Jim had said about my incompetence in the media. It was something I'd have to think about.

"Then I got a phone call from Jim Garner asking me to come and do it for him."

Roy said, "Gee, Jim. Let me consider it. Let me think

about it. But what about Meta? I thought she was producing the show."

"She's out," he told Roy. "We're not speaking now."

After agreeing to think it over, Roy hung up the phone and shortly thereafter received a second call from his agent. "Roy, Warner Brothers would really like to have you come on the show."

"It was now obvious to me," Roy declares, "that Garner talked to those people and *he* wanted me. At this point in his career he was in a position to ask for the people he wanted on a series."

Roy said to his agent, "Jesus, Lee. First of all they're not doing 'Maverick.' There's no way I could do 'Maverick' on that show. The series is located in one town. All in one place, like 'Nichols.' I don't see how I could save that show. I'd have to go back to the original concept. 'Maverick' was a wanderer and I don't know how to say this, because I don't want to hurt Jim's feelings."

The agent said, "Roy, I'll tell them you're giving it some thought. I'll tell them you're not feeling too positive, but I won't say no to them just yet."

"I didn't want to say no," Roy says, "because I hadn't said no to Jim when he called. Three days later they canceled the show, and I was never put in the position of having to turn Jim down. I'm pleased about that."

The series was canceled and Meta Rosenberg was gone. Meta's version was different. She says she quit Cherokee, that Garner did not drop her. "I never expected that 'Brett Maverick' would be canceled," she said, explaining her exit from the company. "I got the show going, was certain it would be on for years, and decided it was time to go out on my own. I'm getting a lot of offers and right now it's a matter of deciding which to choose." The implication is that she did not have another job lined up when she left Cherokee.

Meta Rosenberg wasn't the only person shocked by NBC's canceling the series. Alan Shayne, president of Warner Brothers TV, declared that "Brett Maverick" was "NBC's seventh-ranked show. James Garner has been ranked eighth most popular out of 490 stars in the country. I have to say this is a crushing blow. I'm simply shocked."

He said that NBC chairman Grant Tinker and NBC Entertainment president Brandon Tartikoff (who had earlier declared that "Brett Maverick" fit right in with NBC's new format) were looking for shows that appealed to a "young urban audience." "Brett Maverick" didn't fit into *that* new format.

James Garner, more relaxed than he had been in years, refused to become depressed. "I went through all that crap with 'Rockford,' and I don't need any more of it," he declared, and that was his last public comment on the subject. He went behind the big wrought-iron gates of his estate and closed out the world without malice. He had more important things to consider than television—like his family.

He was extremely proud of his daughter Gigi, who was making quite a splash in England as a country-western singer. "Sort of country-western," he says with fatherly admiration. Gigi, in fact, was lucky to be alive. At the height of Jim's personal problems his younger daughter had crashed her BMW into a parked vehicle and had gone through the windshield. For a long time it was doubtful whether she would be able to use her mouth or jaw without distortion. Permanent paralysis was a definite possibility. It took over one hundred stitches to repair her shattered face, and she has been left with a slight paralysis in her lower face. That has only made her more determined to do something with her life besides, as she told a writer in London, "being just another spoiled Hollywood brat."

She had plenty of time to reflect on just who she was during the three weeks she was hospitalized and the months of therapy that followed. Right out of the hospital, she was invited by her father—who hoped to cheer her up—to visit him in London, where he was completing *Victor/Victoria*. Jim had always discouraged his children from getting involved in show business. He knew all the liabilities and was very protective—sometimes too protective—of his daughters, wanting to make sure that they did not suffer the agonies he had suffered. Still, while she was in London a record producer heard a tape of her voice and signed her to a contract, and she soon had a hit record, "Love Hurts."

As much as she loves her father, she says that Hollywood is no place to live. Growing up behind iron gates with watchdogs is her father's life-style, not hers. "I'd change my name," she said, "if so many people didn't already know me. I just want to be me." Most parents would smile at that slightly rebellious statement. It isn't limited to Hollywood.

XXIII

Jim's February 1981 fracas with William Stewart of Laguna Beach at the Bing Crosby Pro-Am Golf Tournament at Pebble Beach brought him back into the courtroom early in 1983. Stewart had filed a $2.2 million suit against Jim, claiming that he had suffered "severe mental anguish" over the incident. The case was heard in Superior Court at Salinas, California, during the second week of March.

Both sides presented cases and witnesses. The press treated the trial as a media event rather than serious litigation. Jim testified that he had indeed slugged Stewart in an effort to "educate him on golfing etiquette." Witnesses for Jim testified that Stewart had been drinking and somewhat disorderly. Stewart admitted that he had gone to the tournament to "have a few beers and a good time."

The jury took less than an hour to bring in a verdict against Stewart. Outside the courtroom Stewart told the gathering of reporters, "I was very surprised that I lost the suit." He added that he felt James Garner had been favored by the jury because "everybody likes him."

Jim seemed destined to spend a great deal of his life in a courtroom. In July he was involved in litigation again. This time he was not being sued. He was suing Universal Studios for a whopping $22.5 million in connection with his ongoing dispute over profits from "The Rockford Files." The suit charged Universal with "breach of contract, failure to deal in good faith and fairly, and fraud and deceit."

Jim's attorney, William A. Masterson, stated in an aside, "Universal claims it ["The Rockford Files"] never made a profit. If that is true they must be like the used car dealer who said he lost a bit on each sale but made it up on volume."

Asked why he hadn't brought the matter to court in 1980 when he first discovered the discrepancy in the figures, Jim said, "I was going to file suit then but decided not to because Universal asked for more time in order to give me an accounting of the show's revenue." Nothing worthwhile had been forthcoming, and he felt that time had run out.

It might have been mere coincidence but the timing raised eyebrows in the film community. The suit was filed just a few days after Universal reached a secret settlement with producer Harve Bennett, who was suing the studio for his share of the profits from the two series "The Six Million Dollar Man" and "The Bionic Woman." Bennett had taken his case all the way to trial in Superior Court. Universal offered its settlement during the second day of trial, before the trail was actually underway. As part of the settlement, which Bennett accepted, Universal insisted that the terms of the settlement never be revealed.

Jim took leave of absence from his legal entanglements in April to travel to Georgia, where he was making a film on location with Shirley Jones. Even though he was suing Universal Studios, he did not hesitate to appear in a Lorimar-Universal production. Shirley Jones hadn't made a motion picture for theatrical distribution since *Beyond the Poseidon Adventure* some four years earlier and was delighted to be back on the screen again, particularly as Jim's co-star. She played Jim's gutsy wife in the picture, *Tank*, a different kind of role for her. "I love the role," she said. "It gets me away from that Miss Goody Two-Shoes rut that has plagued me for years. And I love working with Jim." She said they had known each other for years but had never worked together. "We even dated once when we were both new to Hollywood."

The film, shot mostly at Fort Benning, Georgia, stars Jim as a "good ol' boy" professional soldier who comes into conflict with a corrupt local sheriff who has an intense, almost pathological abhorrence of anything military. The plot thickens when the sheriff (played admirably by G. D. Spradlin) frames Jim's son (played by C. Thomas Howell) on a drug charge and hauls him off to the local version of a chain gang. Garner declares a personal war—thus the tank.

When the film was reviewed, both Jim and Shirley Jones received the kind of praise—warm but not adulatory—suited to Jim's kind of picture (the film had the usual reception of a Garner film by most critics). The director, Marvin J. Chomsky, was faulted as "a straight-on director" who "flattens out the film as surely as if it had been run over by the Sherman tank of its title."

Kevin Thomas of the *Los Angeles Times* said, "*Tank* turns out to be a rabble-rouser, but were it not so broad, it could have been more than that."

It was another picture, another review. Jim had long ago ceased keeping count of either. He had other commitments to fulfill. His family life had never been better; he beamed whenever someone asked how Mrs. Garner was. He seemed delighted to relate some recent humorous anecdote involving his family and appeared to be totally secure in his marriage.

Even his trips away from home to film on location no longer seemed to cause tension or misgivings for him or Lois.

During the latter part of the year he left Hollywood again, heading north to Vancouver, British Columbia, where he would be starring with Margot Kidder in Joseph Wambaugh's "novel-to-film" *The Glitter Dome* for Home Box Office cablevision. At that time he did an interview with New York writer Robert Ward, declaring, "I only give one interview a year, kid, and this is it."

Jim was having a good time, and it was obvious that he was in his element. He was playing poker every day with burly members of the crew. He talked about his years in television and movies, the friends he had made along the way, and the people he had worked with, some of whom were no longer around. "I'm a lead sinker in deep water," he contended, "totally out of my league with the business people who run the industry. My friends—the actor friends—have all paid a tough price. This is no easy business. I grew up in the industry with David Janssen. We were close friends. I saw what the pressures did to him. The drinking. He was no drunk, but in the end it killed him. A television series is a man-killer, believe me."

He never wanted to be a big star, he said. "I never had the drive to be on top of the heap. Not really. I've been lucky to always work, but I don't yo-yo up and down like some guys. I've seen them go up the ladder and then come back down while I stayed just about at the same position all the time." After thirty years, he says he feels comfortable being "just part of the pack that hangs in there."

Jim doesn't like change. He doesn't mind moving about to work, but real change frightens him. He had too many abrupt changes in his youth and consequently never quite felt rooted despite the love offered to him by his extended family. He put down roots when he got married and hopes never to pull them up.

He has managed to keep the same crews for years. Now, even up in the cold north, he was being directed by his old pal Stuart Margolin. People who have stayed with Jim Garner over the years have prospered in the industry, if that's what they wanted. He is proud of their accomplishments and lets them know it. A generous man, he is delighted to have helped so many people but doesn't boast about it.

James Garner is fifty-six at this writing and has apparently become larger than the industry he has been a part of since the early fifties. He is not afraid to move away from the stereotyped roles in which he has been cast and has at times cast himself. In the spring of 1984 he acted in *Heartsounds*, a true-life story opposite Mary Tyler Moore for Norman Lear. A made-for-television film (ABC), it was not just another exercise in James Garner's humor. It was far more serious. Based on the best-selling book by Martha Weinman Lear, it was the story of her husband, Dr. Harold Lear, Norman Lear's cousin.

Dr. Lear died from heart disease. The film does not so much concern his death as the five-year battle he waged against incompetence on the part of the medical establishment in its treatment of disease.

This was the most dramatic role Jim had ever played. Dr. Lear's wife, Martha, was on the set almost every day while the picture was being shot in New York, and she was often spellbound by Jim's portrayal of her husband. In one scene, when Garner was arguing with Mary Tyler Moore, who was playing Mrs. Lear in the story, the real Mrs. Lear was asked if she would like to be an extra in the picture. In this particular scene, Jim and Mary are on the sidewalk in front of a building. Just as Mrs. Lear is walking by as part of the passing crowd, Jim says to Mary, "Martha, stop it!"

The scene was so vivid and real, says Mrs. Lear, that instead of walking on by, she "stopped, whirled around, and stood dead in my tracks. It was as if the whole thing was happening all over again for the first time. I tell you, it was eerie."

Jim commented about the seriousness of the role. "Nobody has ever wanted to hire me as a dramatic actor. I'm a comic actor. All the *producers* know that." He made the statement with no small amount of sarcasm. He was aware that he had been typecast and that he had fostered the stereotype by not demanding more versatility in the parts he played from the very beginning. But he does not seem to be embittered by the past. "I don't know what I can do and what I can't do," he stated candidly, "until I do it. We'll find out if I can do something else. It's all a mattter of concentration and confidence. If you have the confidence that you're doing what's right, then the concentration will be there."

Everything about the picture was first-class. Big stars; a prominent producer; and a screenplay by Fay Kanin, a recent president of the Academy of Motion Picture Arts and Sciences and an award-winning writer. The film, Miss Kanin, explained "is probably not as hard on the medical profession as the book was. This is a two-hour movie. In a four-hundred-page book you can recite a great many more instances than in a two-hour movie. The failings of hospital care are readily discernible in the film, however. It says a lot about our medical establishment."

Director Glenn Jordan stated that his intention was "not to indict the medical profession, but to present a love story centered around a couple who have to deal with heart disease. I hope to communicate that terminal illness can bring people together. Dying is a part of living, and in a way it enriches their lives. I find it a wonderfully moving and uplifting story, and I hope people laugh and cry their way through it."

Jim brought more realism to the character than he had to any previous role. When required to act out a heart attack he gave a vivid portrayal. He understood that heart attacks are painful, and nobody in films knew more about pain than Jim. He needed only to draw on his own experiences to understand what was required of him, and his performance was brilliant. He had grown so much as an actor that without realizing it he had stepped across the threshold from comedy to drama. A whole new world lay ahead of him. It was exciting, and he felt renewed.

In 1982 James Michener's novel *Space* was published by Random House and quickly became a number one bestseller. Michener's books not only have a record of shooting directly to the top of the best-seller list but many of them have been brought to the screen as major motion pictures. *Tales of the South Pacific* became a long-running Broadway musical and then one of the great musical films of all times. Other films based on Michener's novels include *The Bridges at Toko-Ri*, *Sayonara* (in which Jim had his first important role, opposite Marlon Brando), and *Centennial* (which became an award-winning television mini-series).

It seemed reasonable to believe that, with such emphasis since the sixties on space travel and exploration, Michener's account of four men who had been involved in the space program since 1944 would be subject to film presentation. When Paramount Pictures and Stonehenge Productions purchased the film rights to *Space*, the producers realized that this would be a major production with immense impact and would require the best possible talent on both sides of the cameras. Both production companies were experienced, and Paramount had been responsible for the spectacular success of three mini-series: *Winds of War*, *Shogun*, and *Washington Behind Closed Doors*.

Projected as a thirteen-hour, five-part mini-series, *Space* would be aired on the CBS Network "sometime in 1985." Such a large undertaking, it was decided, required two active producers instead of one. Allan Marcil, Stonehenge's vice-president in charge of creative affairs, would personally co-produce with producer Martin Manulis. Marcil had been responsible for the television productions of *Johnny Belinda* and *Invasion of Privacy* and had been associate producer on *A Rumor of War*, each a successful television movie. Martin Manulis had been a legend in Hollywood since the early fifties, when his "Playhouse 90" television dramas were produced live and electrified the country with their crispness and quality. Manulis had recently produced the television mini-series *Chiefs*, which received great critical acclaim as well as high Nielsen Ratings.

Directing segments one and five was Joseph Sargent, who had directed the Emmy Award–winning *Marcus-Nelson Murders*, *Amber Waves* (which proved that Kurt Russell was more than a Disney pin-up), *Memorial Day*, and *Choices of the Heart*.

Lee Philips, who began his Hollywood career as an actor on the television series "The Adventures of Ellery Queen," would direct shows two, three, and four in sequence. Philips had made the transition from actor to director and had directed many excellent television dramas, including *The Red Badge of Courage*; *Louis Armstrong, Chicago Style*; *The War Between the Tates*; and dozens of other television shows. Tough, seasoned, and an actor's director, he brought total understanding of the medium to the production.

Stirling Silliphant and Dick Berg, whose writing credits include dozens of high-caliber scripts, were assigned to transfer Michener's story from novel to screenplay.

James Garner was the first to be cast. He won the plum

part of a U.S. naval hero from World War II, Norman Grant, over all comers—and every actor in the proper age group wanted that part. The role was considered to be a model by which male actors would be judged throughout the eighties. That placed great pressure on the producers to cast it correctly and equal if not greater pressures on the man selected to perform it.

Certainly Jim will go on to other roles in other films and perhaps other mini-series, but getting this role is the crowning achievement of his long, sometimes brilliant, often average career. He will be one of the most talked-about actors around. He will be taken more seriously than ever before. After all his years in films and television, it was actually his very human portrayal of Dr. Lear in *Heartsounds* that gave him the opportunity to be considered when serious drama is discussed.

Jim's role is that of the courageous American navy commander from a small midwestern town who comes home after the war, runs for the U.S. Senate, is elected as a war hero, and goes on to become a powerful force in the American space program. His is a key role. It embodies all the changes in America after World War II.

Jim was joined by an outstanding cast that included Susan Anspach, Beau Bridges, Blair Brown (director Sargent's wife), Bruce Dern, Melinda Dillon, Harry Hamlin, Barbara Sukowa, and Michael York. Fortunately, shooting on location was nothing new to him. He would travel extensively for *Space*, with shooting at several locations in California, the NASA space agency in Houston (the first time commercial movie cameras were ever allowed to film there), Cape Canaveral, Washington, D.C., and England.

The picture began shooting on May 29, 1984, in San Diego and is still in the final days of production at this writing.

Executives who have viewed the completed film to date use superlatives when describing Jim Garner's performance. Such praise is generally reserved for actors destined to be nominated for an Emmy and most likely to win.

James Garner's career is no fluke. It is going stronger than ever after thirty years in the business. He has been relatively unscathed by gossip or by adversaries. His enemies are few; close friends, limited. Yet he is lauded by those who have fought with him professionally.

Any summation of Jim's life and career would be remiss if it did not include the opinions of James Garner by those who have known and worked with him—and by the man himself.

Mariette Hartley: Polaroid was only paying me scale for the first six or seven commercials I did for them with Jim. At that time, Jim's contract was up and he stipulated in his new contract that I was to be paid more. I would love to make a movie with him, and a friend of mine wrote a wonderful script for us. But Jimmy said no. He's a fascinating, very talented man, but he has specific ideas about what he wants to do and when he wants to do it. I think he's a little afraid that we'll become too much of a team. I don't think that will happen. I'd love to do a full-length feature with him. . . . But he doesn't seem to agree.

Stephen Cannell: With regard to "The Rockford Files," Jim was always totally supportive. He did not cause one ripple in five years. I never had to go down to the set because he was causing trouble or because he didn't like the material—and, believe me, we had some pretty iffy scripts. Jim knew when a show was not good, but with Jim, it's "You are my guys. I trust you. If it's a bad script this week, it's because it's the best you can do under the circumstances, and I know next week it will be better, so I'm not going to call you on it." It was always that way.

Gigi Garner (Jim's younger daughter): I mother him; I'll go out of my way one hundred miles for him.

Luis Delgado: Jim sees to it that I am financially taken care of. I had a heart attack while he was making *The Children's Hour*. He visited me in the hospital every day after work.

Roy Huggins: I really had stumbled onto something wonderful, the rarest thing there is in Hollywood, an actor with an unerring instinct for a funny line. Some lines are funny no matter how they are read—punch lines, joke lines—but the kind of humor I have always liked is the kind that comes out of character and is funny only if the actor understands how that character would read the line and why. Garner understood, and his understanding was absolute. I am pleased he is now getting roles to which he brings his real talents. *Heartsounds* insured his place as an actor.

Dr. Irene Kassorla (psychologist and writer): Women react to James Garner like they would a pop star. He's a startling combination. . . . You just know you could sit down and talk with this man.

Les Martinson: If Jim Garner had left "Maverick" at the end of the second year, along with Roy Huggins, there would have been no third year. Garner was the only man in the world for that role. I'm sorry, but I do not remember a series called "Nichols."

Jack Kelly: I first met him twenty or twenty-five years ago— it's been a while. Jim Garner is the same man today that he was twenty-five years ago. Hasn't changed. Not a nuance.

Nothing. I would come running if he asked me to do a walk-on in one of his pictures. I love the guy.

Stuart Margolin: He's getting better and better as an actor. The next ten years should be interesting. He's turning the corner into what you call the leading character man.

Jack Bumgarner (Jim Garner's brother): Jim does take care of an awful lot of people. He pays a lot of the bills. Nobody hears about that.

Robert Altman: I have long thought that Jim Garner was one of the best actors around. I don't know anyone in the business with his charm and charisma who can act as well.

Bill Robinson (a Garner agent): Jim is a low-key guy, unimpressed with material things, who, in my opinion, has gotten little joy out of what you can buy with a dollar. His greatest thrill is getting to sit on the Raiders bench and cheer for the quarterback.

George Seaton (director-producer): Jim Garner is that rarity among actors—one who cannot be typed.

Jimmy Lydon: Jim has a sense of humor about life and it shows in his work. He may seem very laid back and very casual about his profession and his work, but he is not. He works very hard. On a television show that has been running four or five years he'll relax from time to time and learn the words about ten minutes before he shoots the scene, but by that time he has a knack for character and everything else.

I've always respected the way he deals with his family. When things were not going well with his brother, Jim always found a spot for him and it was always legitimate money because Jack worked for whatever the money was. He was useful. Jim has a good relationship with his brother.

Meta Rosenberg: His comprehension is absolute. Working with him was a joy.

Garner on Garner

I like people around me that I know. People that know me. People I can trust.

"Rockford," I believe, has been the most successful series I ever had. It was the most fun and to come out with a total loss really dimmed my eagerness. It broke my heart. They're bad people. I don't like to work with bad people. It hurt me physically, financially, and mentally.

Actors' salaries are blown out of proportion by the media.

I directed one "Rockford." I like to direct. I just don't have the conviction. I can communicate with actors but I think I'll be too easy. I won't be able to force them.

They don't teach you anything in schools. It's common sense. The best way to learn is to be on the set: You make one mistake and you won't forget it.

I don't like compliments. I can't accept them well for one reason or another. I feel either that they are not deserved or that I can't fully believe them.

I don't like being number one or two. Seven is about right for me.

When I'm not working I want to get off and hide away. I want to get off to my house. I take one isolated road and then veer off to another and finally I approach an iron gate. Behind it is a German shepherd. I walk inside, close the gate, and do my thing. I like popularity but also like being left alone.

Sometimes I get depressed. I don't want to go anywhere. I don't want to see anyone. I don't want to do anything. I don't talk much. I don't know what I'm doing."

I prefer a car to a horse. I've ridden horses all my life. We lived out in the country. I've had 'em bite me, kick me, stomp on me, throw me, run me into trees, walls, corrals, barns, whatever.

You couldn't be around somebody as good as Henry Fonda without learning something. I'll tell you one thing I did get from him, I hope, and that is, he treated everybody equally. He was good to people.

Oh, Ronnie, Ronnie, isn't he wonderful? Listen, I was vice-president of the Screen Actors Guild when he was its president, and we used to tell him what to say. He can talk around a subject better than anyone in the world. He's never had an original thought that I know of, and we go back a hell of a lot of years. Do you realize *I* could have been your president?

I loved "Nichols." The show lasted one year, but I swear to you, if they would have left it on another year, it would still be running. It was just too damned original for some Chevrolet executive's wife. She wanted "Maverick."

I quit drinking when I was 26. I had this habit of trying to drink all there was, but I found out that the liquor boys could produce more bottles than I could down—not that it stopped me in my drinking days.

I don't consider myself a sex symbol at all. I was a total introvert until I was twenty-six years old. I was afraid of girls. I never dated or even danced. I was a wallflower. Women still scare the hell out of me.

I didn't begin to accept any kind of responsibility until I was twenty-six and about to get married to Lois. Before that, I didn't care. All I did was eat, sleep, and do whatever I wanted. And I didn't want anything.

What I'd really like to do is get a nice ranch or farm where I could go through my daily chores of taking care of my animals or vegetables or whatever you do on a farm and not have business pressures every day. My wife was born and raised in Los Angeles and that's what she prefers. So I think we're probably going to buy a place outside Los Angeles. I can keep an apartment in the city where I can go when I work. She'll have easy access to the city and we'll both be happy.

Author's Note: In twenty or thirty years Hollywood will remember James Garner as some kind of legend—he has the charisma from which legends grow. His fans will remember him as a Hollywood maverick.

Index